The task of the theologian is two-fold. First, the theologian must seek to understand the Scriptures. Second, the theologian must seek to understand the realities, issues and challenges which the Christian faces. This book, *African Contextual Realities*, is a serious study by theologians who have an intimate grasp of African Christianity. The theologian in each of these chapters intentionally seeks to make the Christian message relevant without compromising its meaning. I believe that the authors of this exciting book have met the goal of the book, namely to contextualize the Christian message. I enthusiastically recommend this book to church leaders, pastors, mission students, missionaries, etc. It is a book that scratches where the church is itching!

Samuel Waje Kunhiyop, PhD
Professor of Systematic Theology and Ethics,
ECWA Theological Seminary, Kagoro, Nigeria
Author of *African Christian Ethics* and *African Christian Theology*

African Contextual Realities showcases an outstanding collection of contextually oriented theological essays. The authors consider local histories of Christianity, prior failures in contextualization, and dilemmas posed by cultural practice (like widow cleansing) and ethnicity. They analyze spiritual and pastoral challenges of everyday life and suggest models for healthy contextual theological engagement and formation. Highly recommended.

Robert J. Priest, PhD
Professor of Anthropology, Taylor University, Upland, Indiana, USA
Former President, American Society of Missiology

ASET Series

We often hear these days that the center of Christianity is moving toward the Global South and Africa is a key player in that movement. This makes the study of African Christianity and African realities important – even more so when it is being done by Africans themselves in their own context. The Africa Society of Evangelical Theology (ASET) was created to encourage research and sustained theological reflection on key issues facing Africa by and for African Christians and those working within African contexts. The volumes in the ASET series constitute the best papers presented at the annual conferences of ASET and together they seek to fill this important gap in the literature of Christianity.

ASET Series

African Contextual Realities

GLOBAL LIBRARY

African Contextual Realities

General Editor

Rodney L. Reed

© 2018 Africa Society of Evangelical Theology (ASET)

Published 2018 by Langham Global Library
An imprint of Langham Publishing
www.langhampublishing.org

Langham Publishing and its imprints are a ministry of Langham Partnership

Langham Partnership
PO Box 296, Carlisle, Cumbria CA3 9WZ, UK
www.langham.org

ISBNs:
978-1-78368-473-1 Print
978-1-78368-474-8 ePub
978-1-78368-475-5 Mobi
978-1-78368-476-2 PDF

The Africa Society of Evangelical Theology have asserted their right under the Copyright, Designs and Patents Act, 1988 to be identified as the Author of this complete work, and the Contributors have asserted their right under the same act to be identified as the Author of their portion of the Work.

All rights reserved. No part of this publication may be reproduced, stored in a retrieval system or transmitted, in any form or by any means, electronic, mechanical, photocopying, recording or otherwise, without the prior written permission of the publisher or the Copyright Licensing Agency.

Scripture quotations, unless otherwise indicated, are taken from the Holy Bible, New International Version®, NIV®. Copyright ©1973, 1978, 1984, 2011 by Biblica, Inc.™ Used by permission of Zondervan.

British Library Cataloguing-in-Publication Data
A catalogue record for this book is available from the British Library

ISBN: 978-1-78368-473-1

Cover & Book Design: projectluz.com

Langham Partnership actively supports theological dialogue and an author's right to publish but does not necessarily endorse the views and opinions set forth here or in works referenced within this publication, nor can we guarantee technical and grammatical correctness. Langham Partnership does not accept any responsibility or liability to persons or property as a consequence of the reading, use or interpretation of its published content.

CONTENTS

Preface xi
Acknowledgments xiii

Part I: Contextualizing Theory and Theology for Africa

1   Holiness, *Missio Dei* and the Church in Africa 3
     Gift Mtukwa

2   A Theology of Spiritual Power in African Christianity. 19
     Johana Kariuki Gitau

3   Contextualization of Pastoral Theology in African Christianity: Theory, Models, Methods, and Practice 31
     Ndung'u J. B. Ikenye

4   The Significance of Johann Ludwig Krapf's Mission Work in East Africa. 57
     David Kimiri Ngaruiya

Part II: Addressing African Realities

5   Syncretism in African Christianity: A Boon or a Bane?. 75
     Joseph D. Galgalo

6   Dependency's Long Shadow: Mission Churches in Kenya and Their Children 97
     Joseph William Black

7   The Impact of an Essential African Christian Theological Reconciliation Schema in Peace-Building in Africa 113
     Fredrick Amolo

8   Widow Cleansing in Rural Kenya: Toward a Critically Contextualized Theological Response. 127
     Mary Thamari Odhiambo

9   Religion, a Means to Disobedience: A Reflective Analysis of the Story of the Golden Calf in Exodus 32 143
     Hermann Mvula

10 Interfaith Dialogue between Christians and Muslims as a
    Response to Religious Radicalization in Kenya 165
    Patrick Mburu Kamau

Part III: Christian Education in the African Context

11 African Christian Universities and the Old Testament
    Concept of the *Lev* 189
    Daryll Gordon Stanton and Rickson Nkhata

12 A New Model of Theological Training in Nairobi: Tyrannus Hall
    at the Nairobi Chapel 209
    David Bawks

13 From the Classroom to the Pulpit: Navigating the Challenges 227
    Elizabeth Mburu

14 Toward the Propagation of KAG Christian Schools in Kenya:
    An Investigation of Stakeholder Perceptions 249
    Rev Isaac Kasili

15 Spirituality, Work Conditions, and Job Satisfaction of
    Distance Education Personnel in Kenya's Christian Institutions
    of Higher Education 267
    Rosemary Wahu Mbogo

    List of Contributors 287

Preface

Whenever Christianity encounters a new culture, the need for contextualization arises. The "faith once delivered" must be communicated and lived out in the thought forms, language, and traditions of that new culture if it is to take root there. This is certainly true of African Christianity. In fact, one could argue that the history of Christianity in Africa could be effectively written using as its interpretive principle the success or failure of those propagating the faith to contextualize it. Yet it is not so simple to conclude that the tremendous growth of Christianity across Africa is the result of the effective contextualization of the faith. Colonization, Westernization, education, and global technologies are among the many intervening variables that make that conclusion less certain. Consequently, one could alternatively argue that in many quarters of Africa effective contextualization is yet to happen, resulting in the often-used saying that "Christianity in Africa is a mile wide but an inch deep" – a saying that itself needs some metric contextualization! Nevertheless, Christianity is spread widely across the African continent. From Cape Town to Cairo and from Dakar to Dar es Salaam, one can easily see the impact of Christianity on the African context, but the question is, "In what ways should the African context impact Christianity?"

This book explores what it means for Christianity to think and speak "African." It does so not just in theory, but also by addressing some of the "nuts and bolts" issues of Christianity as it is experienced in Africa today. It represents the best of the papers presented at the 6th Annual Conference of the Africa Society of Evangelical Theology on the topic of "African Contextual Realities," held on the campus of Africa Nazarene University in Nairobi, Kenya, on 4 and 5 March 2016. The contributors, though not all African by birth, reflect on the topic of contextualization from the perspectives of their own ministry contexts in Africa.

It wrestles with such questions as:
- In what ways should the mission of God be universally recognizable in every cultural context?
- What lessons can we learn from those who contextualized the gospel before us?
- In our efforts to contextualize, how do we avoid compromising the very gospel we are to proclaim?

- How can the African church wean itself away from dependency on the Western church?
- How does Christianity speak into some of the cultural and social issues arising out of the contemporary African setting – issues like widow cleansing, Christian-Muslim relations, and peace-building?
- How should Christian ministry and Christian education and the training of Christian ministers be carried out in the African context?

Together, the chapters in this book represent what might be called the "next phase" of the contextualization of Christianity in Africa, after the initial phases of evangelism and church planting. After Christianity's existence in much of sub-Saharan Africa for decades, if not a full century, there are still areas where the alignment between Christian faith and African realities is not complete. This book addresses those issues. The chapters are independent units and so readers are encouraged to scan the table of contents and find something that interests them and enjoy the reading! If you are from or ministering within Africa, another way of saying that is, "Look for a chapter that scratches where you are itching, and hopefully find some relief!"

Rodney L. Reed
Chair, ASET Editorial Committee

Acknowledgments

There are many people to thank who have been part of the production of this work. I wish to thank the Executive Committee of the Africa Society of Evangelical Theology for their commitment to see the research of African Christian scholars of religion gain a wider hearing. Thanks also go to the Publication and Communication Committee and the Editorial Committee of ASET for their contribution to this volume. Special thanks are due to Prof. Melitus Wanyama, who read these papers for style and form editing and whose attention to detail is much valued. Most of all we give thanks to God, without whom the publication of this volume would never have come to pass.

Part I

Contextualizing Theory and Theology for Africa

1

Holiness, *Missio Dei* and the Church in Africa

Gift Mtukwa
Lecturer and Chair, Department of Religion, Africa Nazarene University, Nairobi, Kenya

Abstract

There is no doubt that the *missio Dei* is one of the overarching theological concepts that interlaces the biblical story into a single story. It is a story of a missional God who calls people to be with him on a mission. Consequently, the church is unequivocally missional, and its mission is defined by the God who calls it into existence. This paper proposes that if the church in Africa is to be truly missional, it cannot avoid being a holiness church. Pope John Paul II supported this connection between holiness and mission when he said, "The universal call to holiness is closely linked to the universal call to mission. Every member of the faithful is called to holiness and to mission."[1] The paper traces the connection between the concepts of holiness and mission in both the Old and New Testaments of the Bible; it then proceeds to provide a biblical synthesis of these twin concepts. After that, a picture is painted of where the African church stands in relation to these two concepts, and conclusions with some practical recommendations for the African church are made.

Key words: holiness, Christlikeness, mission of God/*missio Dei*, missional, church, African church.

---

1. John Paul, "Redemptoris Missio," Encyclical letter on the permanent validity of the church's missionary mandate, Vatican website, 7 Dec 1990, http://www.rcan.org/evangelization/Redem_Missio_JPII.pdf. 90.

Definition and Concepts of Mission and Holiness

This paper defines holiness as "the state or condition of being holy, whole, healed."[2] A cognate of the word "holiness" is "sanctification," which has its roots from "*sanctus*, meaning 'holy' or 'set apart for the service of the gods,' and *facio*, 'to make.' Hence 'to sanctify' is defined as 'to make holy or sacred; to set apart for holy or religious use; to hollow; to purify from sin; to make the means for holiness.' *Sanctus* is also the source of 'saint,' a term applied in the New Testament to all the people of God."[3] Therefore, holiness is a result of sanctification, the purging of sin from a person or people.

Holiness in the Bible is essential to the nature of God. According to James Muilenberg, it is "the 'given' undergirding and pervading all religion; the distinctive mark and signature of the divine . . . It is, therefore, to be understood, not as one attribute among other attributes, but as the innermost reality to which all others are related."[4] God, whose essential nature is holiness, desires that the people he created be in a relationship with him, and become holy as he is holy. People and things are holy only as they relate to the God of holiness, hence the phrase "derived holiness."[5] John Wesley, in his *Explanatory Notes upon the New Testament*, said that, "When God is termed holy, it denotes that excellence which is altogether peculiar to himself; and the glory flowing from all his attributes conjoined, shining forth from all his works, and darkening all things besides itself."[6]

Mission, on the other hand, is defined as "our committed participation as God's people, at God's invitation and command, in God's own mission within the history of God's purpose for the redemption of God's creation."[7] The mission human beings participate in is not their mission; it is God's mission. In Wright's words, "Our mission flows from and participates in the mission of God."[8] Those on God's mission are the sent ones; Karl Henrich Rengstorf concludes his examination of the term *aposteleo* by defining it as "to send forth

---

2. W. T. Purkiser, *Exploring Christian Holiness*, 3 vols. (Kansas City: Beacon Hill, 1983), 1:13.

3. Purkiser, *Exploring Christian Holiness*, 14.

4. James Muilenberg, "Holiness," *The Interpreter's Dictionary of the Bible*, ed. George Arthur Buttrick (Nashville: Abingdon Press, 1962), 616–625.

5. Purkiser, *Exploring Christian Holiness*, 19.

6. John Wesley, *Explanatory Notes upon the New Testament*, quoted in Purkiser, *Exploring Christian Holiness*, 27.

7. Christopher J. H. Wright, *The Mission of God: Unlocking the Bible's Grand Narrative* (Downers Grove: IVP Academic, 2006), 23.

8. Wright, *Mission of God*, 23.

to service in the kingdom of God with full authority (grounded in God)."[9] Rengstorf goes on to note that "the one who is sent is of interest only to the degree that in some measure he embodies in his existence as such the one who sends him."[10]

As to the purpose of mission, the words of Pope John Paul II remind us that "The ultimate purpose of mission is to enable people to share in the communion which exists between the Father and the Son."[11] This was the mission of Jesus Christ: to reconcile men and women to God. Whatever the church does, this ought to be its central mission, to ultimately present men and women to God "without stain or wrinkle or any other blemish, but holy and blameless" (Eph 5:27). For the apostle Paul and his co-workers, that was their reason for existence: "so that we may present everyone fully mature in Christ. To this end I strenuously contend with all the energy Christ so powerfully works in me" (Col 1:28–29).

The Old Testament Witness

The people of God in the Old Testament were chosen by God to be a blessing. When God called Abram he told him, "I will make of thee a great nation, and I will bless thee, and make thy name great; and be thou a blessing" (Gen 12:2 ASV). Abram was called specifically to be a blessing to the nations. God also said to Abram, "I am God Almighty; walk before me faithfully and be blameless" (Gen 17:1). There is no doubt that Abraham was to be holy/blameless and at the same time be a blessing to the nations. The children of Abraham, now the family of Jacob, moved to Egypt because of famine, and there they settled until Pharaoh, who had not known Joseph, came to power. Pharaoh oppressed these people (now known as the children of Israel), and they cried out to God, who came down to rescue them with a mighty hand. God called Moses to the task of leading these people from Egypt to the promised land. Through God's mighty hand, the people of Israel were freed from bondage, and when they got to Sinai, God formed a covenant with them. They now become the people of God in a way not known before in the history of God's relation to the world. God told them through Moses, "Now therefore, if ye will obey my voice indeed, and keep my covenant, then ye shall be mine own possession from among all

---

9. Karl Henrich Rengstorf, "apostoleo," in *Theological Dictionary of the New Testament* (Grand Rapids: Eerdmans, 1985), 406.

10. Rengstorf, "apostoleo," 406.

11. Pope John Paul II, *Redemptoris Missio*, 90.

peoples: for all the earth is mine: and ye shall be unto me a kingdom of priests, and a holy nation" (Exod 19:5–6 ASV). Purkiser's comment is worth noting: "While ethical and spiritual ideas are never completely absent, the major stress is on ceremonial cleanness."[12]

This passage links holiness and mission in a way not seen anywhere else in the Old Testament. Israel was to be a kingdom of priests and a holy nation. As priests, they were in a way doing the mission of God: representing the nations to God, and Yahweh to the nations. Israel preferred to be God's holy people and neglected the mission part of their calling. According to Kent Brower, "As soon as Israel began to see its separateness as an end in itself, the people's holiness became a barrier rather than a means to God's mission in the world."[13] Holiness was never intended to be a barrier for mission. It was in fact intended to facilitate the mission of God.

According to Gordon Thomas, "the mirroring of God . . . is a crucial aspect of the mission of the people of God."[14] He goes on to say that, "corporately, collectively, communally in their shared living, Israel is called to model the life of the Godhead, to live out the love and goodness and justice of God for the nations to see and be drawn to it. But they can only be a kingdom of priests in so far as they are also a holy nation"[15] J. C Rylaarsdam attests that "The essence of the covenant is the promise of God, backed by the gift of deliverance already given, that Israel will be his special possession and instrument . . . [a] promise [that] depends on the faithfulness and obedience of Israel."[16]

The prophet Isaiah's experience with the Holy God in Isaiah 6 is crucial for this discussion. Isaiah says, "And one called out to another and said, 'Holy, Holy, Holy, is the LORD of hosts, the whole earth is full of His glory' . . . Then I said, 'Woe is me, for I am ruined! Because I am a man of unclean lips. And I live among a people of unclean lips; for my eyes have seen the King, the LORD of hosts'" (Isa 6:3, 5 NASB).[17] After the prophet Isaiah lamented his condition, it was time for the Lord to act. Purkiser captures what happened succinctly.

---

12. Purkiser, *Exploring Christian Holiness*, 43–44.

13. Kent Brower, *Holiness in the Gospels* (Kansas City: Beacon Hill, 2005), 25.

14. Gordon J. Thomas, "A Holy God among a Holy People in a Holy Place: The Enduring Eschatological Hope," in *Eschatology in Bible and Theology*, ed. K. E. Brower and M. W. Elliott (Downers Grove, IL: InterVarsity, 1997), 59.

15. Thomas, "A Holy God," 60.

16. J. C. Rylaarsdam, "Revelation in Jewish Wisdom Literature," in Purkiser, *Exploring Christian Holiness*, 45.

17. Scripture marked NASB is taken from the New American Standard Bible®, Copyright © 1960, 1962, 1963, 1968, 1971, 1972, 1973, 1975, 1977, 1995 by The Lockman Foundation. Used by permission.

> When touched with the heavenly coal (v. 7), Isaiah's lips became his greatest asset... The cleansing of the lips symbolizes the purging of the heart: "Your iniquity is taken away, and your sin is forgiven" (v. 7, NASB, better, as KJV, "purged"; the term used literally means "covered, atoned for")... When the prophet's lips were touched, his ears were opened and he "heard the voice of the Lord saying, 'Whom shall I send? And who will go for us?'" His reply was immediate, "Here am I. Send me!"[18]

Here the link between holiness and mission is quite evident. Isaiah felt unclean, and YHWH responded by cleansing his lips. God followed that with a call for Isaiah to go; Isaiah was ready to go wherever God would send. Isaiah was sent to his people, who had neglected the covenant. The entire prophetic tradition demonstrates a loving God who reaches out to his people so that they can be his holy people, on his mission.

Morna Dorothy Hooker summarizes Israel's call: "God had called Israel to be his people and made a covenant with her. Now Israel is herself a covenant – the means of binding together God and the nations ... to open blind eyes, release prisoners, and establish justice on the earth."[19] However, Israel was not successful in becoming God's instrument in the world. Jeremiah and Ezekiel saw a time coming when God would make a new covenant, a covenant which would include even the Gentiles. Let us now turn to the New Testament to investigate the link between holiness and mission.

New Testament Witness

The New Testament is much clearer on the connection between holiness and mission. Jesus, who was sent from God, gathered men and women around him and sent them. The Gospel of John shows the clearest connection between holiness and mission. The shepherd's prayer of John 17 is important in this regard. Jesus's plans for the world are accomplished by the disciples; as his mission on earth ends, the disciples' mission is about to start.[20] J. Ramsey Michaels states on John 17, "Just like the Son glorifies and is glorified by the Father, so are the disciples to glorify the Son and be glorified by him ... The

---

18. Purkiser, *Exploring Christian Holiness*, 63.

19. Morna D. Hooker, "Be Holy as I Am Holy," in *Holiness and Mission: Learning from the Early Church about Mission in the City*, ed. Frances M. Young and Morna D. Hooker (Norwich: SCM, 2010), 4–19.

20. J. Ramsey Michaels, *John*, New International Commentary on the New Testament (Grand Rapids: Eerdmans, 2010), 865.

disciples of Jesus are also to be consecrated in the Truth of his Word (v. 17). This consecration is to make holy, and God is the one who does the consecration. He consecrated Jesus."[21] The connection between consecration and sending cannot be overlooked, especially in John 10:36: Jesus was set apart and sent into the world.[22]

In John's perspective the purpose of sanctification is mutual indwelling. Michaels observes, "The purpose of consecrating the disciples, or giving them glory, is indistinguishable from the purpose of the prayer itself: 'so that they might be one just as we are one – I in them and you in me – so that the world might know that you sent me and loved them just as you love me' (vv. 22b–23)."[23] Kent Brower's comment is worth noting: "Separation is important in the fourth Gospel, but it is not insulation from the world. Rather, it is essentially mission-related."[24] Mutuality and the relationality of the Trinity are related concepts, according to Brower: "The mutuality of the Holy Trinity has always been outward-looking, creative, and redemptive love . . . it is because 'God so loved the world that he gave his only Son' (3:16). God, whose holiness is expressed through his seeking love, has made it possible for his alienated creation to be brought back into that intended relationship with him."[25]

The New Testament witness is that salvation is not complete until men and women reflect the divine image. Brower asserts concerning the fourth Gospel, "Jesus does the work of the Father, fulfilling his purposes in the world and acting in complete unity with the Father. The consequences of mutuality for the disciples are the same. If the holiness of the triune God is manifest in his seeking love, the holiness of those who dwell in him will find expression in love for each other. Keeping the love commandment is the primary way in which the world will know of this mutual indwelling."[26]

In this case, what applies to Jesus is also true of his disciples; they can only be useful to the Master if they are in him, and he in them. It is important to note the temptation to inward-looking love; the Holy Trinity exists as a community of persons with an outward-looking love, and the disciples are to be outward-looking like their Lord.[27]

---

21. Michaels, *John*, 869–872.
22. Michaels, 872.
23. Michaels, 877.
24. Brower, *Holiness in the Gospels*, 79.
25. Brower, 79.
26. Brower, 79.
27. Brower, 80.

The book of Acts of the Apostles presents the Holy Spirit at work in the lives of the disciples of Jesus. On the day of Pentecost, the promised helper was given. His coming evokes memories of John's baptism – he will baptize with the Holy Spirit and fire. The Spirit of God does cleansing work, as well as empower for mission. Jesus, after his resurrection, said, "For John baptized with water, but in a few days you will be baptized with the Holy Spirit" (Acts 1:5). In Acts 2, Luke says that all of them were filled with the Holy Spirit; according to Purkiser, this "becomes a normal way of describing the spiritual endowment of believers . . . Baptism tends to emphasize the epochal or momentary aspect of the Spirit's work while 'fullness' tends to emphasize the ongoing or continuing ministry of the Spirit . . . Both fit the normal Christian experience."[28] Lawrence W. Wood captures the dual role of the Spirit when he says,

> The "power from on high" which Jesus promised to his disciples was divine energy (*dynamis*) which empowered them to live truly and completely as disciples and to become effective witnesses of God's reality in a hostile world. This power of the Holy Spirit is purifying power (Acts 15:8–9) which cleansed the disciples from . . . fears . . . and allowed them to be released from the threatening fear of their enemies. This "power from on high" was a power to love God truly and fully (Rom 5:5). No longer did they "follow afar off," but boldly and with deep devotion and commitment they became witnesses of their Lord. The power of the Holy Spirit given at Pentecost is the power to be true disciples (John 14 – 17).[29]

The church in Acts is a church on the move; this is seen after persecution. It is a church that is keen on hearing what God is doing and joining him, the church at Antioch being an example. As the Antiochene church prayed and worshiped, the Holy Spirit spoke: "Set apart for me Barnabas and Saul for the work to which I have called them" (Acts 13:2b). The church responded: "they placed their hands on them and sent them off" (Acts 13:3b). Pope John Paul says of these early Christians, "Underlying this missionary dynamism was the holiness of the first Christians and the first communities."[30] It was in Antioch that the first disciples were named Christians (those who act like Christ).

---

28. Purkiser, *Exploring Christian Holiness*, 107.

29. Laurence W. Wood, "Third Wave of the Spirit and the Pentecostalization of American Christianity: A Wesleyan Critique," *Wesleyan Theological Journal* 37, no. 1 (Spring 1996): 125.

30. Pope John Paul II, *Redemptoris Missio*, 48.

The letter of Peter also highlights the connection between mission and holiness. The apostle quotes from Exodus 19:5–6 when he says, "But you are a chosen people, a royal priesthood, a holy nation, God's special possession, that you may declare the praises of him who called you out of darkness into his wonderful light" (1 Pet 2:9). Peter is saying that what was true of Israel is now true for the church of Jesus Christ. The idea of being set apart for a task is clear; they are holy so that they can be a priesthood declaring the praises of him who called them from the darkness.

In conclusion, the Bible is clear that God created humankind in his image to exist in relationship with him. Sin disrupted that relationship, and God went out in search of humankind, starting in the garden of Eden. That is God's mission, and that mission is not complete until men and women reflect the divine image in all their relationships. Becoming like God is not an end in itself; once we become like him, he sends us out into the world that is in darkness. In essence, there is no dichotomy in Scripture between holiness and mission.

Toward a Theological Synthesis of Holiness and Mission

The nature of Christian mission demands that those who participate in it be holy as God is holy. The mission of God requires "resemblance to him – representing him accurately."[31] According to Clark Pinnock, "Spirituality is a vital part of witness. Each believer should focus on the power of God at work in his or her life and expect God to make him or her an instrument of the Kingdom. As the Spirit leads the church into mission, he leads each believer too. We need to be sensitive to divine appointments day by day."[32] It is important to note that the Spirit who gives guidance in mission is the one who makes holy. When the Spirit of God indwells an individual, that person becomes a temple of God, and the temple of God cannot be anything but holy. Pinnock goes on to state, "The goal is vocation and mission. We need the power of the Spirit to be disciples of Jesus Christ. We are chosen not to privilege but to service, to be God's partners in the mending of creation. For this, we need an abundant supply of power and spiritual gifting."[33]

Pope John Paul II remarked in his Encyclical Letter *Redemptoris Missio*, "Through holiness of life every Christian can become a fruitful part of the

---

31. Gordon Thomas, "A Holy God," in *Eschatology in Bible and Theology*, 68.
32. Clark Pinnock, *Flame of Love: A Theology of the Holy Spirit* (Downers Grove, IL: InterVarsity, 1996), 164.
33. Pinnock, *Flame of Love*, 171.

Church's mission."[34] He went on to quote the Second Vatican Council, which called all "to a profound interior renewal, so that having a lively awareness of their personal responsibility for the spreading of the Gospel, they may play their part in missionary work among the nations."[35]

Bryan Stone, in his paper "Christian Mission as Ecclesial Holiness," declares emphatically that "Christian missiology is fundamentally ecclesiology, and . . . the most missional thing the church can do today is to be the church – to live together as a worshiping, reconciling, forgiving, non-violent, compassionate, just and inclusive community that bears visible, embodied and corporate witness to God's reign in public. It is thus the very shape and character of the faith community as God's 'new creation' that is the source and aim of Christian mission."[36] He continues:

> Because the formation of a "people" with distinctive character is so central in this understanding of the *missio Dei*, I believe that we should talk about Christian mission as ecclesial holiness . . . The waning of modernity and the crumbling of Christendom, however, afford us an opportunity to rethink holiness in fresh, new ways – ways that take seriously the fundamental role of the faith community as the embodied locus of holiness and the (theologically) prior reality out of which both personal and social holiness make any proper sense . . . It is out of calling to be a people that mission arises.[37]

Concerning the missionaries who participate in the mission of God, Pope John Paul urged, "The renewed impulse to the mission *ad gentes* demands holy missionaries . . . What is needed is the encouragement of a new 'ardor for holiness' among missionaries and throughout the Christian community."[38] Here John Paul II was using the term "missionaries" in a narrow way, referring to those who do cross-cultural mission work. We argue here that all God's people have a missional reason for existence, not just a few who do mission work in a culture other than their own.[39] What Pope John Paul says about the missionary applies to every Christian:

---

34. John Paul II, *Redemptoris Missio*, 41.

35. John Paul II, 41.

36. Bryan Stone, "Christian Mission as Ecclesial Holiness," paper presented at Global Nazarene Theology Conference (Guatemala City, 2002), 1.

37. Stone, "Christian Mission," 1.

38. John Paul II, *Redemptoris Missio*, 48.

39. Wright, *Mission of God*, 25.

> The missionary is a person of the Beatitudes. Before sending out the Twelve to evangelize, Jesus, in his "missionary discourse" (cf. Mt 10), teaches them the paths of mission: poverty, meekness, acceptance of suffering and persecution, the desire for justice and peace, charity – in other words, the Beatitudes, lived out in the apostolic life (cf. Mt 5:1–12). By living the Beatitudes, the missionary experiences and shows concretely that the kingdom of God has already come, and that he has accepted it.[40]

The Christian does not only use words to represent the kingdom of God; he or she also embodies the kingdom. The embodiment of the kingdom of God is nothing short of holiness or holy living. Following this argument, we can conclude that every Christian is a missionary, always active and not passive.

The mission of God also entails upholding and defending the values for which the kingdom stands. Such values include justice, mercy, and loving our enemies. The holy people of God should "act justly and . . . love mercy and . . . walk humbly with [their] God" (Mic 6:8b). The apostle James combines practical religion with consecration when he says, "Religion that God our Father accepts as pure and faultless is this: to look after orphans and widows in their distress and to keep oneself from being polluted by the world" (Jas 1:27). The question of whether evangelism or compassion should take priority should never arise when the people of God are living like their Father who is in heaven.

Let us now turn to an assessment of the African church concerning holiness and mission.

The African Church in Light of Holiness and Mission

The African church south of the Sahara was established as a result of the nineteenth-century missionary movement in which missionaries, mostly from Europe and North America, established mission stations on the African continent. At that time Africa was considered a mission field and hence missionaries came not from Africa but from the West, to the extent that in most countries in Africa even today, a missionary is equated to a *muzungu* ("white person" in Kiswahili). This is an area which missiologists need to explore to see how the African church can change this perception and recognize those men and women who serve God in cultures other than their own. This section

---

40. John Paul II, *Redemptoris Missio*, 49.

of the paper explores issues which confront the African church affecting its ability to be a missional–holiness church.

Much has been written on the African church and negative ethnicity.[41] In some countries, this is a heritage the church received from the missionary enterprise. Most denominations ended up working in a particular ethnic community, to the extent that the denomination became a tribal church. Stephen Mutuku Sesi refers to these churches as "church tribes."[42] Sesi reports that in Kenya the church took sides, and even contributed to the causes of ethnic clashes. A pastor is reported to have affirmed that it was right for people to have been "killed and displaced in Rift Valley Province over the December 2007 election results."[43] Even though missionaries divided and shared territories according to denominational lines, that reality ought not to exist in the church today. The African church cannot continue to do what it knows is a contradiction to the life Jesus calls the church to live. The church has to portray in its leadership structures that it is a church for all people, not just for those of a particular tribe or community. A "church tribe" cannot be a holy–missional church, and neither can it reconcile a divided nation.

People have died in tribal clashes, religious wars, and civil wars, in some parts of Africa on a daily basis. Fighting for resources is the most common cause of conflict in Africa,[44] and the church has been shown to be an active participant even in these activities. Churches have created militias of their own in some of these conflicts, as Neils Kastfelt points out concerning the civil war in Eastern Nigeria of the 1960s: "Churches . . . played an active role in the war. Roman Catholic missionaries stayed with their parishes in the war zones inside Biafra, organizing fasts and prayer meetings and reporting to

---

41. The issue of tribal church has been written about in Kenya, South Africa, and Angola: Leonard Verduin, "The Great South African Divide," *Reformed Journal* 20, no. 6 (July 1970): 13–15, accessed 23 January 2016, ATLA Religion Database with ATLASerials, EBSCOhost; Lawrence W. Henderson, "Protestantism: A Tribal Religion: Ethnic Units of the Protestant Churches in Angola," in *Windows on Africa: A Symposium* (Leiden: Brill, 1971), 61–80, accessed 23 January 2016, ATLA Religion Database with ATLASerials, EBSCOhost; Robert T. Parsons, "Toward One People: A Study of Ethnic Relations in Eleven African Churches in Nairobi, Kenya," in *Windows on Africa*, 133–175.

42. Sesi adds that "the Methodist Church is dominant among the Meru people, Legio Maria is dominant among the Luo, and Africa Inland Church is greatly associated with the Akamab and Kalenjin tribes. The Presbyterian Church of East Africa and the Kenya Assemblies of God are associated with the Kikuyu tribe, and the Seventh Day Adventists are largely associated with the Kisii tribe." Stephen Mutuku Sesi, "Ethnic Realities and the Church in Kenya," in *African Missiology: Contribution to Contemporary Thought* (Nairobi: Uzima, 2009), 27.

43. Sesi, "Ethnic Realities," 26.

44. Stephen Mutuku Sesi, "Ethnic Conflicts in Africa: Underlying Paradigms," in *African Missiology*, 2.

the outside world on conditions there."[45] The situation was no different in the Rwandan genocide, in which Rwandese Christians took part, and in which approximately 800,000 people were killed. Priests are said to have identified those who were to be killed and presided over masses to pray for them before going on to kill.[46] While the New Testament has much to say about non-violent resistance to evil (Rom 12:17–21), this clearly has not been the response of the church in some parts of Africa. A church that forms militias cannot claim to be in the mission of Jesus, who called his followers to pray for their enemies.

Africa suffers from the problem of bad governance; those in political office steal resources from the state coffers without regard for the *mwananchi* (ordinary citizen). Africa, a continent endowed with many resources, is home to some of the world's poorest people who live on less than a dollar a day. Paradoxically, Africa also has very wealthy people who keep their money – some of it looted from the government – in foreign bank accounts. The gap between the rich and the poor is enormous. The African church has remained silent despite such injustices inflicted by the business class and political elite. George Kinoti perceptively comments, "the African church continues to contribute substantially to bad governance. She does so mostly by default, through silence and inaction. Silence in effect means approval of the regime in power or specific political actions. Failure to resist evil means accepting evil, with all the consequences."[47] The church in Africa should realize that its mission is not just evangelization but entails the transformation of the social order. Andrew J. Kirk speaks to this issue when he observes, "The church is called . . . to be an anticipation of the kingdom; to show in its internal life the values of justice and supportive love."[48]

Recently, African pastors have made trips to Nigeria and Ghana in order to get healing powers.[49] In September 2014, 116 people, the majority of whom were South Africans, died when a building they were in collapsed. It is reported

---

45. Niels Kastfelt, "Religion and African Civil Wars: Themes and Interpretations," in *Religion and African Civil Wars*, ed. Niels Kastfelt (London: Hurst & Co., 2005), 3–4.

46. Timothy Longman, "Churches and Social Upheaval in Rwanda and Burundi," in *Religion and African Civil Wars*, 86.

47. George Kinoti, *Hope for Africa and What the Christian Can Do* (Nairobi: AISRED, 1994), 40.

48. Andrew J. Kirk, *What Is Mission? Explorations* (Minneapolis: Fortress, 2000), 36.

49. Rachel Ncube, "Fetish: 1700 Pastors and Prophets Visits [*sic*] Ghana's Sangoma for Supernatural Powers," *9ja Informant*, 23 February 2013, https://9jainformant.wordpress.com/2013/02/23/1700-pastors-and-prophets-visits-ghanas-sangoma-for-supernatural-powers/.

that they had visited the prophet T. B. Joshua to receive the powers he has.[50] Sesi says that "One church leader is known to have been carrying his power object (a big snake in a briefcase) from his indigenous belief to church, to draw a large congregation and outsmart his competitors while preaching to his congregation to believe in miracles from Jesus."[51] Church leaders in Africa feel the pressure to solve all the problems which come their way in the same manner the medicine men did in traditional Africa. As a result, they resort to anything that can help them meet the demands of their office. Such practices are not consistent with a holy-missional church.

Related to this issue is the use of evangelistic methods which are designed to be attractive to the audience, particularly the youth. A Nairobi pastor was quoted saying, "We want to connect with teens using the language they are using. We always start with where people are in culture, and we lead them to where God wants them to be."[52] This was in response to a controversial poster the church had produced to advertise its program "Sex Conversation." Most people in church and even outside were outraged by this, considering it as going too far to make the gospel attractive to a pagan culture. Even as the church seeks to be relevant, it should not become like the world it seeks to reach. Kirk asserts that, ultimately, *missio Dei* must also be *missio Christi*, and "following in the way of Jesus Christ (discipleship) is the test of missionary faithfulness."[53] Any mission endeavors which do not start with discipleship are wrong-headed.

We have pointed out issues to do with negative ethnicity, tribal clashes, bad governance, syncretism, and unchristian methods of evangelism. These behaviors are not in conformity with what it means to be a holiness–missional church. God embraces all people; those who are like God – that is, holy people – do not discriminate against those who are not from their tribe, and neither will they desire that anything bad should happen to them. Issues of social justice ought to be of concern to the church of Jesus Christ. A holiness church cannot mix in elements from African traditional religions if it is to follow Jesus Christ faithfully; it must embrace those elements which do not contradict its commitment to Christ, and it must set aside those elements which are in contradiction with following Christ. As the church reaches out to those who

---

50. Samson Omale, "Pastor TB Joshua Expected in Court over Nigeria Collapse," n.d., Eyewitness News, http://ewn.co.za/2015/11/30/TB-Joshua-expected-to-appear-in-court.

51. Sesi, "Ethnic Realities and the Church in Kenya," 31.

52. "Mavuno Church Defends 'Explicit' Poster," n.d., *Daily Nation*, http://mobile.nation.co.ke/counties/Church-defends-explicit-poster/-/1950480/2220590/-/format/xhtml/-/ufe9av/-/index.html.

53. Kirk, *What Is Mission?*, 39.

do not know Christ, the end does not justify the means; the means we use to draw people to Christ must not contradict the gospel of Christ. Our methods of evangelism must be compatible with the gospel.

The above portrayal of the African church seems gloomy. However, just as in all places where the church is or has been, God still has his people. There are those who have not bowed down to the Baal in the African church; they follow Christ as best they can. A few bad apples do not mean the whole sack should be thrown away; we need to address the bad elements in the church so that the church of Jesus Christ can truly be a holy–missional church. Those who malign the name of Christ are still part of our story and so we should care about what they do in the name of Christ. To use Warren Carter's words, the church ought to present itself as an alternative community.[54]

Conclusion

Holiness and mission are like Siamese twins; you cannot separate one from the other without losing both. The Bible testifies to this connection, starting in the Old Testament, the people of Israel, and continuing in the New Testament, the church of Jesus Christ. We are called to be holy and at the same time are sent on a mission. God is our example; he is a holy God on a mission. Some practices in the African church are not consistent with a holy-missional church. This is not to say that the African church is not holy or that it is not missional, but there are issues that need to be addressed so that it can truly be the bride of Christ. "As the Father has sent me, I am sending you" (John 20:21).

Practical Recommendations for the Church

In light of the discussion in this paper, the following are some practical recommendations for the church in Africa, which could also apply to the universal church.

1. The church needs to uphold both holiness and mission; we ought not to pursue one at the expense of the other.

2. The church should realize that being holy is not an end in itself; we are not to be holy for the sake of being holy. We are to be holy so that we can join God on his mission.

---

54. Warren Carter, *The Roman Empire and the New Testament: An Essential Guide* (Nashville, TN: Abingdon, 2006).

3. Evangelism is essential for the fulfillment of *missio Dei*. However, it is only a part of it. *Missio Dei* involves a transformation of the social order. The church should address structures that oppress and keep people in poverty.

4. The church needs to demonstrate its commitment to holiness by the kind of community it is; this means that the church cannot be an exclusive community, but should be an all-inclusive community that embraces all, regardless of tribe and race.

5. The African church should present not only the doctrine of justification but that of sanctification as well. We should proclaim not only the forgiveness of sins but also the cleansing which God offers to those who come to him.

6. As we disciple men and women, we should ensure that biblical stewardship is taught properly. Proper stewardship teaching will result in Christians who commit themselves and their resources to the *missio Dei*, rather than buying into the materialism and consumerism of the day.

Bibliography

Brower, Kent. *Holiness in the Gospels*. Kansas City: Beacon Hill Press, 2005.
Carter, Warren. *The Roman Empire and the New Testament: An Essential Guide*. Nashville, TN: Abingdon, 2006.
Henderson, Lawrence W. "Protestantism: A Tribal Religion: Ethic Units of the Protestant Church in Angola." In *Windows on Africa: A Symposium*, 61–80. Leiden: Brill, 1971. Accessed 23 January 2016, ATLA Religion Database with ATLASerials, EBSChost.
Hooker, Morna. "Be Holy as I am Holy." In *Holiness and Mission*, edited by Frances Young and Morna Hooker, 4–19. Norwich: SCM Press, 2010.
Kastfelt, Niels. "Religion and African Civil Wars: Themes and Interpretations." In *Religion and African Civil Wars*, edited by Niels Kastfelt, 1–27. London: Hurst & Co., 2005.
Kinoti, George. *Hope for Africa and What the Christian Can Do*. Nairobi: AISRED, 1994.
Kirk, Andrew J. *What Is Mission? Explorations*. Minneapolis: Fortress, 2000.
Longman, Timothy. "Churches and Social Upheaval in Rwanda and Burundi." In *Religion and African Civil Wars*, edited by Niels Kastfelt, 82–101. London: Hurst & Co., 2005.
"Mavuno Church Defends 'explicit' Poster," n.d. http://mobile.nation.co.ke/counties/Church-defends-explicit-poster/-/1950480/2220590/-/format/xhtml/-/ute9av/-/index.html.
Michaels, J. Ramsey. *John*. The New International Commentary on the New Testament. Grand Rapids: Eerdmans, 2010.

Muilenberg, James. "Holiness." *The Interpreters Dictionary of the Bible*, edited by George Arthur Buttrick, 616–625. Nashville: Abingdon, 1962.

Mutuku Sesi, Stephen. "Ethnic Conflicts in Africa: Underlying Paradigms." In *African Missiology Contributions of Contemporary Thought*, edited by Caleb Chul-Soo Kim. Nairobi: Uzima Press, 2009.

———. "Ethnic Realities and the Church in Kenya." In *African Missiology: Contributions of Contemporary Thought*. Nairobi: Uzima, 2009.

Ncube, Rachel. "Fetish: 1700 Pastors and Prophets Visits Ghana's Sangoma for Supernatural Powers." *9ja Informant* (blog). 23 February 2013. https://9jainformant.wordpress.com/2013/02/23/1700-pastors-and-prophets-visits-ghanas-sangoma-for-supernatural-powers/.

Omale, Samson. "Pastor TB Joshua Expected in Court over Nigeria Collapse," n.d. Eyewitness News. http://ewn.co.za/2015/11/30/TB-Joshua-expected-to-appear-in-court.

Parsons, Robert T. "Towards One People: A Study of Ethnic Relations in Eleven African Churches in Nairobi Kenya." In *Windows on Africa*, 133–175. Leiden: Brill, 1971.

Paul, John. *Redemptoris Missio*. Encyclical letter on the permanent validity of the church's missionary mandate, Vatican Website, 7 December 1990. http://www.rcan.org/evangelization/Redem_Missio_JPII.pdf.

Pinnock, Clark. *Flame of Love: A Theology of the Holy Spirit*. Downers Grove, IL: InterVarsity, 1996.

Purkiser, W. T. *Exploring Christian Holiness*. 3 vols. Kansas City: Beacon Hill Press, 1983.

Rengstorf, Karl Henrich. "Apostoleo." In *Theological Dictionary of the New Testament*, 398–447. Grand Rapids: Eerdmans, 1985.

Stone, Bryan. "Christian Mission as Ecclesial Holiness." Paper presented at Global Nazarene Theology Conference, Guatemala City, 2002.

Thomas, Gordon J. "A Holy God among a Holy People in a Holy Place: The Enduring Eschatological Hope." In *Eschatology in Bible and Theology*, edited by Kent E. Brower and Mark W. Elliot, 53–69. Downers Grove, IL: InterVarsity, 1997.

Verduin, Leonard. "The Great South African Divide." *Reformed Journal* 20, no. 6 (July 1970): 13–15. Accessed 23 January 2016, ATLA Religion Database with ATLASerials, EBSCOhost.

Wood, Laurence W. "Third Wave of the Spirit and the Pentecostalization of American Christianity: A Wesleyan Critique." *Wesleyan Theological Journal* 37, no. 1 (Spring 1996): 110–140.

Wright, Christopher J. H. *The Mission of God: Unlocking the Bible's Grand Narrative*. Downers Grove, IL: IVP Academic, 2006.

2

A Theology of Spiritual Power in African Christianity

Johana Kariuki Gitau
Doctoral Student, International Leadership University, Nairobi, Kenya

Abstract

When formulating an African Christian theology, the concept of spiritual power is an important issue. This paper gives a brief analysis of that concept and looks at how the biblical issues of power can be contextualized in African Christianity. This is done with an African traditional worldview and a Western missionary background in mind. When we talk of spiritual power (sometimes referred to as mystical power), we are referring to the ability to perform certain acts which are beyond the scope of a normal human being in the natural setting of scientific explanations. These acts can only be explained in terms of the supernatural.

Key words: power, African Christian theology, Western missions, worldview, magic, charms, spirits.

Introduction

When formulating an African Christian theology, the concept of spiritual power is one important issue which should be thoroughly addressed if the theology is to make a meaningful impact in the lives of Africans. This paper briefly analyzes the concept of spiritual power as seen in the African worldview and as expressed in the Bible. The purpose is to look at how the biblical principles concerning issues of power can be contextualized in an African environment which has been dominated by an animistic concept of power for many centuries.

It is important to note that African peoples have their own established forms of religion and culture which took centuries to develop and are therefore deeply rooted among them. The practices of religion do vary from place to place and from one tribe to another within the continent of Africa, but, in spite of this heterogeneity, we can still make general observations of the concept of power which we can use as representative of the African Traditional Religion (ATR). Examples from different parts of the continent reflect a general view of the spirit world which forms the backbone of the concept of mystical power within the African worldview.

Missionaries who came to the African continent from a Euro-American background between the eighteenth and the twentieth centuries had their own conceptions of power which were influenced by their Western Christian theology. This theology had also been developed over a long period of time in an environment completely different from that of the Africans they were trying to Christianize. As a result, the Western theology which had been tailored to address the needs and aspirations of the Westerners failed to adequately address African needs, especially in the area of spirituality. The missionaries tried to impose their Western way of looking at theology onto the Africans, who either rejected it altogether, embraced it as a whole and unquestioningly, or syncretized it with what they already knew. Hence the African Christians adopted an approach of exclusivism, inclusivism, or universalism.

The exclusivists reject African traditions and religion in their totality and prefer the Western style of theology and culture. The inclusivists have adopted Western theology but tend to look at biblical revelation as a fulfillment of African hopes and aspirations. The universalists hold that all religions, including Christianity and ATR, are just different expressions of a person's relationship with the supreme God, such that none can justly claim superiority over the others. Though they don't reject biblical Christianity, the universalists are more concerned about the unity of humanity than the clarity of doctrine. It is in light of these views that we examine the African concept of power in the context of the changing phenomena of world religiosity and especially the Christian impact on the continent.

African Worldview

The African view concerning the world of the spirits is very different from the Western view. Systematic theology in the West is based on a two-tier dualistic perspective which developed from early Greek philosophy. This perspective has two spheres: the supernatural and the natural. The supernatural is addressed in religious terms while the natural is addressed in scientific terms. These two are separate and compartmentalized in the Western worldview. The African understanding is very different. In the African worldview the supernatural and the natural are joined together by the sphere of the spirits, a one-tier monopolistic perspective. There is no clear-cut demarcation between the supernatural and the natural. Hence, power can flow freely from the supernatural to the natural as long as certain religious functions are performed properly. Western Christian theology has failed to address this middle zone of spirituality, thereby failing to adequately theologize an important area in the African concept of Christianity.

One issue in this area which needs to be properly addressed is power. We shall limit ourselves to what is sometimes referred to as mystical power. John Mbiti observes that, when it comes to the issue of mystical power among African Christians, there are two camps: there are those who ignore and belittle mystical power, and there are those who pay attention to African views, fears, uses, and manipulation of power.[1] This depends on the influence of the Western missionaries who evangelized the continent. When we talk of mystical powers we are referring to the ability to perform certain acts which are beyond the scope of a normal human being in the natural setting. These are activities beyond scientific explanations which can be explained only in terms of the supernatural. As Idowu Bolaji observes: "Man has been confronted with a sense of need with which he knows that his own unaided power cannot cope. The complications and riddles of life have been such as urge upon him the need for succor, for deliverance, and for mastery over environmental circumstances . . . He recognizes that behind phenomena is a power 'wholly other' than himself."[2]

Members of African traditional culture have tended to interact with this power, which is not strange to them. Mbiti stresses that every African who has grown up in the traditional culture will no doubt know something about this mystical power. The power manifests itself in the form of magic, divination, witchcraft, and mysterious phenomena that seem to defy even immediate

---

1. John S. Mbiti, *African Religions and Philosophy* (London: Heinemann, 1969), 194.
2. E. B. Idowu, *African Traditional Religion: A Definition* (London: SCM, 1973), 189.

scientific explanations.³ However, Geoffrey Parrinder observes that the use of mystical powers is found in every country of the world and is not limited to Africa.⁴ Our interest here is to see how and why this mystical power is used in Africa.

It is important to note that the concept of deity and religion in the African context is utilitarian. By this we mean that Africans worship the deity not for the sake of the deity but for what they can gain from the deity. In the same way, the mystical powers are utilized by Africans for their personal benefit. Africans have therefore learnt to relate to these powers in a way that helps them to achieve their goals. They will either yield to the powers in religious submission or manipulate them in magical performance. Hence, for Africans, religion is a matter of a reciprocal relationship between a human being and the deity for the fulfillment of personal needs, whether spiritual or material. "Religion implies trust, dependence, and submission . . . magic is an attempt by man to tap and control the supernatural resources of the universe for his own benefit."⁵

John Mbiti states that mystical power is not a fiction but a reality which Africans have had to reckon with.⁶ He argues that Western systematic theology has failed to address a real-life issue, and that the missionaries could not really reach the African heart without addressing this pertinent question. He narrates several stories and African myths that authenticate this power concept, adding that "There is mystical power which causes people to walk on fire, to lie on thorns and nails, to send curses to harm, including death, from a distance, to change into animals, to spit on snakes and cause them to split open and die; power to stupefy thieves so that they can be caught red-handed . . ."⁷ This could be the case in a phenomenological sense but may not necessarily be so on the ontological plane.

What is this mystical power? It has already been stated that it is power beyond normal human ability. It is power that transcends the scientific laws of nature as understood in the West. Such powers are not attributed to the sovereign God or the Supreme Being in the African context, but to lesser spirits. These spirits can be good or bad, benevolent or malevolent, controllable

---

3. Mbiti, *African Religions and Philosophy*, 194.
4. Geoffrey Parrinder, *West African Religion* (London: Epworth, 1949), 156.
5. Idowu, *African Traditional Religion*, 190.
6. Mbiti, *African Religions and Philosophy*, 198.
7. Mbiti, 197.

or uncontrollable, but nevertheless they have the ability to do things and to make things happen.

Mystical power is expressed in different ways. It can be used for good or bad purposes and the motive behind the use of mystical power reflects a war-like attitude where one is either on the offensive or the defensive. Here we can talk of spiritual warfare. In the African context, people are not only physical beings but also spiritual creatures. They are therefore connected with the living dead, the ancestral spirits, other spirits, and the Supreme Deity in a spiritual sense. For this reason, the concept of intermediaries is widespread in African society. People feel unable to approach the Supreme Being or higher spirits alone or directly, so must do so through the mediation of special people or special spirits who are higher than them in the spiritual hierarchy. Such mediatorial roles are performed by priests, prophets, seers, witches, sorcerers, medicine men, rainmakers, diviners, necromancers, elders, kings, ancestors, and perhaps some animals or even inanimate objects. The mediators are said to have the ability to venture into the realm of the spirits on behalf of individuals and either plead their course or manipulate the spirit world, which comprises demons, the living dead, or other spirits. Medicine men, elders, kings, and rainmakers interact with the spirit world for the benefit of society, while witches and necromancers serve destructive purposes. Diviners and ancestral spirits can be used for either harmful or helpful purposes, depending on the circumstances and beliefs of a particular society.

Africans are so sensitive to the spiritual world that they must always protect themselves. The use of charms is therefore extensive, whether for offensive or defensive purposes. Noel King states that "charms are batteries for storage of power (*tumi*) that comes from the spirit of the materials from which the charms are made."[8] The charms are often made by the intermediaries and are offered to the people either for protection or for attack. Geoffrey Parrinder observes that witches and sorcerers use things like bones, hair, nails, spittle, sweat, urine, sleeping mats, dirty clothes, and sticks for offensive purposes to cause harm.[9] Other things used as charms include skins, metals, beads, stones, leaves, necklaces, and coins. Some charms, sometimes called talismans, are worn on the body for protection, while others are placed in strategic positions in the homestead to protect it. Witches may plant certain charms in homesteads to destroy those homes. On the positive side, mystical power can be utilized for curative, preventive, and productive purposes.

---

8. Noel Q. King, *African Cosmos* (Belmont, CA: Wadsworth, 1986), 73.
9. Geoffrey Parrinder, *West African Religion* (London: Epworth Press, 1949), 163.

An African Christian man may have been converted through evangelization by Western missionaries who either ignored or discarded these beliefs in mystical powers. He still struggles with his African background and the new concepts he has acquired. He has an African worldview but is also supposed to look at issues from a Western perspective. He is therefore not sure what to believe and keeps oscillating from Western theology to African Traditional Religion and back, depending on the circumstances. He might trust Jesus for physical healing, and apply Western medication, but when this does not seem to work he will revert to the traditional healer, who invokes the spirit world. He uses whichever option seems most convenient to serve his purpose. This switching between the two worlds does not augur well for Christianity; a solution is to seek and apply a biblical perspective that is neither Western nor African, but which is authoritatively universal for all people everywhere.

Biblical Worldview

The concept of power in the Bible has a close relationship with the African view of power. The Bible acknowledges God as the sovereign, transcendent power above every other being. God is the creator while every other thing is created. God is therefore the source of all power, but he also delegates some power to created beings, including angels and human beings. God created things by the power of his word whereby he said, "Let there be . . ." and things came into being.

All power is used at God's discretion, and as the ruler and controller of all things he determines the course of life and nature. He is the Lord over all, whether natural or supernatural. God allows power to be exercised by created beings, but only to a certain extent. We can sometimes see spiritual beings doing things that exceed the natural course of events; for example, angels were given the responsibility to guard the garden of Eden. Human beings have a level of power they can freely exercise, but we also see that they have limitations. Power variations between human and spiritual beings are obvious, but they are all subject to the sovereign power of God.

Many scriptural passages talk about power, but we will look at just a few to see how we can formulate a biblical theology of power within the African context. In Exodus 8:19, the magicians of Pharaoh recognized that there was a power beyond that which they were used to manipulating, saying, "This is the finger of God." Pharaoh had juridical authority over the Egyptians but he consulted his magicians in that polemical war between Yahweh and the gods of Egypt (Exod 7:1–13). Hence we realize that God recognized the existence of these other powers, but that they are inferior to him and human beings should not worship them. We should worship only God: "I will send the full force of my plagues . . . so you may know that there is no one like me in all the earth" (Exod 9:14). God wrought the miraculous signs in Egypt to show his power so that his name would be proclaimed in all the earth (Exod 9:16).

Proverbs 3:27 acknowledges that human beings have some power to do good to others which they should not hold back. The psalmist calls upon the Lord not to forsake him until he has declared the Lord's power and might to the next generation. He states that the Lord is great, mighty, and powerful, with an unlimited understanding (Ps 147:5). Moses commanded the Israelites to remember the Lord their God, for it was he who gave them the ability to produce wealth (Deut 8:18). We read that the Lord made the earth by his power, wisdom, and understanding (Jer 51:15). Zerubbabel was to accomplish the building of the temple "Not by might nor by power [physical], but by my Spirit" (Zech 4:6), according to the word of God. We should therefore not rely on human strength to accomplish spiritual missions.

In Matthew 22:29, Jesus said that people make mistakes because they don't know the Scriptures or the power of God. The context was the question of the resurrection posed by the Sadducees who didn't believe in the resurrection of the dead. Their beliefs were based on wrong presuppositions about God. In Mark 13:26, we read that the Son of Man will be seen coming in the clouds with great power and glory at his second coming. Jesus gave his disciples power and authority to drive out demons, cure diseases (Luke 9:1), and overcome all the power of the enemy, Satan (Luke 10:19). In Acts 1:8 Jesus promised the Holy Spirit, who would give the disciples power to become effective witnesses; and so "with great power the apostles continued to testify to the resurrection of the Lord Jesus. And God's grace was so powerfully at work in them all" (Acts 4:33). Jesus had God's anointing and power that enabled him to heal all those who were under the devil's power. A man by the name of Simon, who used to practice sorcery, was referred to by people as "the Great Power of God" (Acts 8:10). In Romans 8:38 Paul reckons that there is nothing, not even spiritual powers, that can separate him from the love of Christ.

Paul says he preached by the power of the Holy Spirit which helped him to do signs and wonders (Rom 15:19). He also recognizes the administrative power of government officials, saying that they should be respected (Rom 13:1; Titus 3:1). Of course, this shows that power can be defined in terms other than spiritual. To Paul, the kingdom of God is not a matter of mere talk but a question of power (1 Cor 4:20). He stresses that believers are involved in spiritual warfare against powers in high places, and that they have weapons not of this world which have divine power to demolish the strongholds of their opponents' power (2 Cor 10:4–5; Eph 6:10–12). There are evil powers of darkness with a spiritual nature in the heavenly realms, which Christians are to fight against (Eph 6:12). Those who continue in sin are under the bondage of the power of the spirits of darkness and of the ruler of the kingdom of the air, who is a spirit of disobedience (Eph 2:2). In Revelation 9:5, 10, 19, we see God giving power to certain creatures to perform particular destructive activities upon the earth.

One thing that is clear from the Bible is that there are powers higher than the natural forces. However, these powers are subject to God and should not be misused by human beings. People are to worship God with reverence for him alone, but not in fear of, or by mediation through, these powers.

An African Biblical Worldview

Given that the biblical worldview concurs with the African worldview, as opposed to the Western worldview, concerning the existence of powers, we can develop an African theology based on biblical principles which addresses the African traditional view concerning the mystical powers. We should start from the understanding that both the African and the biblical worldviews have a one-tier concept of life in which the supernatural is not dichotomously separated from the natural. The two worldviews may differ strongly on how to interact with the spirit world, but we can start from the one point of agreement on its existence.

The African Christian should understand that, unlike in the traditional context, where God was distant and far off, necessitating the mediation of spirits, the Bible reckons that God, though transcendent, is nevertheless very close to human beings, such that they can have close, intimate fellowship. Tokunboh Adeyemo observes:

> To the Biblical worshipper, God is not some far-off deity, too high and holy to take notice of him. Rather, He is his father who has demonstrated his love by reaching out through wonders and mighty works and prescribed sacrificial systems in the Old Testament and finally in his son Jesus Christ in the New Testament, sanctifying and building up his own family, a royal priesthood, and a holy nation, and accepting them into the beloved through Jesus Christ their High Priest.[10]

---

10. Tokunboh Adeyemo, *Salvation in African Tradition* (Nairobi: Evangel, 1997), 46.

With the God-human being relationship so close, the use of mediator powers becomes unnecessary. We have already mentioned the African concept of power in terms of utilitarian values. It was in pursuit of these values that Africans found God unable to be manipulated and so resorted to lesser powers. The biblical view is that men and women should live in faith and obedience to God, worshiping God for who he is and not for what they can gain from him. However, God is not a mean but a loving God, and so he will bless those who are faithful and obedient. We cannot use faith and obedience to purchase God's blessings, but we should expect them as the promises of a trustworthy God. Africans seemed to lack the patience of waiting for God's blessings at his discretion, instead wanting to cajole him if possible through the lesser spirits. This reflects the anthropocentric nature of African worship, which tried by all means possible to make the supernatural power beneficial for human interests.

Biblical theology is God-centered, and human beings are to serve God rather than be served by God. There is a need for Africans to change their attitude toward God and to make allowance for his supreme will to be done. Instead of resorting to lesser powers, Africans must learn to adjust themselves to God's sovereign power. Here the issue of our sinful nature arises. The African people are as sinful by nature as is any other race, hence Scripture is proved right when it says that all have sinned and fall short of the glory of God (Rom 3:23). It is because of this sinful nature that traditional African culture resorted to spiritism by way of witchcraft and magic.

In the Bible, God warned the Israelites against spiritism, stating that such practices were not only an abomination but would hinder fellowship between him and them. In Deuteronomy 18:9–13 the Lord said to his chosen people:

> When you enter the land the LORD your God is giving you, do not learn to imitate the detestable ways of the nations there. Let no one be found among you who sacrifices their son or daughter in the fire, who practices divination or sorcery, interprets omens, engages in witchcraft, or casts out spells, or who is a medium or spiritist or who consults the dead. Anyone who does these things is detestable to the LORD; because of these same detestable practices the LORD your God will drive out those nations before you. You must be blameless before the LORD your God.

It is explicitly clear that the Lord abhors spiritism, and African Christians must adjust in accordance with the standards of the Bible rather than try to use the Bible as another charm in their manipulation of the deity.

How, then, can we contextualize biblical theology in the African situation? The answer lies not in denying the existence of mystical power, but in countering it on the basis of biblical theology. Jesus never denied the existence of these powers but he combated them, freeing many demoniacs, advising his disciples on how to face them, and even assuring them of victory against the powers. When commissioning the disciples, Jesus said he had all authority in heaven and on earth (Matt 28:18), and that he was building his church, against which the gates of hell would not prevail (Matt 16:18).

Biblical worship is directed to God alone, and in Old Testament times no sacrifices were to be offered to other spirits. The once-for-all sufficient sacrifice of Christ on the cross is enough for New Testament believers. Thus African Christians must discard the idea of sacrificing to spirits and other mediators, as this is contrary to the Bible. Instead, the easier and only acceptable way of worship is to worship God in truth and spirit, as stated in John 4:24. The first of the Ten Commandments was that Israel should not have any other god; the second was that they should not worship any idol, for this would provoke God's jealousy (Exod 20:3–4).

The African use of charms is a form of idolatry in which the charm is believed to have some power either to harm or to protect. The Bible states that nobody except the true God – not even good or evil spirits – should be worshiped. Seeking the mediation of charms is worshiping them, for it is recognizing their authority over some other person or being. Even the angel of the Lord commanded John not to bow to him on the island of Patmos in Revelation 19:10. African theology should therefore endeavor to explain biblical principles. African Christians shouldn't beg elementary spirits for help, but should use their position in Jesus Christ to take charge over them. However, this must always be done in submission to God and in full cognizance of our natural helplessness against the mystical powers without the greater power of the Lord Jesus.

Conclusion

In the African worldview, mystical power is above human, natural means. However, the Bible claims that there is supreme power in the triune God, and it is upon him that African Christians should exclusively depend to counter the lesser opposing powers. They don't have to attempt to appease all other spirits, such as of the ancestors, which would bind them in bondage. It is because of this divine power that the apostle Paul could confidently say, "In all these things we are more than conquerors through him [Christ] who loved us" (Rom 8:37).

Bibliography

Adeyemo, Tokunboh. *Salvation in African Tradition*. Nairobi: Evangel Publishing, 1997.

Browne, Neil M. and Stuart M. Keeley. *Asking the Right Questions: A Guide to Critical Thinking*. 4th edition. Englewoods Cliffs, NJ: Prentice Hall, 1994.

Crusius, Timothy W., and Carolyn E. Channell. *The Aim of Argument: A Brief Rhetoric*. 3rd edition. Mountainview, CA: Mayfield Publishing, 2000.

Gehman, Richard. *Doing African Christian Theology*. Nairobi: Evangel Publishing, 1987.

Geisler, Norman L., and Ronald M. Brooks. *Come Let Us Reason: An Introduction to Logical Thinking*. Grand Rapids, MI: Baker, 1990.

King, Noel Q. *African Cosmos*. Belmont, CA: Wadsworth, 1986.

Mbiti, John S. *African Religions and Philosophy*. London: Heinemann, 1969.

Mugambi, J. N. K. *African Christian Theology*. Nairobi: Heinemann, 1989.

Osadolor, Imasogie. *Guidelines for Christian Theology in Africa*. Achimota, Ghana: African Christian Press, 1983.

Parrinder, Geoffrey. *West African Religion*. London: Epworth Press, 1949.

Weston, Anthony. *A Rulebook for Arguments*. 3rd edition. Indianapolis: Hackett, 2000.

3

Contextualization of Pastoral Theology in African Christianity: Theory, Models, Methods, and Practice

Ndung'u J. B. Ikenye
Professor, St Paul's University, Limuru, Kenya

Abstract

The problem with African Christianity is not the use of Scripture or the use of historical Christian tradition in pastoral theology, but its application in daily life. This problem needs to be given attention in multiple dimensions. The African pastor seeks to meet Christians at their points of need in their contexts of embeddedness, but the issues experienced at a communal level and within African ethnic and cultural meanings, including African Traditional Religion, remain unattended to. The African pastor trained in the classic systems of care and counseling uses healing, sustaining, guiding and reconciling, prayer, Scripture, and church tradition to solve these problems. This paper argues for contextualization and particularization in African pastoral theology, emphasizing that the pastor's and the Christian's contexts intersect (faith in Christ) and at other points are distant and disconnected (personal and communal, ethnic and cultural meanings, African traditional spirituality) to the point that both face pastoral issues and cannot complete the circle of problem-solving. This paper is an analysis of classic pastoral theology in theory, models, methods, and practice, with a special focus on the biblical, church tradition, church reasoning, and experience of persons (in faith and personal development) and classic mandates for the pastor as a person and as a holder of pastoral office. The paper recommends the reframing method of pastoral theology and its models, methods, and theory of practice for the African Christian context. This reframing will expand the functions of pastoral care and counseling to include empowerment, liberation, faithing, decolonization, prophesying, healing, sustaining, guiding, and reconciling.

Key words: Protestant, pastoral theology, pastoral care, counseling, contextualization, tradition, classic, African Christian, ethical boundaries, ethnic, cultural factors, problems of living.

Introduction

The missionary paradigm holds that African Christianity is challenged in the use of Scripture, the use of Christian tradition, and the classic role and office of the pastor. Yet the problem any Christian or pastor faces is the lack of contextualization in the use of Christian beliefs, Scripture, and Christian tradition in daily life after church on Sunday or following a Bible study session. The African pastor (whether in office or role) seeks to meet Christian persons in pastoral care and counseling at their multiple points of need as they face the problems of life. The African pastor trained in the classic Protestant pastoral paradigm and functions will focus on the goals of pastoral care and counseling – healing, sustaining, guiding, and reconciling[1] – and will also use prayer and Scripture in seeking to solve the problems of daily life.

However, the contemporary container of African care and counseling has been experienced as distancing and disconnecting. The desire of both the African pastor and the Christian parishioner is for indepth connection as they share their stories of faith (the meaning and purpose of grace, divine acceptance) and experience regard and genuine empathy[2] for and with one another. Yet the caring contexts (pastoral relationships and working relationships) experienced by the African pastor and those in his congregation, are distant, contradicting, and have empathic failure, to the point that both face pastoral issues (using self, Scripture, the classic tradition of method, model, and theory in pastoral care

---

1. William A. Clebsch and Charles R. Jaekle, *Pastoral Care in Historical Perspective* (New York: Jason Aronson, 1975), 36–66.
2. Carl R. Rogers, *Client-Centered Therapy* (Boston: Houghton Mifflin, 1951), 65–196.

3

Contextualization of Pastoral Theology in African Christianity: Theory, Models, Methods, and Practice

Ndung'u J. B. Ikenye
Professor, St Paul's University, Limuru, Kenya

Abstract

The problem with African Christianity is not the use of Scripture or the use of historical Christian tradition in pastoral theology, but its application in daily life. This problem needs to be given attention in multiple dimensions. The African pastor seeks to meet Christians at their points of need in their contexts of embeddedness, but the issues experienced at a communal level and within African ethnic and cultural meanings, including African Traditional Religion, remain unattended to. The African pastor trained in the classic systems of care and counseling uses healing, sustaining, guiding and reconciling, prayer, Scripture, and church tradition to solve these problems. This paper argues for contextualization and particularization in African pastoral theology, emphasizing that the pastor's and the Christian's contexts intersect (faith in Christ) and at other points are distant and disconnected (personal and communal, ethnic and cultural meanings, African traditional spirituality) to the point that both face pastoral issues and cannot complete the circle of problem-solving. This paper is an analysis of classic pastoral theology in theory, models, methods, and practice, with a special focus on the biblical, church tradition, church reasoning, and experience of persons (in faith and personal development) and classic mandates for the pastor as a person and as a holder of pastoral office. The paper recommends the reframing method of pastoral theology and its models, methods, and theory of practice for the African Christian context. This reframing will expand the functions of pastoral care and counseling to include empowerment, liberation, faithing, decolonization, prophesying, healing, sustaining, guiding, and reconciling.

Key words: Protestant, pastoral theology, pastoral care, counseling, contextualization, tradition, classic, African Christian, ethical boundaries, ethnic, cultural factors, problems of living.

Introduction

The missionary paradigm holds that African Christianity is challenged in the use of Scripture, the use of Christian tradition, and the classic role and office of the pastor. Yet the problem any Christian or pastor faces is the lack of contextualization in the use of Christian beliefs, Scripture, and Christian tradition in daily life after church on Sunday or following a Bible study session. The African pastor (whether in office or role) seeks to meet Christian persons in pastoral care and counseling at their multiple points of need as they face the problems of life. The African pastor trained in the classic Protestant pastoral paradigm and functions will focus on the goals of pastoral care and counseling – healing, sustaining, guiding, and reconciling[1] – and will also use prayer and Scripture in seeking to solve the problems of daily life.

However, the contemporary container of African care and counseling has been experienced as distancing and disconnecting. The desire of both the African pastor and the Christian parishioner is for indepth connection as they share their stories of faith (the meaning and purpose of grace, divine acceptance) and experience regard and genuine empathy[2] for and with one another. Yet the caring contexts (pastoral relationships and working relationships) experienced by the African pastor and those in his congregation, are distant, contradicting, and have empathic failure, to the point that both face pastoral issues (using self, Scripture, the classic tradition of method, model, and theory in pastoral care

---

1. William A. Clebsch and Charles R. Jaekle, *Pastoral Care in Historical Perspective* (New York: Jason Aronson, 1975), 36–66.
2. Carl R. Rogers, *Client-Centered Therapy* (Boston: Houghton Mifflin, 1951), 65–196.

and counseling) and thereby do not complete the circle of problem-solving. This results in disconnected and weak pastoral and working relationships.

This paper is, first, an analysis of pastoral theology, theory, and practice, with a special focus on the biblical mandates and on the Protestant traditional models and methods for the pastor as a person and as a holder of the pastoral office. The paper argues for contextualization using the reframing model[3] as a necessary tool for the completion of the African Christian problem-solving cycle, both in theory and practice, as informed by the Bible, the Word of God and divine mandate and qualifier. The previous missionary and classic paradigm of dealing with crises and life problems in African pastoral care and counseling was informed by the historical understanding of Scripture, church tradition, and denominationalism. This pre-colonial, colonial, and post-colonial paradigm was used in classic pastoral theology, and the training and appointing of clergy was male and Westernized (Eurocentric) in its cultural underpinnings (core values and value systems of the West).

This paper then discusses pastoral theology from the perspective of classic Protestant biblical care and cure, and with the critique of that classic model as used by un-cultured African pastoral theologians. The last section of the paper proposes a reframed model of African pastoral theology, and, specifically, of African pastoral care and counseling as an integrative model.

To answer the question "How can African pastors meet their parishioners at their multiple points of need within their contexts of embeddedness?," this paper contextualizes both theory (pastoral theology) and practice (pastoral care and counseling methods) as informed by the Bible, the Word of God, the primary and core mandate and qualifier for clergy. Contextualization will also use ethnicity, culture, and pastoral psychology to expand the repertoire and resource base to understand the needs of persons and their communities. The paper argues that contextualization of pastoral theology, pastoral care, and counseling (the pastor as a person and as a steward of the pastoral office with tasks, goals, and ethical boundaries) requires the consideration of both Protestant pastoral ethics and African ethnic and cultural factors affecting pastoral theology. It argues for models and modalities of delivery (contextualization) of an African Christian pastoral ministry which is effective, efficient, and competent to meet African Christians at their points of need.

---

3. Donald Capps, *Reframing: A New Method of Pastoral Care* (Minneapolis: Fortress Press, 1990), 9–51.

Pastoral Theology, Contextualization, and Reframing Method

Pastoral theology is defined as "that part of Christian theology that deals with the office and functions of a pastor."[4] This paper's concern is the contextualization of the office and functions of a pastor in the African Christian context. The focus therefore is on pastoral theology and the "consequences of God's self-disclosure,"[5] in proclamation, witnessing, and mediation of divine acceptance, in calling and using a Christian pastor in meeting persons at their multiple points of need. Pastoral theology gives special attention to "the systemic definition of the pastoral office and its functions."[6] Pastoral theology in Africa is concerned with the theory and its practice in ministries carried out by those who are called and set apart to preach, teach, discipline, disciple, care for, edify, and comfort, and to preserve Christian identity and teaching, and administer the sacraments of baptism and Holy Communion. The classic definition of pastoral theology[7] focuses on the tasks and roles of the pastoral office in terms of reflection, witness, mediation, critical reasoning, and embodiment, all in the context of Scripture, tradition, reason, and experience. Oden[8] argues that it would be dangerous for the church to practice ministry "without good foundation in Scripture, tradition, reason and experience." The outworking of these classic definitions is seen in the pastoral goals of discipling, discipline, guidance, sustainment, reconciliation, edification, and faithful living.

African definitions of pastoral theology and its functions add the personal and communal experiences of empowerment, liberation, prophetic acceptance, justice, and freedom.[9] The functions and role of the pastoral office also speak to witnessing and mediation of God's acceptance. But the question that this paper addresses is the theory and practice of pastoral theology in African contexts, especially pastoral care and counseling, with attention given to ethnic

---

4. Thomas C. Oden, *Pastoral Theology: Essentials of Ministry* (New York: Harper & Row, 1983), x.

5. Oden, *Pastoral Theology*, x.

6. Oden, 18–63.

7. Oden, 79–81; Don S. Browning, *Religious Thought and the Modern Psychologies* (Philadelphia: Fortress Press, 1987), 61–93; Browning, *A Fundamental Practical Theology* (Minneapolis: Fortress Press, 1991), 2–12; S. Hiltner, *Preface to Pastoral Theology* (Nashville: Abingdon, 1958), 8–18.

8. Oden, *Pastoral Theology*, 52–65.

9. Ndung'u Ikenye, *Pastoral Theology: Rediscovering African Models and Methods in the Care and Cure of Souls* (Eldoret, Kenya: Zapf Chancery Research Consultants, 2008); Ndung'u Ikenye, *Modeling Servant-Leaders for Africa* (Eldoret, Kenya: Zapf Chancery Research Consultants, 2010), 9–21; Douglas W. Waruta and H. W. Kinoti, eds., *Pastoral Care in African Christianity: Challenging Essays in Pastoral Theology* (Nairobi: Acton, 1994), 12–86.

and cultural values and African Traditional Religion and spirituality; thus it seeks to move to a consistently African theory of the pastoral office and role and an African system of implementing (putting into practice) pastoral tasks and functions.

Pastoral care and counseling is concerned with the "care and cure of souls."[10] Care and cure is a ministry of the church[11] as "all ministry is a sharing in Christ's ministry" (see 1 Cor 12:12). With personal experience of divine acceptance and grace in Christ, the pastor comes as an empathic and interpathic connection; from the inner self of the pastor, a relationship with God and an incarnational connection of love originate from the personal experience of God's love and acceptance. This experience of the pastor with a Christian under his or her care is what is described by the metaphor of a shepherding God and a shepherding pastor.

The implication for pastoral care and counseling is that it is an act, a ritual, an experience, and a conversation within the context of "Ultimate Concern," a fostering of faith in and relationship with God.[12] Contextualization of pastoral care and counseling for the African context addresses the questions of establishing, fostering, strengthening, deepening, and practicing faith with the support of the pastor as the compassionate neighbor, following the example of the Good Samaritan. Pastoral care and counseling is defined as "communicating the inner meaning of the Gospel through a relationship . . . toward holistic and wholistic salvation."[13]

Contextualization of Pastoral Theology (Theory and Practice) for Africa

Contextualization has the thesis of relevance and understanding of God's purpose for the world in the contexts of culture and ethnicity in the African experience. The world and worldviews are enshrined in culture. The African worldview is enshrined in ethnicity and culture, languages for communication purposes, and African Traditional Religion. The arguments about mission and

---

10. Dictionary of Pastoral Care and Counseling, 867–872.

11. John Patton, *Pastoral Care in Context* (Louisville, KY: Westminster John Knox, 1993), 3–12.

12. Patton, *Pastoral Care in Context*, 6.

13. Ndung'u Ikenye, *African Pastoral Counseling* (Thika, Kenya: Joroi Counseling Consultants, Researchers and Publishers, 2014), 52.

colonization[14] and God's attitude toward culture (in, against, above, above but through, and supra)[15] are relevant to contextualization of African pastoral theology and pastoral care and counseling.

Contextualization of pastoral theology in Africa is also concerned with professionalism, communication of empathy, care ethics, sociopolitical concerns, and justice and freedom for individuals and communities. With the intrusions of secularism, revisionism, and liberalism, African pastoral theology seeks to keep the evangelical and integrative stance in theory and practice, thus maintaining a balanced stance of orthodoxy – submission to the complete authority of the Word of God – while still allowing ethnic, cultural, and the African traditional ethos to have a voice in delivery of effective, efficient, and competent care. The strength of the missionary paradigm of pastoral theology in Africa is the emphasis on Scripture and the mediation of the knowledge of God through church tradition. This Christo-centric focus must be lived out in contextualization of pastoral theology and its practice in pastoral care and counseling. The downside of the missionary paradigm is the disregard for definitions, and for the role and functions of the pastoral office and the pastor seen from an ethnic and cultural perspective – hence the call for contextualization.

Contextualization "is rooted in dissatisfaction with traditional models."[16] Contextualization of African pastoral theology focuses on models, methods, techniques, personal and communal experiences, relevance, and ethnic and cultural core values and value systems.[17] Following the Pentecostal paradigm (Acts 2) and the proclamation, witnessing, and mediation of divine acceptance (Rom 10:17), the African pastoral theologian must make sure that pastoral theology speaks to the African soul.[18] But the African pastoral theologian must be warned not to collapse or fuse ethnic and cultural heritage and give them the same authority as Scripture; and not to alter the integrity of the gospel by adding to, subtracting from, or complicating by multiplication.[19]

---

14. Lamin Sanneh, *Translating the Message: The Missionary Impact on Culture* (Maryknoll, NY: Orbis, 1989), 15–28.

15. Charles H. Kraft, *Christianity in Culture* (Maryknoll, NY: Orbis, 1988), 103–115.

16. David Hesselgrave, and E. Rommen, *Contextualization: Meanings, Methods and Models* (Grand Rapids, MI: Baker, 1989), 144–157.

17. Ikenye, *Pastoral Theology*, 21–29.

18. Ndung'u Ikenye, *African Christian Counseling: Method, Theory and Practice* (Nairobi: Envoy Graphic and Print Systems, 2002), 85–92.

19. Ikenye, *Modeling Servant Leadership*, 16.

Theological Background to an African Pastoral Theology: Models, Methods, Theory, and Practice

The beginning point is contextualization as a theoretical problem (problems in the system of pastoral theology regarding the role and functions of pastoral office) and a practical problem (problems in the use of classic Westernized models, methods, and contexts to meet the needs of African Christians in pastoral care and counseling). Second, Africans have a faith that affects their lives, yet at moments of personal and communal crisis[20] their Christian faith is not enough, hence they are known to revert to using systems of African Traditional Religion. The African, therefore, lives in three worlds, as proposed by Ngewa: Christian faith (Christian self); African culture and modern culture (cultural self, spiritual self); and African traditional self (African traditional spirituality).[21] Ikenye adds the world of ethnic norms (ethnic self, relational self), mental processes (mental self), and environmental processes (environmental self) as systems that inform African Christians at their points of need in life.[22] The African pastoral theologian (pastor as a person and as a professional) has to address himself or herself to an African Christian as a complex living human document.[23] The African is living with a complicated ethos of life (traditional, modern, and postmodern), including contexts of embeddedness (colonial and neo-colonial), lived experience, broken relationships, moral problems, language constructs and meaning, and capacity for interpretation. This means that the pastor and counselee must read and interpret the multiple levels of the African Christian soul. Ikenye[24] discusses the broad definition of the African soul from biblical, ethnic, and cultural perspectives. The observations by Galgalo in Chemorion and others[25] indicate that the blood of ethnicity is thicker than the water of baptism – raising the question of resources used by the African pastor and Christian in dealing with the problems of life.

---

20. John Mbiti, *African Religions and Philosophy* (Nairobi: Heinemann, 1969), 18–228.

21. Samuel Ngewa et al., eds., *Issues in African Christian Theology* (Nairobi: East African Educational Publishers, 1998), xi–xiv.

22. Ndung'u Ikenye, *African Psychological Anthropology: Ethnicity, Culture, and Personality* (Thika, Kenya: Parkside Counseling Services, Consultants, Researchers and Publishers, 2015), 35–41.

23. Charles V. Gerkin, *The Living Human Document: Re-Visioning Pastoral Counseling in a Hermeneutical Mode* (Nashville: Abingdon, 1984), 37–54; Ikenye, *African Pastoral Counseling*, 56.

24. Ikenye, *African Christian Counseling: Method, Theory and Practice*, 8–13.

25. D. C. Chemorion et al., eds., *Contested Space: Ethnicity and Religion in Kenya* (Limuru, Kenya: Zapf Chancery Publishers, 2013), 1–6.

The evangelical African practical theologian[26] argues that the primary resources for pastoral theology and its practice in pastoral care and counseling are the Bible as the prescriptive and descriptive authority for Christian living; the experience of walking with Christ as Lord and Savior (divine acceptance); and the empowerment of the Holy Spirit. African pastoral theology (the office and role of the pastor) as a systematic theology and as a theory of the practical care and cure of African souls has to contextualize, indigenize, and cross over to an authentic, genuine, and effective African system of thinking, reflecting, responding, and acting.

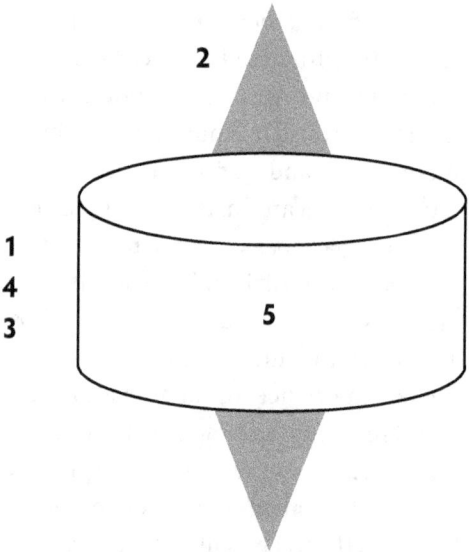

Figure 3.1: Care and Cure of Complex African Christian Souls

The pictorial system for the issues at hand for our discussion is shown using the two realities in Figure 3.1 on the multiple dimensions of the needs of an African Christian who needs pastoral care and counseling: (1) The interior, represented by the holon of the African Christian reality, is the authority of Scripture and the classic Christian tradition of pastoral care and counseling. This holon speaks to African Christian first-level change brought by the missionary paradigm of proclamation and missionary pastoral care and counseling. (2) The second reality is the multiple levels of conversion, encounter with Christ, and personal apprehension within the parishioner's and pastor's own personality content and structure. (3) The third reality of this

---

26. Ikenye, *African Christian Counseling*, 22–24, 38–40.

holon speaks to the classic Westernized models and psychology systems of care and counseling as rooted in Western culture, core values, and value systems. The disconnect of this classic model, techniques, and modalities with African Christianity and African pastoral care is due to the Western worldview, with its culture-bound and class-bound systems of pastoral care and counseling. (4) The fourth reality is the problems of living the African Christian life, and their multiple dimensions, and the traditional and modern worldview and post-colonial life. (5) The fifth reality is the ethnic, cultural, economic, political, religious, and spiritual contexts of living and their challenges. The exterior four and interior realities are shown in Figure 3.1 and are concerned with the theory, method, techniques, and goals of African pastoral care and counseling.

Pastoral Theology and Its Practice in Care and Counseling in Africa

Our concern in this paper is African pastoral theology and its practice in the pastoral office, the functioning of the pastoral office (roles, tasks, duties), and, more specifically, the systems of responding during moments of pain and suffering (care and cure) in the lives of African Christians. God has called particular persons (with particular biblical standards, gifts, and graces) and the church has affirmed the call and sent these persons into the field (the marketplace and its contexts and needs – of individuals and community). The question for African contextualization of the pastoral role and office is the question of capacity to meet persons at their multiple points of need. Ikenye[27] argues that, to respond meaningfully, the pastor responds in the context of faith in Christ (empathically, within divine acceptance) and crossing over (interpathically) in the context of ethnicity, culture, and African Traditional Religious ontology. As noted above, Oden gives attention to knowledge of God as (1) witnessed to in Scripture; (2) mediated through tradition; (3) reflected upon by a systematic system of reasoning; and (4) embodied in personal and social (communal) experience.[28]

In terms of practice in pastoral care and counseling, African pastoral theologians have neglected the African complexity of being;[29] this paper therefore proposes a paradigm shift.

---

27. Ikenye, *African Pastoral Counseling*, 59–76.
28. Oden, *Pastoral Theology*, 18–25.
29. Ikenye, *African Pastoral Counseling*, 155–169.

Paradigm Shift for African Pastoral Care and Counseling

The paradigm shift reflects the missionary paradigm and its effects on the theory of pastoral theology and its practice in pastoral care and counseling. This reflection will expand the definition of classic pastoral theology and its practice in the African pastoral office and will raise questions and answers for liberation, empowerment, decolonization, faith-building, pastoral ethics, prophesying, and telling the truth. This shift will affect not only pastoral theology but also the roles, functions, and duties of the pastor to give birth to genuine African care and cure. The focus of the paradigm does not shift from the African experience of Scripture and tradition in the care and cure of African Christian souls. The exegetical and historical materials (African historical scripts, written inner-world experiences and their connections with stories of meaningful life in traditional systems and meanings of pain; and systems of colonial abuse, injustice, oppression, and exploitation) of the Christian inheritance are brought to bear in our definition as well as in our theory and practice. African proclamation and witness (in line with the Great Commission), use of two sacraments of Protestant theology (baptism and Holy Communion), and use of church order and discipline have direct implications for the care and cure of African souls. Pre-colonial, colonial, and post-colonial systems of care and cure have not been integrated – though they need to be not integrated, but decolonized. Rather, African practical theologians have been cynical, ignorant, reactive, and critical (in their loss of African groundedness in the African Christian soul). African practical theologians have been left without solutions in their search for meaningful African definitions, theory, and practice in seeking to deliver effective, efficient, competent, and in-depth care and cure. There are scandals facing the pastoral office in Africa today[30] in spite of manifold religious freedoms. In response, the Kenyan Government,[31] for example, has been seeking to discipline church organizations and clergy.

The African practical theologian is left with further questions to help in the paradigm shift:

1. Can we have religious freedom without accountability in pastoral roles, tasks, and functions?

2. Can we have a pastoral theology and practice that is without a divine call, commissioning, and empowerment by the Holy Spirit?

---

30. Ikenye, *Pastoral Theology*, 159.
31. Ikenye, *Modeling Servant Leadership*, 55–62.

3. Can we have a pastoral theology that is concerned with culture and ethnicity and focused on social ministries and political advocacy?

4. Can we allow modernity and postmodernity to unbalance the systems argued by Oden[32] and abandon the pastoral theology which was previously balanced by Scripture, tradition, reason, and experience?

5. Can we continue with a theory and practice that is monocultural, Eurocentric, and egocentric, and does not consider the African communal reality, thus practicing a disconnected pastoral theology?

These five critiques need consideration in our definition and development of an African Christian theodicy, where God speaks justly to African Christian souls and thereby heals, sustains, guides, empowers, liberates, and decolonizes persons and their communities. God's mercy, compassion, justice, and love must speak care and cure to individuals and communities today on the African continent. The prophetic voice of pastoral theology must speak clearly in African definitions, theory, and practice. The call for African pastoral care and counseling is the second-order change and, as a paradigm shift, is liberation and decolonization while maintaining the biblical and church tradition of Protestant contexts, thereby expanding the definitions and systems of classic pastoral care and counseling.

Theoretical Frameworks of Pastoral Theology: Classic Models

As already noted, Oden described pastoral theology as office, functions, and practice that are informed by Scripture, Christian tradition, the reasoning of the Western church, and the personal and communal experience of the Westernized Christian.[33] Wise defines pastoral counseling "as a process through which people are helped to grow, to meet and solve problems, and to achieve mature religious lives."[34] This classic process of pastoral theology, care, and counseling is affected by four factors: (1) the attitude of the pastor toward the Christian person and his or her multiple points of need, and the relational dynamics; (2) the role of religious and biblical anthropology, the role of faith in care, cure, and redemption, and the role of truth in the transformation of

---

32. Oden, *Care of Souls*, 26–42.
33. Oden, *Pastoral Theology*, x–xii.
34. Carroll A. Wise, *Pastoral Psychotherapy: Theory and Practice* (New York: Jason Aronson, 1980), 3–20, 25–47.

the soul; (3) the processes of communication of empathy (and interpathy); and (4) the self-understanding of the pastor as representative of the church and Christ (demonstrating saving grace as servant, judge, lover) and living out the reality of the ministry of presence (as coach, midwife, shepherd).

African Christianity has found fertile ground; Mbiti says, "Africans are notoriously religious."[35] Yet African traditional beliefs, ceremonies, rituals, and trust in traditional religious officials have not helped Christianity to permeate all departments and dimensions of personhood.[36] That is to say, Africans who are "homo-religious" have not become "Christo-centric" in life and practice; the public culture of religion and ethnicity in the African context has not translated to receiving and integrating the core systems of the Western/Eurocentric functions of pastoral care and counseling. Reconciliation, healing, sustaining, and guiding are not enough for the care and cure of African Christian souls.[37] The biblical model of pastoral care and counseling, following the mandates of Matthew 9:35–10:16; 1 Corinthians 12:4–13:13; and 2 Corinthians 5, and the central principles of faith, love, and hope, have not been deeply rooted in the consciousness of African Christians. The biblical model and method affirms the authority of Scripture and the necessity and the adequacy of Christ.[38] This classic model also affirms the classic sins as deadly – bitterness, guilt, worry, resentment, anger, self-pity, envy, and lust – hindering spiritual growth and spirit life.[39] This model and method emphasizes that God through his pastors, prophets, apostles, and the church, is able to deliver and restore persons and communities to full, productive, vibrant, and creative lives in which service and fellowship are emphasized. But what we see in African Christians is that their lives are not deeply involved in this message, model, and method.

The classic models and method of pastoral care and counseling are defined by Wise as "the art of communicating the inner meaning of the Gospel to persons at their point of need."[40] What is at stake in the classic theory, model, and method is pastoral functioning, pastoral relationship, and pastoral ways of being that effect realization and incarnation of the gospel. This is because Christians have problems of living which are connected to their systems of

---

35. Mbiti, *African Religions and Philosophy*, 1–5.
36. Mbiti, 1.
37. Clebesch and Jaekle, *Pastoral Care*, 32–66.
38. Lawrence Crabb, *Basic Principles of Biblical Counseling* (Grand Rapids, MI: Zondervan, 1975), 15–19.
39. Donald Capps, *Deadly Sins and Saving Virtues* (Philadelphia: Fortress Press, 1987), 11–18.
40. Carroll A., Wise *Pastoral Psychotherapy: Theory and Practice* (New York: Jason Aronson, 1980), 23–48.

thinking, feeling, relating, connecting, participating, and their personality contents and structures. The question that remains unanswered is: Does the communication of the meaning of the gospel become confused with other voices and messages? Another question that arises from systems of entry in classic pastoral care and counseling is: Are the pastor's integrity, trustworthiness, pastoral relationship, genuine empathy, positive regard, and interpathy systems not enough in incarnating the gospel? Issues of immature personality are shown in personal mental deficits and conflict, personal and communal problems of conflict (genocide in Rwanda and Burundi; post-election violence in Kenya; civil war in South Sudan and Congo), and other problems such as dependence, passivity, manipulation, apartheid, and colonization clouded by abuse, marginalization, oppression, racism, and exploitation.

The incarnation work of communicating the inner meaning of the gospel through pastoral relationships also has to do with the work of the Holy Spirit and the use of the gifts of the Holy Spirit (Gal 5). Encountering Christ has a transformative effect on the pastor and parishioner (1 Cor 2:10–13). There are personal development issues that come into play in the pastoral care and counseling encounter:[41] trust vs. mistrust; autonomy vs. shame and doubt; initiative vs. guilt; industry vs. inferiority; identity vs. identity diffusion; intimacy and distantiation vs. self-absorption; generativity vs. stagnation; and integrity vs. despair and disgust. The world, the flesh, and the devil work against competent, effective, and efficient pastoral care and counseling (Matt 8:28–29). An African Christian practical theologian will keep asking questions that will derail the work of incarnating the gospel in African pastoral theology. The goals and functions of pastoral care and counseling in the African model and method (see Table 3.1 below) are forgiveness and producing faith, reconciliation, healing, guiding, resolution, empowerment, decolonization, discipling, disciplining, transformation of situations of conflict among persons and their communities of embeddedness, and bringing together the isolated, separated, abused, and marginalized.

---

41. Erik H. Erikson, *Childhood and Society* (New York: W. W. Norton & Co., 1950, 1963), 247–274.

44 African Contextual Realities

Table 3.1: The Classic Model and Method

Problems of Living	Classic Solutions	Pastoral Stance
Sin: world, flesh and the devil SPIRITUAL WARFARE	Commitment to Scripture Tradition, reason, and experience in the context of prayer, and the goals of healing, reconciliation, guiding, and sustaining	New Paradigm: pastoral call, focus on the mission of the church (tasks, functions, roles) Genuine pastor in care and counseling
Problems of living Christian lives: distorted and disconnected Behaviors Thinking Relationships FUNCTIONAL PROBLEMS	African experience: Pastoral care and counseling out of context Disconnected Christianity: there is no difference between a colonialist and a priest; disconnected pastoral care and counseling	New Paradigm: Personal and communal liberation, empowerment, freedom with justice and abundant living

Paradigm Shift: Critique of Classic Models by Western-Hemisphere Theologians

As African pastoral theologians import the classic model and method of contemporary Westernized pastoral care and counseling, they must be aware of the critique from among Westernized practical theologians. Oden criticizes the American model and method for pastoral care and counseling for its lack of integration of theological and pastoral wisdom, claiming it has (1) an anti-historical view of pastoral theology; (2) an anti-pastoral approach to historical theology; and (3) an anti-theological style of pastoral care and counseling.[42] This spirit, he argues, has come from the perspective of individualism, naturalistic reductionism, narcissistic hedonism, and modern chauvinism.

---

42. Oden, *Care of Souls*, 13, 21–24.

Oden concludes that there is a pastoral crisis of identity.[43] The solution he proposes is twofold: pastoral-theological integration and contextualization of pastoral care and counseling. Oden also proposes a balanced Christian anthropology, corporate responsibility, mutual accountability, moral self-examination, and social commitment which will be undergirded by Scripture and historical Christian tradition; and the integration of pastoral care and counseling with the pastoral office, roles, and functions.

Patton addresses two erroneous assumptions about pastoral care and counseling: (1) that all counseling done by a pastor is pastoral counseling; and (2) that a pastor making use of knowledge and methods from the psychotherapeutic field ceases to be a pastor.[44] Patton's solution is to develop a theory of pastoral care and counseling based on the pastoral relationship and thereby claim (and reclaim) pastoral care and counseling as an authentic ministry of the church. Wise argues that pastoral care and counseling is the gospel communicated at the point of personal need.[45] Hinkle laments that Wise's approach, which is pastoral, clinical, and empirical, lacks cross-cultural concerns.[46] Wimberly argues that the spiritual values and inner healing used by the pastor need to be articulated in the context of a parish base.[47] The solution to African importation of classic pastoral theology and its practice is an integration of pastoral identity, integrity, and passion in meeting Christians as complicated human documents in their cultural and ethnic contexts, and using the resources of the incarnation of the gospel, the pastoral tradition as rooted in Scripture and church tradition, and functional interpersonal relationships with clear pastoral ethics while clinical in method and drawing from a psychological understanding of persons and their contexts.

Critique by African Pastoral Theologian

According to Parrinder, African Traditional Religion wields great power in the African mind; he argues that despite ancestral worship, divine rulers,

---

43. Oden, 13, 21–24.

44. John Patton, *Pastoral Care in Context: An Introduction to Pastoral Care* (Louisville, KY: Westminster/John Knox Press, 1993), 6–12.

45. Carroll A. Wise, *The Meaning of Pastoral Care*, with revisions and additions by John Hinkle, Jr. (New York: Harper & Row, 1966, 1989), 8–12.

46. John E. Hinkle in Carroll Wise, *The Meaning of Pastoral Care*, 34–60; John E. Hinkle in *At the Point of Need: Living Human Experience*, eds. James B. Ashbrook and John E. Hinkle, Jr. (Lanham, MD: University Press of America, 1988), 185–199.

47. Edward Wimberly, *Pastoral Counseling and Spiritual Values: A Black Point of View* (Nashville: Abingdon, 1982), 135–155.

personal and communal rituals, magic, sorcery, and witchcraft, the worship of the "Supreme Being" connects all Africans.[48] Despite the fact that African Traditional Religion has no sacred writings, it affects the lives of the living and the dead like any other religion. Nevertheless, as noted above, this depth of religiosity has not been tapped by Protestant missionaries and the African heirs to their ministries. Ikenye raises the issue of the environmental self and African spirituality which can be called animism;[49] this dynamism or vital force is exercised and used in the daily lives of African Christians, in incantations for blessing, justice, vengeance, or good omens. For example, in offering pastoral care and counseling after the death of a loved one, the pastor can go only to a certain point; the other details are left to the family, clan, and ethnic community. The burial of the late father of the nation of South Africa, Nelson Mandela, was a mixture of Christian and African Traditional rituals and rites. This also means that in African Christianity, there is no division between the sacred and the secular; hence in pastoral theology, the Traditional Religious beliefs, moral norms, religious symbols, customs, and rites are not in the custody of the clergy only but are also in the community.

Magesa discusses five problems within African Christianity which are not dealt with by African pastoral theology.[50] The first problem from her African school of thought is that of adaptation and acculturation: the wrappings of Christianity require the African Christian to adapt and acculturate (accommodation and second enculturation, as Christianity came with modernity). The meaning of Christianity has not fully developed or grown to the point of it becoming second nature for African Christians. This means that an African practical theologian will experience this disconnect with the client.

The second problem is that of internalization and transformation, when the external systems are taken in to become part of one's own way of life. Christianity is still an external reality to most African Christians.[51] Galgalo calls Christianity "the stranger within" in African Christian life.[52] Conversion to Christianity has not yet entered the conscious level to inform every aspect of life. The African environment has not grown Christianity to effect transformation of the wholistic and holistic self. The pastoral theologian in Africa will work with a fragmented Christianity in dealing with life crises and problems.

---

48. Geoffrey Parrinder, *African Traditional Religion* (London: SPCK, 1962), 9–20.
49. Ikenye, *African Psychological Anthropology*, 35–41.
50. Laurenti Magesa, *Anatomy of Inculturation: Transforming the Church in Africa* (Nairobi: Paulines Publications Africa, 2004), 13–16.
51. Magesa, *Anatomy of Inculturation*, 14.
52. Galgalo, *African Christianity*, 23–30.

The third problem is that of perception whereby the reality of Christianity is reflected on and articulated in a pragmatic way that affects life decisions. In pastoral theology, reflection informs thought systems, conversation, correlation, and interpretation.[53] There has been a one-sided reflection, and African Christians as narrative- and story-oriented persons have not reasoned out their faith and its practical implications. Ikenye[54] argues for a narrative- and story-oriented pastoral theology to be incorporated within the theory and practice of pastoral care and counseling.

The fourth problem is that of ambivalence, paradox, and contradictions in reactions and attitudes toward the incarnation and inculturation of Christianity. Total or partial denial of the ethical and cultural underpinnings of African Christianity and Westernized coatings of the cultural core values of individualism and independence and their connections with colonization make the pastor and Christian parishioner live and discuss life problems in an unrealistic, distant, and distorted pastoral relationship. The solution is "differentiation and distinction," and to consider the problematic issues of life without fusion of thought, relationships, and facts.

The fifth argument is that of Christian growth. African Christian faith has remained at a fixed position. The struggles of pre-colonial and colonial Christianity wrapped with the missionary mentality have continued into post-colonial Christianity to the extent that Christianity is still suspect and is like a "potted plant" planted in a foreign soil. In discussing personal and communal problems, the pastoral theologian uses a "foreign language and mentality." Christianity has to be fully incarnated, accepted, and used in daily living. Ikenye discusses the problems of leadership in the African church, an issue Magesa raises because moral issues, heresy, and deceit undermine servant leadership.[55] Genuine positive regard in African pastoral theology (pastor as a person and a professional) is engaged in the care and cure of relationships.[56] Meaning that the pastor respects the congregation in delivering pastoral care and counseling and by genuinely understanding their worth and dignity, and their capacity and right to self-direction.

---

53. Galgalo, 41–43.

54. Ikenye, *Pastoral Theology*, 50–54.

55. Laurenti Magesa, *African Religion: The Moral Traditions of Abundant Life* (Maryknoll, NY: Orbis, 1997), 1–34.

56. Rogers, *Client-Centered Therapy*, 20–64.

Contextualized African Pastoral Theology: African Christian Models and Methods for Theory and Practice

The call for the second-order change for African pastoral theology (reframing) gives rise to a new paradigm that focuses on theory and practice which is sensitive toward and attends to the care and cure of the African soul. This offers a first-level change (conversion of the soul) leading to a second-level change (living abundant life in the Holy Spirit). This new change is a systems change (wholeness defined from the African Christian dimensions of humanness),[57] and righteousness (life of righteous, and African Christian discipline) as incarnational of divine acceptance. The biblical anthropology is applied in the context of African ecopsychology[58] and African ethnocultural psychology.[59]

This second-order change maintains the centralities of Scripture, Christian tradition, reason, and experience of Christ, yet applied within the African context.[60] This second-order change calls for the use of the classic Christian models of pastoral care and counseling,[61] yet changes those models, theories, methods, and techniques to include African contexts and their indigenous perspectives.[62]

Contextual Proposals for Cross-Cultural and Cross-Ethnic Pastoral Care and Counseling

Clinebell argues for the *Maieutic* Model in which pain, suffering, and the crises of life are encountered by presence, listening, reflective empathy, attending, inviting, following and responding, clarification, exploring, confronting, understanding, and confession and absolution.[63] These characteristics must be lived out in all forms of African pastoral care and counseling.

---

57. Ikenye, *Pastoral Theology*, 24–29; Ikenye, *African Pastoral Counseling*, 23–44.

58. Bame Nsamenang, *Human Development in Cultural Context: A Third World Perspective* (Newbury Park, CA: Sage, 1992), 165–208.

59. Ikenye, *African Psychological Anthropology*, 35–42.

60. African Bible and African Bible Commentary (2006).

61. Robert C. Anderson, *The Effective Pastor* (Chicago: Moody Press, 1985), 3–23; Howard Clinebell, *Basic Types of Pastoral Care and Counseling* (Nashville: Abingdon, 1994), 72–102.

62. Gladys Mwiti and Al Dueck, *Christian Counseling: An African Indigenous Perspective* (Pasadena, CA: Fuller Seminary Press, 2006); Ikenye, *African Pastoral Counseling*; Patton, *Pastoral Care*; Waruta and Kinoti, *Pastoral Care in African Christianity*.

63. Howard Clinebell, *Basic Types of Pastoral Care and Counseling* (Nashville: Abingdon, 1994), 46–71.

Sue and Sue argue for a cross-cultural model (from the perspective of counseling and psychotherapy) and argue for working against class and cultural barriers and communication systems that block, break, or hinder genuine pastoral relationships.[64] These authors focus on counselor training and the development of sensitivities toward sociopolitical, class, cultural core value, value systems, and language factors. The African pastoral and practical theologian must be cross-cultural and cross-ethnically competent, and therefore be enlightened, non-defensive, open, and skilled in dealing with differences, prejudice concerning minorities, labeling and stereotyping, and all-encompassing attitudes and beliefs.

Berinyuu and Silva-Netto argue for an African model that is more relevant to the African situation, activities, individual and communal needs, and use of individual and group resources like prayer, religious and biblical studies, and sacraments. This group focuses on the psychoneumatic approach (an integrative approach of counseling using psychology and African spirituality without separating the sacred and the secular).[65]

Ikenye argues for an African theory and model of pastoral care and counseling as an art and science in which sympathy is based on the dimensions of humanness.[66] He calls his model and method the Biblical-Ethnographic-Clinical Method. This means meeting persons in the contexts of their life problems, including the body, mind, spirit, relationships, and environments. Ikenye argues that empathy as a system of feelings must include acceptance, joining, and genuine standing with a client in a hospitable context (church office). Interpathy must mean crossing over to the client's world, in which observation and participation will include differentiation of mental, relational, feeling, and functional relationships.[67]

---

64. Derald Wing Sue and David Sue, *Counseling the Culturally Different: Theory and Practice*, 2nd ed. (New York: John Wiley & Sons, 1990), 27–92.

65. Abraham Adu Berinyuu, "Change, Ritual and Grief: Continuity and Discontinuity of Pastoral Theology in Ghana," *The Journal of Pastoral Care* 46, no. 2 (Summer 1992): 141–152; Abraham Adu Bernyuu, "The Encounter of Western Christianity, Civilization and Islam in Ghanian Culture: Implication For the Ministry of Pastoral Care and Counseling," *African Theological Journal* 17, no. 2 (1988): 18–31; and Benoni Silva-Netto, "Pastoral Counseling in a Multicultural Context," *The Journal of Pastoral Care* 46, no. 2 (Summer 1992): 131–139.

66. Ikenye, *African Pastoral Counselling*, 30–48, 65–74.

67. Ikenye, 49–58.

Reframing Theory, Method, and Model in African Pastoral Theology: Cautions

Contextualization in African pastoral theology and its practice in pastoral care and counseling must consider six cautions from Pobee[68] and Ikenye:[69]

1. Producing an all-African universal theory and practice is not possible unless the values of interdependence and communal and family kinships are considered as fundamental. Ethnic values and rules of life and ethnic language and idioms must be given room with the understanding that there are ethnic definitions of what is optimal and what is pathological in functioning for individuals and their ethnic community.

2. There are universal, continental, cultural, and ethnic personalities and traits; each individual is unique due to differences in personality type and psychology, and African pastoral care and counseling needs to be sensitive to this.

3. African Traditional Religions have strengths, symbols, but also idols. This means that, while African Christianity should not go backwards to idolatry and syncretism, neither can it afford to deny the effect of African spirituality and African Traditional Religions in African ontology.

4. In proposing contextualization of pastoral theology, we are not challenging the authority and authenticity of biblical theology and biblical anthropology.

5. The use of African proverbs, stories, idioms, and symbols is not euphoric (a feeling of vigor or bearing things easily) and does not separate African Christians from Christians around the world.

6. The Westernized Christian world is characterized by divisions concerning the rule of faith, and the role and authority of Scripture. African Christianity and its outworking in African pastoral theology which is used in African pastoral care and counseling will not be another avenue of alienation, disconnection, and departure in African life and/or professional and nonprofessional relationships.

---

68. John S. Pobee, *Toward an African Theology* (Nashville: Abingdon, 1979), 15–42.
69. Ikenye, *African Christian Counselling*, 1–7.

Reframing as Contextualization in African Christianity: A New Paradigm and Second-Level Change in Theory and Practice

The focus of this method of reframing in pastoral theology is communicating the inner meaning of the gospel through pastoral relationships and meeting complicated persons and communities at their multiple points of need within multiple contexts of embeddedness. Table 3.2 demonstrates the new paradigm of African pastoral theology.

Table 3.2: African Paradigm of Pastoral Care

Theory	Pastoral Care	Pastoral Counseling
Goals	Meeting persons and communities at their multiple points of need	Indepth and multidimensional Meeting persons and communities at their points of need
Practice	Pastoral and Personal Identity As a calling from God	Counselor: Stance of Acceptance of Parishioner
Methods, Models, and Techniques	Contact, listening, inquiry, entry, diagnosis, and intervention	Contact, listening, inquiry, entry, diagnosis, and intervention
Transformation	Holistic Self: conversion at justification, righteousness and processes of sanctification and Christian discipline	Wholistic Self: "faithing" as a process of incarnating Christ in all spheres of Christian life as an active faith
Goals	Healing, restoring, guiding, reconciliation, empowerment, liberation, discipling, disciplining, decolonization, and prophesying	Healing, restoring, guiding, reconciliation, empowerment, liberation, discipling, disciplining, decolonization, and prophesying

Conclusion

This paper concludes that contextualization of pastoral theology (theory) and its practice in pastoral care and counseling is an imperative for effective, efficient, and competent pastoral care and counseling. Contextualization must be informed by the Bible, the Word of God, as the primary and core mandate and qualifier for clergy. The classic paradigm of Protestant pastoral care and counseling is also informed by the historical understanding of church tradition and denominationalism. In classic pastoral theology, the training and appointing of clergy was (is) male and Westernized (Eurocentric) in its cultural underpinnings (core values and value systems of the West). It is evident that the goals of pastoral theology were proclamation, witnessing, and mediation of divine acceptance. Furthermore, the goals of pastoral care and counseling as discussed in the chapter are part and parcel of communicating the inner meaning of the gospel through pastoral relationships.

Recommendation

This paper recommends contextualization of pastoral theology (pastor as a person and pastor as a holder and steward of the pastoral office with tasks, goals, and ethical boundaries).

In recommending reframing as a paradigm shift in African Protestant pastoral care and counseling, this paper recommends that African pastoral ethics and African ethnic and cultural factors should influence pastoral theology.

The goals of African pastoral care and counseling should include empowerment, liberation, decolonization, and prophesying. The models and modalities of delivery (contextualization) of an African Christian pastoral ministry will make the ministry effective, efficient, and competent to meet complicated African Christians at their multiple points of need.

This paper recommends the reframing method of pastoral theology as the second-order change in models, methods, theory, and practice for the African Christian context.

Finally, African ethnicity and culture should be a part of the considerations for pastors in training and in delivery of services in ministry.

Bibliography

Anderson, Ray S. *The Shape of Practical Theology: Empowering Ministry with Theological Praxis.* Downers Grove, IL: InterVarsity, 2001.
Anderson, Robert C. *The Effective Pastor.* Chicago: Moody, 1985.
Ashbrook, James B., and John E. Hinkle, eds. *At the Point of Need: Living Human Experience.* Lanham, MD: University Press of America, 1988.

Atkinson, David J., and David H. Field, eds. *New Dictionary of Christian Ethics and Pastoral Theology*. Downers Grove, IL: InterVarsity, 1995.

Berinyuu, Abraham Adu. *Toward Theory and Practice of Pastoral Counseling in Africa*. New York: Peter Lang, 1989.

———. "Change, Ritual and Grief: Continuity and Discontinuity of Pastoral Theology in Ghana." *The Journal of Pastoral Care & Counseling* 46, no. 2 (June 1992): 141–152.

———. "The Encounter of Western Christianity, Civilization and Islam in Ghanian Culture: Implication for the Ministry of Pastoral Care and Counseling." *African Theological Journal* 17, no. 2 (1988): 18–31.

Browning, Don S. *A Fundamental Practical Theology: Descriptive and Strategic Proposals*. Minneapolis: Fortress Press, 1991.

———. *Religious Thought and the Modern Psychologies: A Critical Conversation in the Theology of Culture*. Philadelphia: Fortress Press, 1987.

Capps, Donald. *Reframing: A New Method in Pastoral Care*. Minneapolis: Fortress Press, 1990.

———. *Deadly Sins and Saving Virtues*. Philadelphia: Fortress Press, 1987.

Chemorion, D. C., et al., eds. *Contested Space: Ethnicity and Religion in Kenya*. Limuru, Kenya: Zapf Chancery Publishers, 2013.

Clebesch, William A., and Charles R. Jaekle. *Pastoral Care in Historical Perspective*. New York: Jason Aronson, 1975.

Clinebell, Howard. *Basic Types of Pastoral Care and Counseling*. Nashville: Abingdon, 1994.

Crabb, Lawrence J., *Basic Principles of Biblical Counseling*. Grand Rapids, MI: Zondervan, 1975.

———. *Effective Biblical Counseling*. Grand Rapids, MI: Zondervan, 1977.

———. *Understanding People: Deep Longings for Relationships*. Grand Rapids, MI: Zondervan, 1987.

Erikson, Erik H. *Childhood and Society*. New York: W. W. Norton & Co., 1963.

Galgalo, Joseph. *African Christianity: The Stranger Within*. Limuru, Kenya: Zapf Chancery Publishers, 2012.

Gerkin, Charles V. *Crisis Experience in Modern Life: Theory and Theology for Pastoral Care*. Nashville: Abingdon, 1979.

———. *The Living Human Document: Re-Visioning Pastoral Counseling in a Hermeneutical Mode*. Nashville: Abingdon, 1984.

———. *Prophetic Pastoral Care: A Christian Vision of Life Together*. Nashville: Abingdon, 1991.

Graham, Larry K. *Care of Persons, Care of Worlds: A Psychosystems Approach to Pastoral Care and Counseling*. Nashville: Abingdon, 1992.

Harbaugh, Gary L. *Pastor as a Person*. Minneapolis: Augsburg, 1984.

Hesselgrave, David J. and Rommen, Edward. *Contextualization: Meanings, Methods and Models*. Grand Rapids, MI: Baker, 1989.

Hunter, Rodney J. ed., *Dictionary of Pastoral Care and Counseling*. Nashville: Abingdon, 1990.

Ikenye, Ndung'u. *African Christian Counseling: Method, Theory and Practice*. Nairobi: Envoy Graphic & Print Systems, 2002.

———. *African Pastoral Counseling*. Thika, Kenya: Joroi Counseling Consultants, Researchers & Publishers, 2014.

———. *African Psychological Anthropology: Ethnicity, Culture and Personality*. Thika, Kenya: Parkside Counseling Services, Consultants, Researchers and Publishers, 2015.

———. "A Call for Prophetic Ministry in Kenya." Unpublished paper, St Paul's University Consortium, 21 March 2009.

———. *Modeling Servant Leadership for Africa*. Eldoret, Kenya: Zapf Chancery Research Consultants and Publishers, 2010.

———. *Pastoral Theology: Rediscovering African Models and Methods in the Care and Cure of Souls*. Eldoret, Kenya: Zapf Chancery Research Consultants and Publishers, 2008.

James, William. *The Varieties of Religious Experience*. New York: Penguin, 1958.

Kraft, Charles H. *Christianity in Culture*. Maryknoll, NY: Orbis, 1988.

Magesa, Laurenti. *African Religion: The Moral Traditions of Abundant Life*. Maryknoll, NY: Orbis, 1997.

———. *Anatomy of Inculturation: Transforming the Church in Africa*. Nairobi: Paulines Publications Africa, 2004.

Mbiti, John. *African Religions and Philosophy*. Nairobi: Heinemann Educational Books, 1969.

Mwiti, Gladys, and Alvin C. Dueck. *Christian Counseling: An African Indigenous Perspective*. Pasadena, CA: Fuller Seminary Press, 2006.

Ngewa, Samuel, et al., eds. *Issues in African Christian Theology*. Nairobi: East African Educational Publishers, 1998.

Nouwen, Henri. *The Wounded Healer: Ministry in Contemporary Society*. New York: Image Books Doubleday, 1990.

Oates, Wayne E. *The Christian Pastor*. 3rd edition. Philadelphia: Westminster Press, 1982.

———. *Pastoral Counseling in Social Problems: Extremism, Race, Sex, Divorce*. Philadelphia: Westminster Press, 1986.

Oden, Thomas C. *Care of Souls in the Classic Tradition*. Philadelphia: Fortress Press, 1984.

———. *Pastoral Theology: Essentials of Ministry*. New York: Harper & Row, 1983.

Pargament, Kenneth I. *The Psychology of Religion and Coping: Theory, Research, Practice*. New York: Guilford Press, 1997.

Parrinder, Geoffrey. *African Traditional Religion*. London: SPCK, 1962.

Patton, John. *Pastoral Care in Context*. Louisville, KY: Westminster/John Knox Press, 1993.

Ramshaw, Elaine. *Ritual and Pastoral Care.* Philadelphia: Fortress, 1987.

Rogers, Carl R. *Client-Centered Therapy.* Boston: Houghton Mifflin, 1951.

———. *On Becoming a Person.* Boston: Houghton Mifflin, 1961.

Sanneh, Lamin. *Translating the Message: The Missionary Impact on Culture.* Maryknoll, NY: Orbis, 1989.

Silva-Netto, Benoni. "Pastoral Counseling in a Multicultural Context." *The Journal of Pastoral Care & Counseling* 46, no. 2 (June 1992): 131–139.

Sue, Derald W., and David Sue. *Counseling the Culturally Different: Theory and Practice.* New York: John Wiley & Sons, 1990.

Waruta, Douglas W., and H. W. Kinoti, eds. *Pastoral Care in African Christianity: Challenging Essays in Pastoral Theology.* Nairobi: Acton Publishers, 1994.

Williams, Daniel D. *The Minister and the Care of Souls.* New York: Harper & Row, 1961.

Wimberly, Edward P. *Pastoral Counseling and Spiritual Values: A Black Point of View.* Nashville: Abingdon, 1982.

Wise, Carroll A. *The Meaning of Pastoral Care.* New York: Harper & Row, 1966.

———. *The Meaning of Pastoral Care (with Revisions and Additions by John Hinkle, Jr.).* New York: Harper & Row, 1966; Meyer Stone Books, 1989.

———. *Pastoral Counseling: Its Theory and Practice.* New York: Harper & Brothers, 1951.

———. *Pastoral Psychotherapy: Theory and Practice.* New York: Jason Aronson, 1980.

4

The Significance of Johann Ludwig Krapf's Mission Work in East Africa

David Kimiri Ngaruiya
Associate Professor, International Leadership University, Nairobi, Kenya

Abstract

Scholars have divergent opinions regarding the legacy and effectiveness of Ludwig Krapf's missionary work in East Africa. Some claim that Krapf's work was a failure. Others argue that Krapf's mission work was a success. Using the lenses of civilization theory prevalent at the time of Krapf's mission undertaking, this paper examines the weight of these claims. The author argues that Krapf undertook a significant mission endeavor in East Africa. This paper draws on *Travels, Researches and Missionary Labours* and *Journals of the Rev. Messrs. Isenberg and Krapf.* The significance of Krapf's work is presented in the context of Krapf's early life and initial mission to East Africa, European presence and interests in East Africa in the 1840s, and Krapf and Rebmann's visit to the interior of East Africa.

Key words: mission theory, civilization, Ludwig Krapf, Church Missionary Society, Christianity, Galla, Rebmann.

Introduction

Scholars have divergent opinions regarding the legacy and effectiveness of Ludwig Krapf's missionary work in East Africa. M. Louise Pirouet describes some of the areas of debate among scholars pertaining to "the legacy" of Johann Ludwig Krapf in East Africa.[1] These include Krapf's expulsion from Ethiopia after a brief stay, that Krapf and his "companions" made "only a tiny handful of converts," that his mission "became a backwater," and that his missionary strategy was a failure.[2]

Pirouet notes that while Roland Oliver commends Krapf and Rebmann's "vision, tenacity and boundless energy," Oliver's evaluation of these missionaries is that they had little "evangelistic success" among the Wanika, for example.[3] Pirouet also notes that Adrian Hastings "barely" mentions Krapf in *Church in Africa*.[4] Roy Bridges, on the other hand, commends Krapf as "a remarkable pioneer, a good man, and a notable figure in the history of nineteenth-century Africa."[5] While it is clear that there are differences in appreciating the work of Krapf, it is important to understand Krapf's mission contribution in East Africa through the lens of the theory of civilization.

According to the civilization theory, it was important to educate the heathen to a point where they could comprehend the gospel. Accordingly, "The missionary enterprise thus became part of a much wider benevolent movement in Africa: to elevate the peoples of Africa to 'assume their place among civilized and Christian nations.'"[6] To this way of thinking, Christianity, as a "mighty lever," was the chief means of civilizing. The following kinds of assertions were made: "Let missionaries and school masters, the plough and the spade, go together and agriculture will flourish; the avenues of legitimate commerce will be opened; confidence between man and man will be inspired

---

1. M. Louise Pirouet, "The Legacy of Johann Ludwig Krapf," *International Bulletin of Mission* (April 1999): 69; Roland Oliver, *The Missionary Factor in East Africa* (London: Longmans, Green & Co., 1952).

2. Pirouet, "Legacy," 99.

3. Pirouet, 69.

4. Adrian Hastings, *The Church in Africa, 1450–1950* (Oxford: Clarendon Press, 1994).

5. C. Roy Bridges, "Introduction to the Second Edition," *Travels, Researches, and Missionary Labours during an Eighteen Years' Residence in Eastern Africa*, 2nd ed. (London: Frank Cass, 1968), 65.

6. Kwame Bediako, *Theology and Identity: The Impact of Culture upon Christian Thought in Second-Century and Modern Africa* (Carlisle: Regnum, 1992), 27.

while civilization will advance as the natural effect and Christianity will operate as the proximate cause of this happy change."[7]

That Krapf worked on the basis of the civilization theory of mission can be deduced from his statements, a publisher's note, and his strategy of using the Galla as the "Germans" of East Africa. In other words, just as the Germans were a leading civilizing force in Europe, the Gallas were a leading force in Africa and would become agents of civilizing Africa. Other indicators of his civilizational approach include his modified vision of building mission stations linking the East African coast with West Africa, and his later modified vision of building the apostles street comprising twelve mission stations from the Nile Valley to Ethiopia. Finally, Krapf's work in acquiring local languages and translating Scripture is a telling aspect of his civilizational approach. Krapf's approach had an impact on East Africa which is still being felt today, such as in the need for missionaries to be trained in local languages, the passing on of a mission vision, and the ability to adopt and protect the welfare of nationals.

In this brief paper, it will be argued that Ludwig Krapf made a significant impact toward the growth of Christianity in East Africa. This is important because the church in East Africa has been growing rapidly and it is good to appreciate the pioneers of missions in the region at the humble beginnings of a vision to spread Christianity. The significance of Krapf's impact is presented in the context of the last years of Krapf's mission to East Africa and then through his legacy.

Krapf's Early Life and Initial Mission to East Africa

Krapf was born in 1810 in the village of Deverendigen close to Tübingen, Germany. He was baptized Ludwig, the wrestler. His father was a farmer and well able to provide for his family.[8] At the age of eleven, Krapf was severely beaten by a neighbor for an offense he had not committed. The beating was so severe that Krapf was ill for six months. This experience, however, led him to focus on eternity, and he developed much interest in studying Scripture and devotional literature. Krapf also had a good attitude toward and aptitude for learning as he began his schooling. Krapf's sister was instrumental in leading him to be educated beyond elementary school.

---

7. T. F. Buxton, *The African Slave Trade and Its Remedy* (London: Frank Cass, 1840), 515.

8. J. Ludwig Krapf, *Travels, Researches, and Missionary Labours during an Eighteen Years' Residence in Eastern Africa* (London: Trubner & Co., 1860), 1.

Krapf recalled how he had to travel to and from school three times a day as he had lunch at home; he claimed that this repeated journey helped him grow to be healthy and prepared him to travel in his missionary career.[9] Krapf was provided with an atlas by his father; as he studied it, he wondered why there were hardly any place names in the region of Adal and Somali. Africa fascinated Krapf from an early age. When he was fourteen, he wanted to become a captain of a ship and sail to foreign lands. His parents, however, could not afford the training needed for a sea captain. Instead, Krapf joined a seminary and, through the influence of a missionary and friend by the name of Fjelstadt, Krapf was sent out as a missionary to Ethiopia, having learned Amharic and Ethiopic languages.

In 1837 Krapf began working with the Church Missionary Society (CMS). The CMS's "objectives and methods were suspect" to a significant part of the Anglican Church and its leadership at that time, which made it difficult for the CMS to engage missionaries from England.[10] This was a key factor in why Krapf, a German missionary, was taken on by the CMS. A CMS seminary had been started in Islington in 1825 which served to train foreign missionaries for the CMS. Krapf, however, trained at Basle Seminary, an institution founded by German Protestants in 1815. Krapf, a Christian of millenarian leanings, was influenced by pietism. Basle not only conducted its own missions but also provided men for the CMS,[11] which was how Krapf served under the CMS.

Krapf's missionary work in East Africa marked the beginning of serious work in that region. This is all the more evident when indigenous developments are considered; and Krapf is the only notable source of written information for some "parts of East Africa in the 1840s and 1850s."[12] Although the Portuguese had visited the East African coast, it was Krapf and other missionaries such as Rebmann and Erhardt who brought the interior of East Africa to the knowledge of Europeans. Krapf, for example, visited Ukambani in 1848 and 1852. Rebmann visited Jagga in 1848 and 1852. Erhardt visited Fuga in 1853. It is noteworthy that as David Livingstone was moving toward Mozambique from the south, Krapf and Rebmann were approaching the same place from the north.[13] This reveals that the East African coast was little known in Europe ethnographically, geographically, or in other ways.

---

9. Krapf, *Travels*, 6.
10. Bridges, "Introduction," 8.
11. Bridges, 9.
12. Bridges, 7.
13. Krapf, *Travels*, viii.

The Europeans had a preference for the East African coast over the West African coast because of the better climate, good harbors, less likelihood of fevers leading to death, and a stable political environment.[14] There were drawbacks, however, in reaching the East African coast; it was a long distance from Europe and not even the opening of the Suez Canal would shorten this distance. The Europeans were very eager to promote commerce in the region and Krapf influenced colonial powers to protect East Africa from occupation by the French. As the work of Krapf is considered, the context of rivalry among European nations regarding military and commercial superiority is evident.

Krapf viewed his mission as follows: "My calling, in which through all perils I have been so mercifully preserved and upheld, enables me to set forth in their true light the moral misery and degradation to which the heathen nations of East Africa have fallen, and to point out the various routes by which these benighted populations may be approached, and the means for their elevation to Christian truth and Christian civilization be conveyed to them."[15] According to Krapf, a missionary also needed to contribute toward geographical and scientific knowledge so as to advance the human race. Krapf described East Africa as "overflowing with milk and honey," and as having a great agricultural harvest requiring little labor.[16] Krapf was aware that there were barriers to be overcome in the work among the East African nations. Such barriers included a hostile welcome and a harborless coast, but these could be overcome.

Krapf was not only a man of hope and courage; he was also a man of optimism. In recommending his friend Rebmann for support, he referred to the Wanika among whom Rebmann worked as a "perverse and crooked" generation, words that were used by Jesus in reference to the Pharisees. At the same time Krapf was ready to continue to labor for his fellow Christians who were surrounded by hostile nations. How Krapf longed that such believers would be revived by the Lord to become light to those around them! Krapf envisioned those tribes becoming "spiritual rivers to irrigate the arid wastes of surrounding heathenism."[17] Such was his hope.

From a young age, Krapf had valued education and longed to have Africa known by the European world. He considered himself as a light to the Africa he worked hard to reach and was not deterred by difficulties coming his way. Thus we see Krapf as a man well prepared for his task of bringing the good

---

14. Krapf, xxxiv.
15. Krapf, xiv.
16. Krapf, xvi.
17. Krapf, xvi.

news to East Africa through good education and knowledge of local languages. Moreover, Krapf was also concerned about the consequences of occupation of East Africa by colonial powers.

Krapf's Arrival in Ethiopia

Krapf joined Wilhelm Isenberg in 1837 to continue the work begun by Samuel Godat, who had studied at Islington, revitalized the Coptic Church in Egypt, and extended the work to Ethiopia, then known as Abyssinia. Bridges states that, in general, the CMS work in Abyssinia seems to have been aimed at creating a "Reformation" equivalent to that in Europe, one means being that of using the Gospels in a vernacular language.[18] Krapf joined Isenberg in Abyssinia, but within two months the two missionaries were expelled because they were considered to be enemies collaborating with the English to conquer Abyssinia. This hostility gained particular intensity with the arrival of two Roman Catholic priests accompanied by two French Catholic brothers. The Roman Catholics had given an Abyssinian priest a "present," a practice that Krapf and Isenberg would not condone.

Not only was the church in Abyssinia opposed to Protestantism, but also Islam was spreading very rapidly. Isenberg and Krapf did all they could to continue the work, but opposition would not allow it. Isenberg then left for Europe, traveling through Cairo to have Amharic works prepared for the press. At this time Krapf resided in Shoa and translated the New Testament into the language of the Gallas. Krapf changed the Roman Catholic thinking "Give us China and Asia is ours" to "Give us the Gallas and Central Africa is ours."[19]

Krapf often accompanied the king during the Shoa conquest of the Gallas. Krapf noted that the Abyssinians were extreme monophysites, perceiving Christ as having one nature and will.[20] The Shoans were a rigid people in their fasting practice but immorality was rampant among them. "Krapf's labors and sufferings in Abyssinia" and in Shoa "form one of the most thrilling chapters for missionary history," according to Eugene Stock.[21] Stock also notes that, in a sense, the CMS mission in Abyssinia did not die because it became "East Africa Mission" two years later when Krapf moved to Mombasa. No wonder

---

18. Bridges, "Introduction," 10.
19. Krapf, *Travels*, 27.
20. Krapf, 39.
21. Eugene Stock, *The History of the Church Missionary Society* (London: Church Missionary Society, 1899), 353.

Krapf and Isenberg could assert that "we are pilgrims for him" and rested on the principle that a good reception of the gospel would lead to the flourishing of a nation.[22] Both men can only be commended for their integrity in Ethiopia. In any case, it is not an unknown fact that Christianity thrives even in moments of opposition.

The European Presence and Interests in East Africa in the 1840s

As already stated, not much of East Africa was known by the European world. However, there was considerable British influence to end the slave trade in Zanzibar in the 1840s, partly on account of the fact that the Asian traders known as "Banyans," who were also British subjects, were an economic force that was suited to a growing expansion of the British Empire. Krapf refused to engage in searching for antimony mines in East Africa. It is a well-known fact that in the 1800s and 1900s "colonies existed for the benefit of the mother country."[23] Bridges states that humanitarian and geographical exploration were two key factors that furthered British interests in East Africa.[24]

In the 1820s Mombasa was a British protectorate on the understanding that the slave trade would discontinue in the region. The Mazrui clan, who were the rulers in Mombasa at the time, were ousted by Said Seyyid in 1837. When Krapf visited Zanzibar, he wished to go onto the mainland, but Captain Atkins Hamerton, a British consul, not wishing to arouse Arab hostility, would not allow Europeans to do so. European endeavors to reach the interior of East Africa had failed and this interior remained a mystery up to the middle of the nineteenth century. The previous barriers of unnavigable waters, disease, hostile tribes, and difficulties of terrain were now overcome by concentrating resources of money, effort, and time. Both Europeans and Arabs used African trade routes to penetrate the interior.

The "Germans" of East Africa

The Gallas were of special interest to Krapf because he considered that upon their conversion as Christians they were "destined by providence" to be capable of fulfilling the mission of heaven as pointed out to the Germans in

---

22. Charles W. Isenberg and Johann L. Krapf, *Journals of the Rev. Messrs Isenberg and Krapf: Missionaries of the Church Missionary Society* (London: Seeley & Burnside, 1843), 34, 206.

23. George Frederick Zook, *Japan and Germany* (New York: Carnegie Endowment for International Peace, 1947), 694.

24. Bridges, "Introduction," 20.

Europe.[25] Krapf estimated the Gallas to number about six to eight million. The name "Gallas" means "immigrants" and was coined by Arabs; Krapf and the Abyssinians referred to them as "Ormas." While making attempts to reach the Gallas, Krapf realized that East Africa was a vast mission field and not dominated by Islam as he had previously thought. According to Krapf, had the Abyssinians been united under one leader, they would have conquered the whole of East Africa. Krapf observed that the Gallas were in a "low state of heathenism," spoke a common language, and revered the Sabbath day.[26]

The weapons of the Gallas included swords, spears, and shields. They rode on horseback and considered it beneath their dignity to "go on foot."[27] They were also farmers, producing grain such as wheat and corn, and they reared livestock. Krapf had a great determination to bring them Christianity and the European way of life. Priests and magicians were influential in the Galla traditions. Every year, the Gallas would offer a huge sacrifice of sheep and oxen to Waka, their most powerful deity.[28]

Krapf wished to extend his mission to the Gallas but a Galla insurrection in Yerver made the endeavor unsafe. Two fellow workers were also stranded at Tajua, and Krapf set out to help them. He also had a personal interest in undertaking the trip because he intended to marry Rosine Dietrich. His journey to Massoa was difficult, resulting in the loss of his possessions and his being held hostage. At Massoa he made his way to Aden and finally to Egypt, where he married Dietrich in the autumn of 1842.[29]

Krapf's return to Abyssinia was not a success due to hostility toward Protestant missionaries; to add to his pain, he lost his daughter who was born prematurely. There was such strong pressure to keep going that his wife Rosine could rest for only three days following the loss of their child.[30] Later, Krapf would lose a second daughter and his wife through ill-health. To the committee at home Krapf wrote, "Tell our friends at home there is now on the East African Coast a lonely missionary grave. This is a sign that you have commenced the struggle with this part of the world; and as the victories of the Church are gained by stepping over the graves of her members, you may be the more

---

25. Krapf, *Travels*, 72.
26. Isenberg and Krapf, *Journals*, 162.
27. Isenberg and Krapf, 75.
28. Isenberg and Krapf, 77.
29. Isenberg and Krapf, 106.
30. Isenberg and Krapf, 110.

convinced that the hour is at hand when you are summoned to the conversion of Africa from its eastern shore."[31]

Krapf notes that Protestants had the consolation of knowing that they had distributed 2,000 copies of Scripture, which brought the figure to a total of 8,000 copies distributed since the work had begun in Abyssinia. Although focused, Krapf was by no means a man of narrow vision. He considered it the duty of a Christian missionary to reach not only the heathen, but also the scattered Jews.[32] Scripture was to be propagated by word and writing, and Krapf would later use school books that Isenberg had prepared.[33]

The heart of Ludwig Krapf continued to burn with a passion to reach the Gallas. He feared that if they were not reached, Islam would take root among them and this would hinder the growth of "Christianity and true morality" in Africa.[34] Krapf and his wife arrived in Zanzibar and spent a little time there preaching to the American and English community before moving to Mombasa. At Mombasa, Krapf's strategy was to reach the Gallas with the good news through the Wanika people.

Krapf devoted himself to learning the Swahili language and he considered 8 June 1844 to be one of the most important days of his life: it was the day when he began to translate the book of Genesis into Kiswahili. Krapf continued to envision mission stations connecting East Africa and West Africa, a task that could be completed within four or five years.[35] Having mastered the Swahili language, Krapf translated the whole of the New Testament into Kiswahili and composed a short grammar and dictionary of the language.[36]

One senses the frustration of Krapf because the people begged for much of what he had. Thus he endured poverty, trusting that his generosity would be a testimony to his faith that would draw the people to Christianity. Krapf noted the native belief in *koma*, which were shades or spirits of the dead believed by the Wanika to be powerful. Their main "resting place" was at Kaya, the major town of the Wanika where a hut was built as a habitation for them.[37] Krapf continued to labor at the coast and was joined by Erhardt with a Portuguese servant named Anthony. Anthony died of sickness, but Krapf said of him, "His very death has brought a blessing to the Wanika and although dead he

---

31. Stock, *History*, 461–462.
32. J. M. Flad, *The Falashas (Jews) of Abyssinia* (London: William Mackintosh, 1869), viii.
33. Isenberg and Krapf, *Journals*, 119.
34. Krapf, *Travels*, 122.
35. Krapf, 134.
36. Krapf, 140.
37. Krapf, 176.

still speaks to them; for they have now for the first time seen the death and burial of a Christian."[38]

In 1850, after thirteen years in Africa, Krapf returned to Europe to promote his vision of mission stations in Africa and to have his work published. He returned to East Africa in 1851. The notable difference was that Mringe, a crippled man with whom Krapf had been sharing the good news, had died. However, Mringe had died as a believer and had been baptized by Rebmann.[39] Krapf returned to Europe again in 1853 due to poor health, but the mission in East Africa was reinforced by a new missionary, Deimler, from Bavaria.[40] Having published his English liturgy and Wakuafi dictionary, in 1854 Krapf set out to visit Abyssinia on his journey to Rabai. War in Abyssinia, however, prevented him from proceeding to Shoa, and as he made his way back to Cairo his health deteriorated to such an extent that the only wise thing to do was to return to Europe.[41]

Krapf had not only a vision but also a strategy. His aim was to seek the transformation of a local culture. By devoting his time and effort to translate Scripture into a local language, Krapf was empowering nationals to fully participate in and to benefit from the mission endeavors. Andrew Walls notes that Germans provided leadership in African linguistics.[42] In our day, the work of translation continues, and it is now common practice to have a team working on a Bible translation. Krapf, in spite of not having such a team, commenced the work with urgency.

Rebmann's approach to mission hinged on the strategy of Christianity that is "realized and embodied" in addition to it being taught and preached. For him, being a married missionary and bringing up children would be a powerful and effective witness.[43]

In the next section Krapf's travels to the interior are highlighted.

Krapf's and Rebmann's Ventures into the Interior of East Africa

Krapf made three journeys to Ukambani. On his second journey, he became great friends with chief Kivoi, who had great influence at the coast and on the

---

38. Krapf, 206.
39. Krapf, 211.
40. Krapf, 213.
41. Krapf, 215.
42. Andrew Walls, *The Cross-Cultural Process in Christian History* (Maryknoll, NY: Orbis, 2002), 209.
43. Krapf, 246.

mainland. Kivoi was familiar with Europeans and Arabs, and Swahili, and he gave Krapf the opportunity to share the good news among the Wakambas. Krapf was, however, aware of and careful concerning Kivoi's greed, and he avoided being swayed to join Kivoi's schemes.[44] Krapf identified Yata as the most suitable place for a mission station.

However, there was an attack on Kivoi and his caravan, and Kivoi died. This led to a plan to have Krapf punished by death for not protecting Kivoi from death. Krapf managed to escape back to Yata and to remain alive through much fatigue, hunger, sickness, and the real threat to his life. During his second journey to Ukambani, Krapf compiled an ethnography of the Wakuafi, Maasai, and Wakambas. He concluded that it was best to postpone a mission to the Kamba and establish an intermediate station at either Kadiaro, Ndara, or Buru.

Rebmann visited Jagga three times and sighted the snow-capped Kilimanjaro in addition to visiting Kadiaro.[45] The fact that a mountain so close to the Equator was snowcapped created a lot of controversy in Europe. Some held that the "existence of perpetual snow" had not been proven.[46] Krapf believed that, in general, the good news reaches a nation "on the brink of destruction." He also noted that critics of missions could blame missionaries for the deterioration of morality in a community reached with the gospel.[47]

On his second journey to Usambara, Krapf observed that the kind disposition of the king toward missionaries, the respect and orderliness of the local people toward their leaders, and the prevailing peace were factors conducive to mission in that region. Krapf also noted that it was best for a missionary to keep away from kings and courts as much as possible and to focus on telling the good news to common people. However, a missionary needed to attend to the king and his family if the king expressed interest in being instructed in God's Word. Krapf objected to the Jesuit principle that missionaries should seek to influence a leader and through the leader influence the subjects. Krapf's approach was to appeal to the heart and conscience of anyone because "the poorest and most insignificant when they truly believe in Christ and are born of God are more worthy and contribute more" to the growth of Christianity than those who advance worldly causes by means of the gospel.[48] Krapf's travels and those of his colleagues such as Rebmann

---

44. Krapf, 314.
45. Krapf, 249.
46. William Desborough Cooley, *Inner Africa Laid Open* (London: Longman, Brown, Green & Longmans, 1852), 127.
47. Krapf, *Travels*, 402.
48. Krapf, 407.

yielded helpful and accurate knowledge, such as that of snow on mountains near the Equator.

The Last Years of Krapf's Mission to East Africa

On his voyage from Mombasa to Cape Delgado, Krapf noted that the Niassa country was still the chief seat of the slave trade.[49] Krapf returned to Abyssinia in 1855; this time, the political power was completely anti-Romanist and the Abuna received the Protestant missionaries favorably. It will be recalled that the Catholics had previously hindered the expansion of Protestant missionary work.[50] The Abuna was pleased to learn that artisans would be sent to work in various trades; they spread the gospel by teaching and example. The missionaries arrived in Abyssinia in 1856.

Erhardt's comment that "if the tribes of the coast are to influence those of the interior, they must first be elevated on the social scale"[51] is an important one. This is because missionaries opposed slavery and the slave trade, as Erhardt continued: ". . . thus in promoting the growth of sheep and cotton powerful blows would be dealt to the American slave trade."[52] Such was also the attitude of Krapf in seeking the welfare of those he was reaching.

The Legacy of Ludwig Krapf

"Krapf has long been before the public in honorable connection with the attempts to introduce civilization and Christianity into the benighted continent of Africa, no less than as a pioneer of important geographical discoveries, and a most successful laborer in the field of Hametic philology."[53] It should be kept in mind that Krapf covered a vast territory and his work comprises many volumes. While according to some Krapf could have made more of an impact, Krapf's impact is nevertheless notable. Bridges notes some significant areas where Krapf made a lasting impact both in Europe and in East Africa.[54] Such areas include missionary strategy, politics (though at a limited level),

---

49. Krapf, 424.
50. Krapf, 441, 453.
51. Krapf, 503.
52. Krapf, 504.
53. Krapf, vii.
54. Bridges, "Introduction," 49.

and economics. The number of missions to East Africa grew and there was a scramble for Africa not long after Krapf died.

Although Krapf had made very few converts, the establishment of the Rabai mission was a gateway to the evangelization of East Africa. Later missions would note that "East Africa is emerging into something approaching light, and we can trace successful waves of conquest."[55] Building a case to justify "enlightened Western influence," Keable stated that "the enjoyment of civilization carries with it a moral obligation" of "sharing . . . its benefits with weaker and childlike races."[56] One may agree that Western believers were obligated to share the good news, but some of their perspectives on image-bearers did not resonate with the gospel truth they were propagating. The CMS still has a presence in Kenya, having been joined by many other missions in East Africa, including Africa Inland Mission.

The Anglican Church in Kenya now has a history of 175 years, with theological institutions such as Saint Paul's Theological College, ordained local bishops, and a church membership of over two million. In August 1994, part of the history of the Anglican Church was relived by some of the faithful who walked from Mombasa, Nyeri, and Mumias to Nairobi to commemorate Krapf's journey from Rabai in addition to the journey of the Rev. William Jones in taking the news of Bishop Hannington's death to Mombasa.[57]

The Germans and the French made use of Krapf's work. The Paris Geographical Society gave the work of Krapf visibility while his immense work in Ethiopian languages was recognized by Tübingen University which awarded him a doctor of philosophy degree. Krapf also discerned the immense use of the Swahili language in East Africa, and his publication of a Swahili grammar and New Testament has been a great tool for missionaries working in East Africa. Krapf's book *Travels, Researches and Missionary Labours during an Eighteen Years' Residence in Eastern Africa* is an invaluable work and is the primary source for this paper. For Krapf, the work on the Swahili dictionary was geared toward the propagation of faith and Christian civilization.[58] In the twentieth century, the evangelization of Africa has mainly been undertaken

---

55. Robert Keable, *Darkness or Light: Studies in the History of the Universities Mission to Central Africa Illustrating the Theory and Practice of Mission* (London: Universities Mission to Central Africa, 1912), 23.

56. Keable, *Darkness or Light*, 48.

57. Provincial Unit of Research, Church Province of Kenya, *Rabai to Mumias: A Short History of the Church of the Province of Kenya 1844 to 1994* (Nairobi: Uzima Press, 1994), 183.

58. Ludwig Krapf, *A Dictionary of the Suahili Language* (London: Trubner & Co., 1882), xi.

by Africans.[59] This should be a heartening footnote to the labors of Krapf and others who painstakingly brought the gospel to East Africa. Krapf spent twenty years in the missionary enterprise and a further twenty-five in behind-the-scenes work for Africa and the gospel.[60]

In March 1885, Thomas Wakefield wrote back home to appeal for help in the mission to the Gallas. For Wakefield, "the greatest and most interesting (to me) of all items of progress I have to report this month, is the commencement of the GALLA MISSION."[61] Thomas Wakefield was a missionary of the United Methodist Free Churches Mission at Ribe in Mombasa. It was in the year 1861 that Wakefield and Woodman volunteered for missions to East Africa[62] as a result of Krapf's mission work in East Africa.

Conclusion

Ludwig Krapf made a significant impact on East Africa through his mission endeavor, though there are differences of opinion among scholars regarding the success of this remarkable man. This impact can be traced through the context of Krapf's early life and initial mission to East Africa, the European presence and interests in East Africa in the 1840s, and Krapf and Rebmann's visits to the interior of East Africa. Krapf produced substantial materials that were published and distributed among the Christian community. His work reminds evangelical Christian missions that people of good training, character, and commitment are needed in mission frontiers and that their work may take decades and even centuries to be appreciated. Krapf used his skills in linguistics to translate Scripture for the benefit of nationals. His travels contributed geographical knowledge regarding the interior of East Africa, and he worked with others toward this task. It is, however, true that the theory of civilization has its limitations, and the author of this paper recommends that further work be done to seek to understand its effect in the Kenyan context in the way Krapf and others used it in their undertaking.

The Anglican Church in Kenya today forms the largest Protestant denomination and is continuing to grow. Alongside nationals, the CMS has a place in a region where the church has become indigenous. At the present

---

59. Walls, *Cross-Cultural Process*, 65.

60. Bridges, "Introduction," 8.

61. E. S. Wakefield, *Missionary and Geographical Pioneer in East Equatorial Africa* (London: Religious Tract Society, 1904), 191.

62. Wakefield, 45.

time, when the Anglican Church around the world has been split on doctrinal issues regarding, for example, the ordination of homosexuals and the blessing of same-sex marriages, some Anglican Churches in the West have chosen to align themselves with the Anglican Church in East Africa, where same-sex marriage is not sanctioned by the church. In our time, this very church that Krapf founded stands as a custodian of evangelical doctrine committed to the biblical criteria for ordaining leaders in the Anglican Church. This is a good reflection of what Krapf sought to accomplish: to bring the gospel of hope to the many who needed to hear and embrace it.

Bibliography

Bediako, Kwame. *Theology and Identity: The Impact of Culture upon Christian Thought in Second Century and Modern Africa.* Carlisle, UK: Regnum, 1992.

Bridges, Roy C. "Introduction to the Second Edition." In *Travels, Researches, and Missionary Labours during an Eighteen Years' Residence in Eastern Africa.* 2nd edition. London: Frank Cass, 1968.

Buxton, T. F. *The African Slave Trade and Its Remedy.* London: Frank Cass, 1840.

Cooley, William Desborough. *Inner Africa Laid Open.* London: Longman, Brown, Green & Longmans, 1852.

Coupland, Reginald. *The Exploitation of East Africa, 1856–1890.* Evanston, IL: Northwestern University Press, 1967.

Flad, J. M. *The Falashus (Jews) of Abbysinia.* London: William Mackintosh, 1869.

Hastings, Adrian. *The Church in Africa, 1450–1950.* Oxford: Clarendon Press, 1994.

Isenberg, Charles W., and Johann L. Krapf. *Journals of the Rev. Messrs Isenberg and Krapf: Missionaries of the Church Missionary Society.* London: Seeley & Burnside, 1843.

Keable, Robert. *Darkness or Light: Studies in the History of the Universities Mission to Central Africa Illustrating the Theory and Practice of Mission.* London: Universities Mission to Central Africa, 1912.

Krapf, J. Lewis. *Travels, Researches, and Missionary Labours during an Eighteen Years' Residence in Eastern Africa.* London: Trubner & Co., 1860.

Krapf, Ludwig. *A Dictionary of the Suahili Language.* London: Trubner & Co., 1882.

Latourette, Kenneth Scott. *A History of the Expansion of Christianity.* Vol. 5. Grand Rapids, MI: Zondervan, 1969.

Oliver, Roland. *The Missionary Factor in East Africa.* London: Longmans, Green & Co., 1952.

Pirouet, M. Louise. "The Legacy of Johann Ludwig Krapf." *International Bulletin of Mission* (April 1999): 69–72.

Provincial Unit of Research-Church Province of Kenya. *Rabai to Mumias: A Short History of the Church of the Province of Kenya 1844 to 1994.* Nairobi, Kenya: Uzima Press, 1994.

Stock, Eugene. *The History of the Church Missionary Society*. London: Church Missionary Society, 1899.

Wakefield, E. S. *Missionary and Geographical Pioneer in East Equatorial Africa*. London: Religious Tract Society, 1904.

Walls, Andrew. *The Cross-Cultural Process in Christian History*. Maryknoll, NY: Orbis, 2002.

Zook, George Frederick. *Japan and Germany*. New York: Carnegie Endowment for International Peace, 1947.

Part II

Addressing African Realities

5

Syncretism in African Christianity: A Boon or a Bane?

Joseph D. Galgalo
Vice Chancellor, St Paul's University, Limuru, Kenya

Abstract

This paper begins by painting a broad canvas of the extensive theme of "African contextual realities" but in a rather impressionistic and sketchy way, without dealing with this topic in any length or depth. Attention is then drawn to some key trends and developments in African Christianity, before considering, in a brief but more focused way, the question of whether syncretism is a boon or a bane for the growth and health of African Christianity.

Key words: African Christianity, syncretism, pluralism, Traditional Religion, doctrine, conversational model.

Introduction: African Contextual Realities

Where do we start in painting a broad picture of the contextual realities of our times? It is not an exaggeration to say that we live in the most dangerous of times. The world powers have accumulated for themselves nuclear and other arsenals capable of destroying the world ten times over. Alarm bells are ringing that the world is slowly but surely facing a disaster as a result of continued global warming. The danger presented by climate change aside, the world is experiencing devastating conflicts. The wars in Yemen, Iraq, Syria, Somalia, Nigeria, and several parts of Asia and South America are no longer isolated cases. Each of these conflicts has the potential to engulf the whole world in its scope and intensity.

The European struggle with the refugee crisis caused by unprecedented mass migration of peoples from the Middle East and some African countries has brought home the scale and effect of large-scale geopolitical conflicts and what this means for the whole world. The 2006 Oxford Research Group Report entitled *Global Responses to Global Threats* identified four major areas of global threat – climate change, competition over resources, marginalization of the Majority World, and global militarization. Each of these threats, cumulatively or singly, carries the potential to destabilize the whole world. The report concluded that "Unless urgent action is taken within the next five to ten years, it will be extremely difficult, if not impossible, to avoid a highly unstable global system by the middle years of the [twenty-first] century."[1]

Such is the global context in which we find ourselves. Africa is more vulnerable than most parts of the world because of the internal conflicts, governance and leadership crises, crises of values, economic difficulties (not least because of international trade opportunity imbalances, gross trade deficit, mismanagement, unhealthy competition, and negative exploitation of resources), as well as crises to do with social progress and diseases (with which, besides the biggest killers like malaria and TB, we contend much more than the rest of the world with the threat of HIV/AIDS, water-borne diseases, and, more recently, Ebola). In addition, Africa faces, at all levels of society, the threats of religious and ethnic conflicts, as well as political differences and expediency – which often marginalizes, discriminates against, and abuses the goodwill of the masses.

Kenya, more than ever before, is faced with internal political strife, terrorism, ethnic conflicts, and governance issues. The curse of corruption is perhaps Kenya's biggest challenge. According to a 2016 survey by PricewaterhouseCoopers (PwC), Kenya ranks top of the world in embezzlement, bribery and procurement fraud. Embezzlement is top on the list of economic crimes.[2] Sometimes we do not realize how much corruption costs the common citizen, including the unborn child.

---

1. Chris Abbott, Paul Rogers, and John Sloboda, *Global Responses to Global Threats: Sustainable Security for the 21st Century* (Oxford: Oxford Research Group, 2006), 4, http://oxfordresearchgroup.org.uk/sites/default/files/globalthreats.pdf.

2. Dominic Omondi, "Survey: Kenya Ranked Third Most Corrupt Country in the World," Standard Digital, 27 February 2016, https://www.standardmedia.co.ke/article/2000193065/survey-kenya-ranked-third-most-corrupt-country-in-the-world.

According to the World Bank, in any given year, "Over 250,000 jobs are lost through corruption,"[3] and that corruption puts the affordability of services, including access to basic needs such as water and electricity, and the cost of business and transport, out of reach of many Kenyans. According to the World Bank report, "Economic instability, weaknesses in infrastructure and pervasive corruption limit business growth and job creation," and "Top on the list is public sector procurement system where Sh.35.8 billion out of Sh.298.5 billion was lost through corruption in 2014 alone. The money was enough to employ 87,000 people. The private sector also lost Sh.68 billion in lost sales through corruption, money that is enough to employ 166,000 people."[4]

Kenya is faced with myriads of other problems, including youth unemployment and crime, endemic poverty and a high unemployment rate, food deficit, insecurity, and ethnic balkanization of various communities. The post-election violence of 2007/08 exposed Kenya's soft underbelly, showing its fragility as a nation, but in these contextual realities it is possible to point out two pertinent issues about African Christianity.

Apostasy and Double Loyalty

Kenya is largely, by its own profession, a Christian country, yet it is also a country in a deep crisis of values. What we believe does not seem to define who we are or inform what we can and cannot do. Our values are so impaired that ethics and morality are simply means to an end in a drama of life where wrong or right seems to be neither here nor there. In a world of twisted morality, it seems that ill-gotten wealth is the new moral default, seen as normal and desirable as long as it comes with status and power. This is the way of the world; but, in my view, Christians also have given into corruption and complacency and by doing so are being conformed to the patterns of this world. The net effect of this sad state is an *apostate Christianity*[5] in which the true sense of values is so corrupted that sin has become an ally of sorts – sanitized, cleansed, absolved, "normalized," and accommodated. Thus, our first conclusion is that

---

3. World Bank, *Kenya Economic Update*, December 2012 (Edition No. 7).

4. World Bank Report, "Kenya Economic Update, December 2012; Kenya at Work Energizing the Economy and Creating Jobs," https://openknowledge.worldbank.org/handle/10986/26660.

5. The word "apostasy" comes from the Greek *apostasia*, which is translated "falling away" in 2 Thess 2:3. The word is closely related to the Greek word for "divorce" (*apostasion*). Apostates are those who abandon or neglect the true path. So African Christianity is comparable to a broken marriage, in which the partners live together but both or one is in an adulterous or unfaithful, extramarital relationship.

Kenyan Christianity (if we may generalize) is guilty of apostasy, of having drunk deeply from the well of society's moral deficiency, which has become an absurd new normal.

Second, a qualitative analysis of the health of African Christianity shows a state of spirituality that is comparable to "a psychopathic personality disorder." A standard description of a psychopathic personality runs like this:

> The psychopath is one of the most fascinating and distressing problems of human experience. For the most part, a psychopath never remains attached to anyone or anything . . . They feel little or no regret, and little or no remorse – except when they are caught . . . They see people in terms of how they can be used. They use people for stimulation, to build their self-esteem and they invariably value people in terms of their material value (money, property, etc.).[6]

Religion has been abused by many followers in similar ways. Particular forms of spirituality or religious loyalty are motivated solely by perceived or real gain; a religion is therefore sometimes followed in the search for some "faith-power." Adherents in this category mainly seek success from whatever inspiration religion may afford. Faith, in this case, is sought after as a boost to self-esteem and a means to health, wealth, power, and status. This astonishing reality could be the key reason why African Christianity is bafflingly flexible and hospitably accommodative to irreconcilable religious views. In Africa, Christianity often appears as just another thread in a plural form of religious beliefs and practices. Elsewhere I made the observation that "African Christianity is incurably pluralistic. Africans are generally hospitable to varied religious views. African Christians are capable of participating in Islam, one form or another of Christianity, and African traditional rituals all in one day without fear of self-contradiction."[7] No wonder some popular forms of Christianity seem to embrace the conviction that if the blood of Christ can wash away the curse of sin, such little things as the curse of poverty can be washed away by the sprinkling of the blood of a white cockerel or a goat.

The insatiable search for material wealth and for freedom from the fear of generational curse, bondage to superstitious beliefs, and the fear of witchcraft will continue to enslave such African Christians even if, at the same time, they

---

6. Michael G. Conner, "The Psychopathic Personality," *Bend Psychology*, May 21, 2014, http://www.bendpsychology.com/Handouts/PsychopathicPersonality.htm.

7. Joseph Galgalo, *African Christianity: The Stranger Within* (Limuru: Zapf Chancery Publishers Africa, 2012), 27.

confess "Christ as Lord and Savior." Many examples could be cited to drive this point home. For example, the story is told of a woman from a community that practices female genital circumcision who, against the collective wisdom of the community, refused to be subjected to this practice. Unfortunately, this woman was not able to carry any pregnancy to term, and every time she miscarried she was told that it was because she was under a curse for not having undergone circumcision. Similarly, some communities might attribute troubled marriages or barrenness to the neglect of one or other traditional religious duties, their being Christians notwithstanding.

In some Christian communities, widows must be ritually cleansed through varied means, sometimes including sexual rituals, following the deaths of their husbands, and a widow may be blamed and even punished for subsequent deaths in the family if such deaths happen before she accepts the necessary cleansing. Church-going Christians often bow to popular beliefs, such as blood sacrifices as part of funeral rites to ward off evil spirits, poverty, or sickness that otherwise might easily stalk them. It is because of this that we conclude that African Christianity "suffers from a form of religious schizophrenia,"[8] to use a phrase first used in African theology by Archbishop Desmond Tutu. Most African Christians are happy to carry the cross, profess Christ, and also accept the obligations of their Traditional Religion, even where the beliefs and demands of these two religions are obviously irreconcilable.

Thus we have two negative observations about African Christianity: it is (1) an apostate and (2) a schizophrenic Christianity. We must be quick, however, to add a rider. This is a general observable characteristic of African Christianity but it is by no means the sum total of what African Christianity is or stands for. Again, as I argued elsewhere, "African Christianity is strong, despite many challenges and weaknesses. This is because African Christianity still has sufficient critical mass of [a] true and faithful community of believers who are burning their candle bright, and holding it up, for all to see;" "We may strain to see the wheat from the tare, but there is no doubt that the wheat is thriving and bearing fruit."[9] The biggest threat is from furtive syncretism, a resurgent African Traditional Religion, and, not least, increasing secularism, all of which, if not checked, carry the potential to eclipse African Christianity.

---

8. Desmond Tutu, "Black Theology and African Theology: Soul Mates or Antagonist?" in *A Reader in African Christian Theology*, ed. John Parratt (London: SPCK, 1987), 47–58; cf. Desmond Tutu, "Whither African Theology?," in *Christianity in Independent Africa*, ed. E. Fashole-Luke et al. (London: Rex Collins, 1978), 364–369.

9. Galgalo, *African Christianity*, 29.

We have outlined, albeit briefly, the contextual realities that face African Christianity today. Let us now see some trends and developments shaping African Christianity.

Trends and Developments

Before we address the question of whether syncretism is a boon or a bane for African Christianity, let us first take a closer look at the trends and developments in African Christianity. Besides apostasy and dual belonging, two key things are equally conspicuous in the religious phenomenon we called African Christianity: its *rapid growth* and *diversity*. Many renowned writers have made clear how rapidly Christianity is spreading in places where it was never heard of some two or so hundred years ago. Andrew Walls, widely quoted on this point, draws our attention to a trend that started in the twentieth century: "the composition of the Christian church, ethnically and culturally, has changed out of recognition . . . [with] a massive accession to Christian faith . . . [taking] place outside the west, in southern continents, including many areas where, before the present century, Christians were few in number."[10] Walls further makes this pertinent observation:

> At the beginning of this century, some 83% of those who professed the Christian faith lived in Europe and North America. Now, some 60% (probably) live in Africa, Asia, Latin America, or the Pacific Islands, and that proportion is rising every year. The center of gravity of the Christian church has moved sharply southwards. The representative Christianity of the twenty-first century seems set to be that of Africa, Asia, Latin America, and the Pacific region. These areas look destined to be the launch pad for the mission of the church in the twenty-first century.[11]

The vibrancy and numerical growth of African Christianity is not in doubt. Churches are sprouting everywhere, making the African landscape unimaginable without church buildings and the conspicuous presence of communities of faith. What is equally amazing is African Christianity's diverse expressions. With everything from ancient Egyptian and Ethiopian Orthodox churches to the newest of the new denominations in East, West, South, and Central Africa, Africa is (perhaps) the continent with the greatest number of

---

10. Andrew F. Walls, "The Mission of the Church Today in the Light of Global History," *Word and World* 20, no. 1 (Winter 2000): 17.
11. Walls, "Mission of the Church Today," 18.

Christian denominations in the world. The diversity of African Christianity makes it very difficult to speak of an "African Christianity." We have multiple appropriations of the gospel and numerous forms of faith expression that exist side by side. The multiple forms of African Christianity raise the question of the accuracy of the expression "African Christianity" as opposed to *Christianities.*

In Kenya alone, the State Law Office says that there were about 20,000 registered Christian denominations in 2015. During the 2009 national census, this number stood at about 8,200 legally registered denominations. A total of 4.5 million of the 31.8 million Christians in these denominations did not want to be identified with either Catholics or any of the Protestant denominations.[12] They were happy to be referred to as Pentecostal, or as members of one or other of the house or family churches, or of the many African Instituted Churches. The denominational diversity is not without merit, especially when each can contribute to the overall vibrancy of mission and the extension of the kingdom of God. The downside is that some of these denominations, judged by their teachings and practices, do not sufficiently meet acceptable standards of orthodoxy to be called Christian. The diversity, therefore, is not just about denominations but also about doctrines and practices that put the authenticity of "being Christian" to the test. For example, *Dispatches*, in a YouTube video entitled *Saving Africa's Witch Children*,[13] exposes an extremely dangerous cult, a "Christian" denomination that mixes Christian beliefs and African traditional spirituality and believes that the devil lives among them, embodied in some of their own children. These children are believed to be possessed by the devil, who either works through them or turns them into evil witches. The video captures testimonies of believers, their pastors, and their bishops proudly narrating how they have tortured and even killed some children suspected of being possessed. It is unbelievable that these children – baptized into "Christian" faith and given biblical names like Mary – can be victims of such atrocities committed in the name of Jesus. It is simply baffling that Christian pastors, at least those propagating this brand of Christianity, can endorse murder, torture, and the abandonment of innocent children, all in the name of God. Who would think that Christianity would ever be accused of killing or murder in the name of God? It is even more difficult to fathom how these merchants of death interpret the biblical commandment "Thou shalt not kill." And what could be their view of the biblical gospel of

---

12. Government of Kenya, "State Law Office and Department of Justice on Religious Freedom Report for 2015."

13. Posted 1 November 2013, https://www.youtube.com/watch?v=ooXBMU_06vg.

forgiveness? What about Christ's grand mission, that he came "that all may have life, and have it abundantly?" This kind of Christianity is possible only because of the conflicting worldviews followed by these supposedly Christian adherents. It reveals the dangerous reality that African Christianity is pluralistic to the extent that most Christians do profess Christ but also hold dear other cherished beliefs. The paradox is that such Christians are able to partake of two conflicting worldviews and, strangely, can live by two value systems even where contradictions may be apparent.

The plural nature of African Christianity cannot be overemphasized. The number of adherents grows by the day and so do the cults and diverse denominations that they follow. Various shades of evangelicalism, charismatic sects, and indigenous churches typically give rise to splinter groups, some of which are clearly unorthodox. In Kenya, a denomination led by Michael Wanyonyi, better known as Jehovah Wanyonyi of the "Lost Israelites" Church, is one example of an extremely syncretic and divergent form of African Christianity.[14] Wanyonyi was a self-proclaimed god who believed Mount Elgon to be the biblical Zion. His followers believe that Wanyonyi was God in human flesh, an embodied spirit who lived among them. Wanyonyi died in 2015 and his followers are awaiting his bodily resurrection with unflagging zeal. Stories of his occasional appearances already abound.

The diversity within African Christianity presents various trends today. Points of divergence are not only denominational affiliations or doctrinal differences or practices, but also encompass other emphases such as the faith gospel (prosperity/wealth and health), social envisioning and services (i.e. popular gospel, often called "empowerment" programs or inspirational seminars), models of mission, church discipline, theological and spiritual emphases, ecumenical interests, and ministerial formation. These trends inform and shape theological thought from which the dominant African theologies, such as inculturation, liberation, evangelical, and prosperity theology,[15] arise. The diversity of African Christianity, however, defies any neat theological categorization and spans a bigger spectrum than just these four types.

Other characteristics of African Christianity today include its vibrancy, a pervasive presence and dominant command of public space, particularly through prayer, popular preaching, and social action, increased uptake of

---

14. Daniel Sitole, "In Jehovah's Village," 15 August 2011, https://newhumanist.org.uk/articles/2638/in-jehovahs-village.

15. See, for example, Timothy P. Palmer's perceptive categorization of African Christian theology into four types, in his paper, "African Christian Theology: A New Paradigm," available at: https://tcnn.ng/wp-content/uploads/2017/08/RB56_Palmer.pdf.

theological education, sustained mission trends, the influence of Pentecostalism and the charismatic movement, and, on the negative side, a growing nominal adherence, syncretism, and incipient secularism (although this last trend may be subtle rather than obvious).[16]

Perhaps one of the most shocking trends is the absence of genuine and sustained concern for sound doctrinal correctness in most churches and denominations. A preliminary survey of most mainline churches shows a worrying trend of laxity in the systematic teaching of faith. It is surprising that most churches, for example, have abandoned programmatic teaching of catechisms, usually to younger adherents. Social "Bible clubs" and "cell groups" abound, but these are a poor replacement for systematic or programmatic teaching of faith. In this regard, the demise of eschatological emphases, for example, is particularly notable. Rarely do we hear serious sermons on God's ultimate purpose for the world, or on sin, hell, or heaven in these churches. Teaching on empowerment, success, or personal progress abounds, which explains the avoidance of such doctrines as eschatology which would seem counter-cultural. As we have argued elsewhere:

> On the whole . . . churches downplay eschatological emphasis of the gospel as they concentrate on propagating a strong realist view of a heaven that can be experienced here and now. The hardships in the present life are not simply to be borne bravely, prayerfully endured until completely subjected to Christ the victorious liberator, but they can actually be overcome here and now by the faithful through the power of faith. In a way, eschatology is already realized – and one can enter into a kingdom sphere – where the devil and all his troubles – poverty, sickness, limitations – can be bound, banished, or placed under the feet of the "saints."[17]

Two observations can be made about this Christianity. First, while African Christianity has admirable elements of evangelicalism, at the same time it is materialistic and earthly-oriented. Paul Gifford observes that African

---

16. These three are perhaps the greatest challenges to African Christianity today. Admittedly, these challenges are not new, although with time and a changing context they tend to change form. As early as the 1970s some pioneer African theologians, notably Byang Kato, identified syncretism alongside what he called "universalism and Christo-paganism" as the greatest challenge to African evangelical Christianity. See his *Biblical Christianity in Africa* (Achimota, Ghana, 1985), 11. See also Tite Tienou, "The Theological Task of the Church in Africa: Where Are We Now and Where Should We Be Going?," in *Africa Journal of Evangelical Theology* 6, no. 1 (1987): 3; and Detlef Kapteina, "The Formation of African Evangelical Theology," *Africa Journal of Evangelical Theology* 25, no. 1 (2006): 62.

17. Galgalo, *African Christianity*, 94.

Christianity, in its popular form, is "not concerned with a renewed order or any 'new Jerusalem,' but with a job, a husband, a child, a car, an education, a visa to the West. It [is] about succeeding in this realm . . . [It] is terrestrial rewards that feature so prominently in African Christianity today."[18] The reason for this is not difficult to understand when we see it from the perspective of the African traditional worldview, which holds that blessing from God is not so much about gains in the hereafter but about tangible earthly benefits, especially of health, wealth, prominence, long life, many children, abundance, harmony, and peace. The influence of the African traditional worldview is not obvious here because these blessings, generally speaking, are good things and seemingly biblical. The blending of Christian views with those of the traditional religions is here so subtle that the dangers of materialism are easily entertained.

Second, earthly-oriented Christianity is a veiled form of African Traditional Religion. Beneath the surface of a seemingly vibrant Christianity is a deep-seated African conceptual framing of how God works. There is, for example, an obvious belief in intermediaries and supernatural powers. It is also common to believe that victory over maladies of any sort cannot be won without the help of some "spiritual powers." God is supreme but seems remote, hence the belief that there is still a place for traditional experts such as the medicine men, diviners, and soothsayers or fortune tellers. That a typical African religious (traditional) worldview is here at work is evidenced, for example, by how these "Christians" pray. Most charismatic churches use a formulaic presentation, passionately pleading their petitions in a way that is careful to either bypass or penetrate the intermediary realms of spiritual forces, as Conrad Mbewe's perceptive analysis shows:

> Prayer in the modern Charismatic movement in Africa is literally a fight. The intercessors are called "prayer warriors." Although they begin by addressing God, within the first few seconds they divert from God and begin to fight the spirits in these impregnable layers with their bare knuckles. The language is almost always, "We bind every unclean spirit in Jesus' name! We let loose the Spirit that breaks the yoke in Jesus' name!" The "prayer warriors" scream at the top of their voices and chant the name of Jesus. They sweat as they put up a gallant fight with these spirits, straining every

---

18. Paul Gifford, *African Christianity: Its Public Role* (Bloomington, IN: Indiana University Press, 1998), 339–340.

muscle of their beings until they prevail . . . That is when they reach through to God and his blessings begin to flow.[19]

This analysis draws specifically on the example of the charismatic churches, but the trend is typical to African Christianity generally. There may be nothing wrong with this spirited fight with evil, but the methodology and the theological framing here belong to traditional religion more than to Christianity. It is also telling that most of these churches hardly emphasize core Christian doctrines such as the Trinity, incarnation, hamartiology, theodicy, atonement, and the afterlife. Belief in these doctrines is not denied but they are rarely taught. This means that the ethical implications of these doctrines are also lacking. The demise of doctrinal emphases does not seem to be a loss to a flourishing entrepreneurial Christianity that "peddles" prayers, entertainment, deliverance or breakthroughs, healing, and other such miracles. For too long, African Christianity has ignored working out its relationship with African Traditional Religion, and has simply given its name to a religion that has appropriated much of Christianity but continues to give form, and to some extent its content, to African Traditional Religion.

Are we saying that African Christianity is just another name for African Traditional Religion? Interestingly, African Traditional Religion has no official name and most of its adherents would genuinely see themselves as "Christians," even when they subscribe to Christianity and traditional religious beliefs at the same time. Possible contradictions are not obvious to most believers because traditional religion has taken on the name of Christianity (through a spontaneous interactive process) and clothed itself in Christian language and forms, such as creeds, hymns, and biblical phrases. African Christianity today may as well be just another name for "African Traditional Religion." Critical analysis shows that African Christians often revert to traditional beliefs in critical situations in their lives. In other words, such adherents may have taken on Christianity but they remain deeply attached to those traditional beliefs. Stories abound, for example, of sicknesses that hospitals have failed to diagnose being healed, and of victims being supposedly delivered from the effects of such maladies as the evil eye, curse, broken taboos, and chronic diseases through the intervention of traditional medicine men. The paradox is that Christians also partake of this "deliverance" and would happily testify that it was Jesus

---

19. Conrad Mbewe, "Why Is the Charismatic Movement Thriving in Africa?," *A Letter from Kabwata* (blog), 21 July 2013, http://www.conradmbewe.com/2013/07/why-is-charismatic-movement-thriving-in.html.

who delivered them through *dawa ya kienyeji* (traditional medicine) or some ritual therapies.

It seems that African Traditional Religion may have hospitably taken a subservient role to Christianity, yet it has always arisen to lead African Christianity by the hand when it mattered most to the believer. Acceptance of such traditional beliefs and practices as funeral rites, initiations, fear of curse, and tribal or ethnic loyalty is evidence of a dual loyalty. The two (Christianity and Traditional Religion) are so blended that African Christianity, irresolute under the weight of syncretism, is increasingly becoming a pluralistic religion – capable of accommodating different and conflicting views of doctrine, beliefs, and practices without flinching, proudly claiming the honors of being "the representative Christianity of the twenty-first century."[20] In this situation, Jesus is accepted but only as one among many ways to God, although, admittedly, he is seen as higher up the ladder of prominence in comparison with other ways. This, then, brings us to our main question: Is syncretism a boon or a bane for African Christianity?

Syncretism[21]

I find an analogy by 'Alik Shahadah, although taken from a different context, very helpful in describing the general syncretic nature of African Christianity. Shahadah holds that "Religion is [like] a bottle with a label on it, spirituality is the thing inside. Religion is the culture of spirituality, the container which gives it structure."[22] African Christianity is definitely visible, vibrant, and unequivocally pervasive. But could that just be the bottle, a container so labeled, whose contents, if analytically scrutinized, may turn out to be "Traditional Religion" in substance as a result of the syncretism that so besets it?

---

20. Walls, "Mission of the Church," 18.

21. I find Gailyn Van Rheenen's definition and description of how syncretism works very helpful. He observes that "Syncretism occurs when Christian leaders accommodate, either consciously or unconsciously, to the prevailing plausibility structures or worldviews of their culture. Syncretism, then, is the conscious or unconscious reshaping of Christian plausibility structures, beliefs, and practices through cultural accommodation so that they reflect those of the dominant culture. Or, stated in other terms, syncretism is the blending of Christian beliefs and practices with those of the dominant culture so that Christianity loses it distinctiveness and speaks with a voice reflective of its culture." See his article "Contextualization and Syncretism," *Mission Alive*, http://www.missionalive.org/ma/index.php/resources/articlesmenu/86-contextualization-and-syncretism; see also Gailyn Van Rheenen, "Modern and Postmodern Syncretism in Theology and Missions," in *The Holy Spirit and Mission Dynamics*, ed. C. Douglas McConnell (Pasadena, CA: William Carey Library, 1997), 173.

22. 'Alik Shahadah, "Africa, Religion and Slavery: A New Lens on Agency Africa and Religion," 2011, http://www.africanholocaust.net/islam/africanandreligion.html.

For most African Christians, Christianity is a social garb. They belong to a church and participate in Christian worship, partake of Christian sacraments and other Christian rituals, use Christian idioms (e.g. Jesus is Lord, I am saved, born again, heaven-bound, a believer, a servant-leader, disciple, apostle), perform spiritual acts of prayer, follow a liturgical calendar, learn from the wisdom of Scriptures, and apply biblical teachings – but they can also lay all this aside as and when it may prove inconvenient. This is syncretic and demonstrates a "double loyalty," which confirms our view of African Christianity as pluralistic in nature. It becomes clear that most African Christians are nominal and naturally, then, without having to make any difficult choice between one or the other, belong to two religions – Christianity and the African traditional spiritual world. We also note that in the face of such "double loyalty" or "dual belonging," Christianity "often finds a superficial acceptance and comfortably (amazingly so) stands alongside African traditional religious views and cherished beliefs."[23] For most professing Christians, Christianity is good – very good – and they love Jesus, but Christianity is definitely not the only spiritual home. This becomes very clear during moments of life transition, such as marriages, funerals, or the performing of last rites, when most Christians feel obliged to partake in the traditional rituals.

This means that, for most African Christians, it is African spirituality and traditional beliefs that reference their religious life – and by extension shape their ethical and moral views and choices. As the analogy of the bottle illustrates, Africans are Christians, by and large, by their self-identification (the label), but are African traditionalists by their spirituality. Their true spiritual content is a spirituality referenced by African traditional religious beliefs. In the syncretistic marriage between African Christianity and African Traditional Religion, "Christianity" has given its name to the marriage, but the home truly belongs to the Traditional Religion.

This brings me to the following thesis: African Christianity has failed to inspire a social transformation that can influence a fruitful ethics and moral vision. This is not because Christianity in and of itself is unable to do so, but simply because African Christianity, while operating under the name "Christian," lives by a syncretic value system largely informed by the traditional religious worldview. This explains why large parts of supposedly "Christian" Africa suffer serious ethical or moral deficiencies and are best known for the social ills outlined earlier, such as corruption, endemic ethnic-based conflict,

---

23. Galgalo, *African Christianity*, 6.

political oppression, marginalization of whole communities, and genocide, contrary to Christian teachings and ethos.

What this means in practice is that the moral worldview of most African "Christians" is not necessarily ordered according to biblical ethics or Christian morality, but is guided by African traditional views of morality and ethics. Does that mean we should blame African Traditional Religion for all our ills in Africa? The answer to this question depends on what value system or worldview you would use as the criterion of judgment. We must make it clear that what Christianity may condemn as evil may not necessarily be deemed evil by the standard of the traditional worldview. Let us use the example of the Decalogue (Exod 20:1–17; Deut 5:4–21) to illustrate this point.

Christian moral teachings, generally speaking, encompass two levels of morality – personal and social morality. The Decalogue is part of the Old Testament moral code appropriated by Christians to provide a moral compass with regard to human relationships both with one another and with God. Broadly speaking, the Decalogue can be grouped into three parts: relationship with God, relationship with parents, and relationship with others. As far as relationship with God is concerned, the African worldview conspicuously holds a belief in the existence of one God but who is worshiped by different communities in different ways and known differently by different local names. Among some traditional communities, notably in South and West African groups, the Supreme Being has often been regarded as rather remote. The Supreme God is, as Philip Steyne observes, "not to be intimately involved or concerned with man's world. Instead, men seek out the lesser powers to meet their desires."[24] This explains the reason for beliefs in divinities and the fear of numerous spiritual forces seen as either manifestations of the Supreme Being or intermediaries. Some pioneer African theologians described the mixture of belief in the existence of the Supreme God alongside the belief in a host of divinities and spiritual beings as "diffused monotheism."[25]

Without going into the complexity of this belief vis-à-vis Christian teachings, one thing can be pointed out. The philosophy that God can be related to in different ways gives Christianity a foothold as one way of worshiping

---

24. Philip M. Steyne, *Gods of Power: A Study of the Beliefs and Practices of Animists* (Houston: Touch Publications, 1990), 35; see also Philip M. Steyne, *In Step with the God of the Nations: A Biblical Theology of Missions – Discovering the Heartbeat of God*, rev. ed. (Columbia, SC: Impact International Foundation, 1999).

25. E. Bolaji Idowu, *Olodumare: God in Yoruba Belief* (Ikeje: Longman Nigeria, 1962), 202; also see E. Bolaji Idowu, *African Tradition Religion: A Definition* (Maryknoll, NY: Orbis, 1973), 153.

the one God who is known by many names. The confusing concept of the Trinity does not strike African "converts" as odd, because it strikes a chord with the African worldview of "diffused monotheism," or at least, it resonates with the idea of intermediaries. In this situation we can, then, conclude that the Christian God is definitely accommodated but we have no guarantee that a reordering of the moral worldview will happen in accordance with the moral code of the "Christian" God. A cursory examination of how the second and third parts of the Decalogue are applied can help illustrate this point.

The section of the Decalogue that prohibits murder, adultery, theft, and lying is perhaps the section interpreted and applied with the most latitude. The Old Testament, however, allowed capital punishment. The New Testament "Christianized" all injunctions in light of the gospel of love, forgiveness, and unity in Christ. The African Christian's interpretation of "Thou shalt not kill," or "Thou shalt not commit adultery," when critically analyzed, is more in sync with the Old Testament. Although literal meanings of these injunctions are preached, in practice the reality is different. Most Africans have often been seen to sanction or at least tolerate murder, adultery, lying, and so on, in situations where the African traditional worldview would have no problem with exemptions. The African traditional worldview supports the application of ritual or liminal boundaries within which any ethical injunction applies. Murder is wrong when it is committed among the people who know God by the same name. With a change of context, murder is actually celebrated as a heroic act – for example, if committed against members of a community whose name for God is different from one's own.

This shapes social belonging and allegiances along "tribal" and language lines; it is believed that what is good for the community is moral and therefore acceptable to God. That is why an insider who crosses taboo boundaries, like stealing from his or her own community, is treated as an "outsider" and God is believed to approve of the murder of that person. The community endorsement then becomes the measure of morality or the ethics to judge the right or wrong of a given action. Simply put, in answer to the question, "When is murder not a murder?," a typical African Christian would draw guidance from the traditional worldview rather than from the New Testament. This may help explain behavior such as the "mob-justice mentality," when suspected thieves are burnt alive or beaten to death by mobs, occurrences common in many African Christian countries. In Kenya, for example, politically instigated ethnic conflicts pitting one Christian group against another often result in serious atrocities such as murder, looting, and displacement. Members who are not directly involved are often known to give moral support, make financial contributions, or simply silently endorse these atrocities, agreeing that the "outsider" gets only a deserved punishment.

Similarly, the strange application of "Thou shalt not commit adultery" can best be understood if seen in light of the African worldview. The principles of acceptability and applicability of African taboos are at work here. In the Traditional Religion, it is believed that there are special circumstances when an "extra-marital affair" is a moral duty. For example, it is a cousin or a brother's obligation to sire children for an impotent man. To reject such a duty is seen as a sin, with negative implications for the community; it is believed that a great curse may befall not only the offender and the family, but even the whole community. The fact that this is tolerated and endorsed through a "conspiracy of silence" is an indication of the approval of this and other such African religious practices, and that the ethical and moral norms at play are here governed by the traditional worldview and spirituality – and seen not as contradictory to Christianity, but indeed a solution to questions of life for which Christianity may have a different set of answers.

How "Thou shalt not steal" is interpreted and applied is even more problematic. In most traditional contexts there are different understandings in determining the definition of what constitutes theft. For example, helping oneself to a neighbor's ripe fruit, while the fruit is still out in the farm, is acceptable as long as none is taken away. A particular set of ethics governs the boundaries within which "not stealing" but "taking" is acceptable. Outside the community boundaries, one is seen not as stealing but rather as retrieving what is rightfully claimable. Perhaps this explains why corruption is taken so lightly in the African "Christian" context. The vice is generally seen as "helping oneself" to a resource that does not, strictly speaking, belong to one's community but to a nebulous entity called "the public." Such an entity is, in any case, seen as an "outsider" or "the other," and so lies beyond the boundaries of communal belonging. It is indeed even expected that a person with the opportunity should bring something home to the tribe. One must guard, not against the sin of ill-gotten wealth as such, but only against the shame of being caught out. This turns upside down the understanding of some basic Christian virtues and vices, such as honor, courage and bravery, compassion (toward your needy lot) and integrity (such as following or enforcing procurement procedures), which are subject to a wholly different set of moral or ethical referencing.

These examples show that African Christianity is largely ordered according to the dictates of a traditional religion and worldview that does not always conform to Christian teachings. Whereas the Bible is preached as it is, and often Christians seek to apply it literally, yet, puzzling enough, it is not this preaching that gives guidance. Contrary to expectation, it is the traditional worldview that takes precedence whenever most Christians are faced by hard choices. We propose that this puzzle can be explained in light of the history of missionary Christianity in Africa, when missionaries denounced African beliefs and practices as demonic and uncivilized, and presented Christianity as the religion of the enlightened, civilized, and people of means and status.

At that time, Christianity was embraced mainly as a means to an end, for the benefits it seemed to promise, and not necessarily as an alternative spiritual home to the Traditional Religion. If for this reason the Traditional Religion was seemingly suppressed, the adherents, who in this case were "socialized as Christians," nevertheless remained faithful to African Traditional Religion, which although pushed underground, remained very much alive.[26] This created a dual belonging, in which Christianity might be professed, but Traditional Religion was truly followed, even when such adherence was never emphasized or openly professed. Syncretism is now growing, not least as it provides a solution, as spontaneous as this may be, to the complexity of such dual belonging. Growing secularism is also influencing an ever-increasing number of nominal Christians who rarely attend church or "practice" Christianity, but who do not mind keeping baptismal names or identifying themselves as "Christians" if only for social self-identification, or family or historical (heritage) reasons.

Conclusion: Boon or Bane?

Syncretism is dangerous for the health of authentic, orthodox Christianity. This is especially so when syncretism is implicit and its influence is silently accommodated, as is the case in the African context today. The church in Africa needs urgently to analyze the serious threat that syncretism presents today. This could be done through sustained study and a workable mission strategy to steer the cause and growth of a strong biblical Christianity. Syncretism can be a blessing if its subtle influence and insidious beliefs are identified, understood, and employed for the purpose of contextualizing Christian beliefs and teachings. If carefully thought through, the challenges presented by syncretism can be turned into an advantage for the advancement of the Christian gospel. Exposing syncretism, and engaging with it, is by far the

---

26. For a detailed treatment of this thought, see Paul G. Hiebert, R. Daniel Shaw, and Tite Tiénou, *Understanding Folk Religion: A Christian Response to Popular Beliefs and Practices* (Grand Rapids, MI: Baker, 1999).

wiser option, rather than ignoring the dynamics and even the very existence of African Traditional Religion and its influence on African Christians.

It is in this regard that I propose a tentative and exploratory theological model which I have called the "conversational model." This is a way of doing contextual theology in which contending spiritual and cultural claims, as well as varied ethical and moral norms, can be brought together in a guided interactive interrogation of each other. Basic to this is the identification of workable cultural equivalents that can enrich Christian doctrine or practices in the most African way possible. This process should begin with a critical diagnosis of different elements of spiritual formation. It should then seek to go beyond their similarities and differences to discover the inherent meanings of each practice and belief. For example, belief in one God is a similarity which may be readily embraced as such, but which may also reveal some shocking and irreconcilable differences when critically interrogated beyond the initial seeming similarity. It should not be taken for granted, for example, that a contextual understanding of monotheism or the universality of God necessarily fits with the understanding of God as Trinity. The end goal of a conversational model is to achieve an accurate position of one's belief, and it calls for an honest search for a descriptor who can attend to the painstaking task of separating the tares from the wheat.

The conversational model is different from inculturation. In the conversational model, Christianity should play the role of an active learner but be a perceptive teacher. It should allow the Traditional Religion to determine what should be practiced (family life, church government, last rites, identity, and belonging, etc.), but clearly mark out what is incompatible with the gospel. This process must be preceded by a reflective interrogation of each practice with the sole aim of redefining and, with time, "Christianizing" the practice. The process must also recognize that we are not looking at the traditional practices as though these practices existed only before the advent of Christianity. The present complex situation in which African Christianity is slowly becoming just another name for the African Traditional Religion must be acknowledged and addressed. The conversational model seeks to identify and separate, so to speak, the elements of African Christianity that are mixed up with the Traditional Religion or practiced alongside it. Matters of core doctrine, including the nature and name of God, must be interrogated with the intention of reaching beyond the obvious similarities to unearth the underlying subtle differences.

For example, it is not sufficient – indeed, it is an abdication of a theological responsibility – to simply accept the naming of the Christian biblical God as *Mungu, Ngai, Nyasaye, Tororut, Mulungu, Katonda, Ori, Rugaba, Ruhanga,*

Ondo, Chuku, Olodumare, Olorun, Osowo, Owo, Imana, Inkosi, Khuzwane, Modimo, Kyala, Kyumbi, Chiuta, Nyambe, Yala, Yatta, and so on, without first dealing with the difficulty of ethical and moral referencing that arises from the understanding of a particular "ethnic" God. Or, to give another pertinent example, it must be appreciated that it is no longer sufficient to administer baptism "for the forgiveness" of sin, but it is vital to go beyond this initial thought and ask what "forgiveness of sin" or, even more pressing, what sin really means. With such primary tasks out of the way, the conversational model can then introduce such doctrines as the Trinity, incarnation, soteriology, and eschatology, and shape understanding in a distinctively biblical way.

Whereas syncretism can provide a guide to what pitfalls should be avoided, it can also inspire a theological language that can productively aid the planting and strengthening of the Christian gospel. For example, in explaining how early Christianity evolved a distinctive religious system, Gerd Theissen contends that there was a need for the believers to "build a semiotic cathedral."[27] This basically involved developing a "sign language" for the purposeful ordering and "building" of a distinctive faith that left no foothold for syncretism. The datum from the old religion was no doubt utilized, but was carefully emptied of its old meaning, redefined, and filled with new meaning before being reapplied. Indeed, some key concepts, such as *kyrios* as applied to Christ, were deliberately applied as an antithesis to the existing or known *kyrios*. Departure from growing orthodoxy was never ignored or accommodated, but was instead corrected or consigned as outside the acceptable boundaries of faith. The continuous process of "conversation" between conflicting or even similar values was carefully guided before any doubtful matter could find a role or place in the new "building" that became the new spiritual home.

African Christianity has for too long lived in the African spiritual home and inspired followers who are happy to take on the name of Christ but without much thought of a Christocentric Christianity. It is time for Christianity to redefine itself by addressing the challenges of syncretism. Taking cognizance of its dangers could be the best place to begin. In discharging this task, we must warn of the dangers that come with uncritical enculturation. A conversational method that is wary of apparent similarities, and interrogates the deep-seated meanings and implications of applying such similarities, is the safer path to follow.

---

27. Gerd Theissen, *A Theory of Primitive Christian Religion* (London: SCM, 1999), 121.

Bibliography

Abbott, Chris, Paul Rogers, and John Sloboda. *Global Responses to Global Threats: Security for the 21st Century*. Oxford: Oxford Research Group, 2006. http://oxfordresearchgroup.org.uk/sites/default/files/globalthreats.pdf.

'Alik Shahadah, Owen. "Africa, Religion and Slavery: A New Lens on Agency Africa and Religion." http://www.africanholocaust.net/islam/africanandreligion.html.

Conner, Michael G. "The Psychopathic Personality." *Bend Psychology*. Accessed 21 May 2014. http://www.bendpsychology.com/Handouts/PsychopathicPersonality.htm.

Detlef, Kapteina. "The Formation of African Theological Theology." *African Journal of Evangelical Theology* 25, no. 1 (2006): 61–84.

Galgalo, Joseph. *African Christianity: The Stranger Within*. Limuru: Zapf Chancery Publishers Africa, 2012.

Gilford, Paul. *African Christianity: It's Public Role*. Bloomington, IN: Indiana University Press, 1988.

Government of Kenya. "State Law Office and Department of Justice on Religious Freedom Report for 2015."

Hiebert, Paul G., R. Daniel Shaw and Tite Tiénou. *Understanding Folk Religion: A Christian Response to Popular Beliefs and Practices*. Grand Rapids, MI: Baker, 1999.

Idowu, E. Bolaji. *African Tradition Religion: A Definition*. Maryknoll, NY: Orbis Books, 1973.

———. *Olodumare: God in Yoruba Belief*. Ikeje: Longman Nigerian Plc., 1962.

Kato, Byang. *Biblical Christianity in Africa*. Achimota: Ghana, 1985.

Mbewe, Conrad. "Why Is the Charismatic Movement Thriving in Africa?" *A Letter from Kabwata* (blog). 21 July 2013. http://www.conradmbewe.com/2013/07/why-is-charismatic-movement-thriving-in.html.

Omondi, Dominic. "Survey: Kenya Ranked Third Most Corrupt Country in the World." Standard Digital, 27 February 2016. https://www.standardmedia.co.ke/article/2000193065/survey-kenya-ranked-third-most-corrupt-country-in-the-world.

Palmer, Timothy P. "African Christian Theology: A New Paradigm." https://tcnn.ng/wp-content/uploads/2017/08/RB56_Palmer.pdf.

Sitole, Daniel. "In Jehovah's Village," 15 August 2011. https://newhumanist.org.uk/articles/2638/in-jehovahs-village.

Smith, Tony. "Dispatches Saving Africa's Witch Children." Retrieved from https://www.youtube.com/watch?v=ooXBMU_06vg.

Steyne, Philip M. *Gods of Power: A Study of the Beliefs and Practices of Animists*. Houston, TX: Touch Publications, 1990.

———. *In Step with the God of the Nations: A Biblical Theology of Missions – Discovering the Heartbeat of God*. Revised edition. Columbia, SC: Impact International Foundation, 1999.

Theissen, Gerd. *A Theory of Primitive Christian Religion*. London: SCM, 1999.

Tienou, Tite. "Theological Task of the Church in Africa: Where Are We Now and Where Should We Be Going?" *Africa Journal of Evangelical Theology* 6, no. 1 (1987): 3–11.

Tutu, Desmond. "Black Theology and African Theology: Soul Mates or Antagonist?" In *A Reader in African Christian Theology*, edited by John Parratt, 47–58. London: SPCK, 1987.

———. "Whither African Theology?" In *Christianity in Independent Africa*, edited by E. Fashole-Luke et al., 364–369. London: Rex Collins, 1978.

Van Rheenen, Gailyn. "Contextualization and Syncretism." *Mission Alive*. http://www.missionalive.org/ma/index.php/resources/articlesmenu/86-contextualization-and-syncretism.

———. "Modern and Postmodern Syncretism in Theology and Missions." In *The Holy Spirit and Mission Dynamics*, edited by C. Douglas McConnell, 164–207. Pasadena: William Carey Library, 1997.

Walls, Andrew F. "The Mission of the Church Today in the Light of Global History." *Word and World* 20, no.1 (Winter 2000): 17–21.

World Bank Report. "Kenya Economic Update, December 2012: Kenya at Work Energizing the Economy and Creating Jobs." https://openknowledge.worldbank.org/handle/10986/26660.

6

Dependency's Long Shadow: Mission Churches in Kenya and Their Children

Joseph William Black
St Paul's University, Limuru and Nairobi, Kenya
Makarios III Patriarchal Orthodox Seminary, Nairobi, Kenya

Abstract

Kenyan churches have struggled since their inception with a range of dysfunctions related to finance and self-sustainability. Often, attempts to correct the problems, such as introducing tithing or promoting various health and prosperity heresies, have made matters more complicated if not worse. This paper looks at a third strategy employed by missionaries and subsequent denominational structures whereby financial needs for salaries, property, buildings, and programs are supplied from the outside by well-meaning donors, a strategy that results in short-term gains but long-term postures of dependency in the congregations affected. Such dependency has a long-term detrimental affect, both on the understanding of the gospel and on the way the gospel is lived out in local contexts. Churches that find themselves in the dependency hole often find it difficult to hear Christ's call to commitment and discipleship, much less to find anyone willing to take those sorts of steps in a personal response to Christ's call. Too many in such congregations are there for what they can get, and if there is nothing forthcoming they may disappear from that church and go in search of another that has something to offer. Such "Christianity" produces "fruit" in lives that hardly differs from that of the lives of those who are outside the church, and renders the religion that is being practiced increasingly impotent in terms of individual transformation and congregational impact in the community. After looking at the historical sources of dependency in Kenyan churches, the paper concludes with a consideration of some of the consequences for Christian churches caught in the dependency trap, and the challenges of finding a way out.

Key words: dependency, missionary Christianity, mission churches, health and prosperity "gospel," self-sustainability.

Introduction

It should come as no surprise that Kenyan Christians and Kenyan churches struggle with the concept of stewardship. The absence of a theology of self-reliance and financial independence can be traced back to the beginnings of Christian missionary efforts in Kenya, both Protestant and Catholic.[1] Christianity came into Kenya and indeed to most of sub-Saharan Africa through the efforts of European and North American missionaries.[2] These men and women sacrificed homes, families, careers, and even their lives for the sake of bringing the good news about Jesus Christ to people on this continent who had never had a chance to hear about him. In the early years of the Western missionary movement, tropical diseases were little understood and treatments for those who fell ill were rudimentary and often ineffective. Hundreds of those who came as missionaries died here, far away from their loved ones back home. Their sacrifice is recalled now only by lonely gravestones in forgotten cemeteries that one sometimes comes across in remote corners where an old mission church perhaps still stands.[3] However, these missionaries and their replacements were also viewed as fabulously wealthy by their new neighbors and

---

1. There is a dizzyingly and notably ever-increasing variety of churches present in Kenya and indeed across sub-Saharan Africa. This makes it impossible to generalize about "Kenyan Christians" or "African churches." There are, however, certain issues, one of which is subjectively represented in this paper, that have had a profound effect on the attitudes and practices of Christians across many denominational divides. Even so, with such a plurality of Christian expressions, one will always find exceptions to the rule.

2. The great exception to what is normally presented, of course, is the conversion of the Aksumite Empire's royal family to Orthodox Christianity in the fourth century. Orthodox Christianity subsequently expanded to include most parts of Ethiopia, which today remains an almost majority Oriental Orthodox country.

3. For alternative perspectives on the coming of Western Protestant missionaries, see O. U. Kale, *African Christianity: An African Story* (Pretoria: University of Pretoria, 2005), 1–42. As in all history, whoever controls the narrative controls how the story is understood. The transition from a narrative controlled by a colonial and missionary agenda to one controlled by an African

converts. Missionaries brought with them fantastical technologies, machines designed to get them from one place to another or which made their lives somehow easier. Missionaries had access to astonishing resources that enabled them to build what seemed to be vast palaces when compared with the one-room mud huts with thatched roofs that had been the norm for housing for as far back as anyone could remember. The missionaries somehow possessed the wherewithal to construct other buildings that they called "churches," "schools," and "clinics": buildings that had never before been a part of the local landscape. Although there were still diseases that nobody could prevent, in the building called the "clinic" or "hospital" missionaries often handed out medicines that worked, and when applied in time to the sick these medicines often enabled them to recover.

When a missionary came to a local community, there may have been grumbling by some, while others may have viewed these outsiders as a threat to the traditional way of life handed down from the past. But for most, the arrival of missionaries, with their comparative wealth, their access to technology, their medical marvels, and their willingness to engage and share with their neighbors, got everybody's attention.

Discussion

It is possible that the growing numbers of conversions to Christianity proclaimed by missionaries were motivated by theological concerns and by a desire to be restored to a right relationship with the Creator through what Jesus Christ had accomplished by his life, death, and resurrection. But it is also possible that for not a few of the adherents to this new religious scheme – which had as its centerpiece a need for salvation that had never before been thought necessary in any of the traditional religious systems – other, more mundane motives drew them to the weekly services in the missionary's church. A good relationship with the missionary's god might get one into heaven. But a good relationship with the missionary might get one a job. It might lead to a place in the school for one's children.[4] It might make one the recipient of donated

---

Christian and political agenda is to be welcomed, with the warning that there is no guarantee that the new perspective will not also repeat the old mistakes.

4. Chukwudi A. Njoku argues that the provision of education was a major factor in the success of Christian missions in sub-Saharan Africa: "One of the most powerful extra-doctrinal techniques adopted in virtually every Christian mission, was the introduction of Western-style education." See Njoku, "The Missionary Factor," in *African Christianity: An African Story*, ed. Ogbu Kalu (Pretoria: University of Pretoria, 2005), 241. While his observation is valid, he does not proceed to the next level and discern that the education did not appear from nowhere but

clothing or food. It might open the door for one to receive training on a sewing machine or as a mechanic to fix the never-ending flow of machines which were now coming from overseas. In other words, Christianity became associated with a way up and out of the poverty of subsistence agriculture, into a new life characterized by education, opportunity, betterment, and prosperity. There are exceptions, of course, but only enough to prove the rule.

In Kenya, things were more complex because many more outsiders came to settle on the land other than just missionaries, and their motives were not nearly as unselfish. As a result of late nineteenth-century politics in Europe, Kenya was claimed as a British colony, part of the far-flung British Empire. As word spread in the UK of the desirability and availability of excellent farm land in the Kenyan highlands, many were motivated to leave their own economic struggles behind and start anew as settlers in Kenya. They "acquired" land, built houses, started farms, established businesses, and created a new world for themselves. Never mind that their new world was established at the expense of a long-existing culture and on land that had been taken from those who, from time immemorial, had understood it to be theirs.

So the context of Christianity coming to Kenya was more complicated than in other African settings. Thomas Nganda, for example, arrived as a young man with his mother near Dagoretti in search of more productive land in the 1910s, heard about opportunities, and walked to the new train-stop settler town of Nairobi in search of a job. Nganda writes:

> Arrived in Nairobi very early and met a white person . . . Without wasting any time I asked him whether he would hire me for any work. The white person did not hesitate and he was open-minded. He told me he would hire me if I really wanted to work. He told me to accompany him to his home. When we arrived, he introduced me to his wife and to his domestic employees. He then showed me the work that I would be doing. My job was pulling a rickshaw. He taught me how to pull it until I knew how. Although it was tiresome and difficult work I did not hate it. He bought me jingles to tie around the ankles so that when I am pulling the rickshaw the jingles would act as bells to warn people to keep out of the way. In those olden days it was the responsibility of the rickshaw puller to take his employer wherever he wanted to go. I worked for this white man for one year, taking him from his house to his

---

was *provided* by the missionaries as part of the largesse that became available to Africans as a result of their association with the mission.

workplace in Nairobi and back after work. Although the salary (twenty shillings per month) was small in those days, one did not mind because things were not as expensive as they are these days.[5]

Nganda's experience introduced him to a cash economy and gave him a taste of a kind of life very different from that which he and his mother had come from when they moved from Murang'a district in search of better farm land. After a year, however, his employer returned to the UK and Nganda was without a job. Even so, he had saved enough money to buy the goats he needed for a dowry, so he married and remained without a formal job for some time, though he worked on his *shamba* like everyone else around him. After a while he, along with many others, was pressed by the colonial authorities into forced labor. Because of his skills, he was made a supervisor. But Nganda says, "I thought of quitting that job because I was not happy about it, particularly because I was forced into it. In those days if the chief or an administrator forced people to work, nobody objected to it and nobody refused. I did not like supervising others; I was forced just as they were."[6]

In time, Nganda was able to find another job with a white man, Mr Montgomery, who served as a veterinarian in Kabete. With the money he earned from this job over the course of six years, Nganda was able to purchase outright the land where he and his family had been living. By now, Nganda realized that the way to advance in this new world was to go to school. "Although I was a mature man, I decided to go to school to learn at least how to write my name. I learned what was available those days and up to the level that I could. I learned how to write my name and read letters."[7]

Even though there obviously were missionaries working in the area where Nganda lived and worked, it was only after he attended the mission school associated with the Presbyterian mission in Thogoto that he engaged with Christianity. "While attending school, I got a desire to be baptized. I attended religious classes because I could read the catechism. After completing the course, the class took a test, and I was one of those who passed; I was therefore baptized 'Thomas.'"[8]

The Church of Scotland mission in Thogoto was led by John William Arthur (1881–1952), a medical doctor and Church of Scotland minister from

---

5. Thomas Nganda, "How the Orthodox Church Started in Kenya," in *Yearbook and Review 2009*, ed. Makarios Tillyrides, trans. Eliud Ng'ang'a Mwaura (Nairobi: Greek Orthodox Archbishopric of Kenya, 2009), 182.

6. Nganda, "How the Orthodox Church Started in Kenya," 183.

7. Nganda, 184.

8. Nganda, 184.

Glasgow. Within months of his arrival, the mission's first hospital was opened in Kikuyu and the first of many schools was established in the grounds of the mission station. A young man named Johnstone Kamau (later known as Jomo Kenyatta) was among the early students of this mission station school. Through Arthur's efforts, a church was established, a building erected (which is still standing in Thogoto), and the ground laid for the further expansion of the mission's evangelistic, medical, and educational efforts. Thomas Nganda was only one of many whose lives were affected by the evangelistic strategies of the missionaries in Thogoto.

After his time at the mission school and his baptism, further opportunities opened up, as Nganda reports:

> I was afterwards confirmed; I continued to attend the church, unlike some people who quit the church after they were baptized. I continued being an active member of the church; and helping others in church work, for I was not lazy. When the church elders noticed that I loved working for the church of God, I was appointed chairman of the church and of the school committee for Ruthimitu Church of Scotland Mission. I was also appointed Deacon for baptizing sick children in the absence of the Padre.[9]

Nganda would go on to join a widespread rebellion among the Kikuyu people against the Church of Scotland mission over the mission's attempt to curtail the practice of "female circumcision." This led directly to the establishment of breakaway churches and schools throughout Kenya's central highlands. Many of these churches would ultimately affiliate with the African Orthodox Church, under the leadership of Father and then Bishop George Arthur Gathuna. But that is another story for another time.[10]

However, the model of Christian missions experienced by Nganda and many others in Kenya and across Africa represents perhaps the major strategy used by missionaries across the denominational spectrum, one that has been practiced not just by Protestant missionaries but also by Roman Catholic, Orthodox, and even Coptic Orthodox missions.[11] In recent years, even Saudi-

---

9. Nganda, 184.

10. For example, see my article: Joseph W. Black, "Offended Christians, Anti-Mission Churches and Colonial Politics: One Man's Story of the Messy Birth of the African Orthodox Church of Kenya," *Journal of Religion in Africa* 43 (2013): 261–296.

11. In writing about the early strategy of the Africa Inland Mission (AIM) in Kenya, for example, James Karanja states that "The Missions' predominant and ultimate interest in establishing work among the Africans was to evangelize the people and build a new Christ's Kingdom on Kikuyu soil. [One writer] says that 'this primary objective has always to be kept

funded Muslims have adopted a similar strategy in their attempts to expand the influence of Wahabi Islam into areas that previously had a minimal Muslim presence. The model has many variations but at its core retains the same approach: meet the needs of the local population and use the goodwill established thereby to attract and establish a worshiping community. The worshiping community thus becomes the center of further aid and support by the sponsoring mission. This tactic has proven very effective in drawing a crowd. But the men, women, and children attracted by means of this strategy to the mission and its new community often view themselves as beneficiaries entitled to the opportunities provided by the mission and the church, rather than contributing members. "Church" and "mission" are viewed as something that someone on the outside does for them, rather than as something we are and do.

Oftentimes, missionaries making use of this strategy for "evangelism" and "church planting" are aware of the dangers of the dependency mentality they are creating among their "church members." However, these missionaries are often taking a longer view of their efforts. They acknowledge that the first generation of "converts" may participate in their churches with mixed motives, and that some are there because of the material benefits and opportunities they perceive they will get. But the goal of the missionaries is to establish the church in the community as an ongoing presence and to focus on the next generation – the children – who through their participation in Christian education and school will become more "Christian" than their parents. So the goal of this mission strategy is to establish a critical mass of adherents in the local community to become a platform for further assistance which in turn attracts more people into the church. A clinic may be established to assist with health care.[12] And a school may be started to educate the children of church members as well as to provide further opportunities to bring non-member families into the orbit of the church.

---

in the forefront if we are to appreciate properly the character of the mission.' This meant that medical work, educational programs, and other social concerns were secondary in importance to the overriding consideration and intention of the Mission, and whenever they were carried out, it was for pragmatic purposes; they were, therefore, utilized as methods and strategies to win Africans' allegiance to Christ." James Karanja, *The Missionary Movement in Colonial Kenya: The Foundation of Africa Inland Church* (Göttingen: Cuvillier Verlag, 2009), 199.

12. Again, Karanja notes that early Kenya missions' strategy often involved establishing a clinic. "The medical treatment drew many people to mission stations. People traveled long distances to receive medical attention at the missions. Those who were seriously ill were detained at the missions for closer attention. Not all beneficiaries of missionary medical services became Christians; many continued in their old faith after returning to their homes. But a good number of patients embraced the new faith." Karanja, *Missionary Movement in Colonial Kenya*, 121.

Oftentimes the missionaries following this church-planting strategy had as part of their plan the transformation of the new church from being a community completely dependent on the support provided by the missionaries to becoming a self-sufficient Christian community able to support its own leadership and ministries without outside assistance. Actual experience, however, shows that missionaries were often unrealistically optimistic. Despite the rhetoric, missionaries often found it very difficult to change the rules of the game that, after all, they established. All too often, the relationship between missionaries and the churches they served had already turned into one of patronage, with the missionary dispensing the support, opportunities, and goods as the patron, and the church members receiving the benefits as the patronized.[13]

It shouldn't surprise anyone that local churches receiving support from outside mission sources were not interested in letting go of this help and trying to make it on their own. In most cases where this way of "doing church" was established by the missionaries, at no point did anyone ever inform the first converts or succeeding generations of church members that, actually, being a Christian involves intentional discipleship, self-sacrificing love, as well as personal and corporate stewardship. And one of the challenges faced by missionaries and local Christian leaders when trying to navigate the transition to self-sufficiency was the discovery that Christianity might have come to this population in the form of this "church" or that "ministry," but Christianity and its principles had never been owned by the people.

Individuals and families participated because of what they perceived they could get. Of course there are wonderful exceptions, but they tend to prove the rule. And when the cost of participation became too high, in terms of requiring of them their own efforts or funding, they suddenly were not that interested in participating, or they moved on to a new church or mission that they perceived would meet their needs. Many missions were thus locked into a destructive cycle. Missionaries continued to act as patrons of their churches because they were afraid that they would lose their converts, churches, and ministries if they didn't. But by continuing to drive this patronage model of missions, these missionaries ensured that their "converts" would never mature and become self-sufficient Christian disciples, nor would their "churches" become the body of Christ in their local community that they were called to be.

---

13. Patronage is often discussed in Kenya with regard to politics or economic issues. But because the dynamics and results are similar, I think it is also a useful term to apply to dynamics within twentieth-century mission strategies employed by many of the Christian missions operating in Kenya.

Thus, ironically, the coming of Christianity often had the opposite effect of what one sees occurring in the Christian communities of the New Testament. Instead of producing individuals who were of demonstrable Christian character and who led by their example of self-sacrificing love, individuals in mission and post-mission churches too often viewed positions of responsibility in the church as opportunities to exercise power and authority over the community, or even as a means to gain access to wealth and property. And churches, rather than being communities of people who had experienced mercy and forgiveness and known as islands of love and kindness, were instead controlled by men and women who were seeking any advantage to climb the ladder of power and opportunity. Rather than churches being a safe place for sinners to find mercy and help, sinners were excluded and cast out when discovered in their midst. The result was often a thin veneer of piety on display at worship services, but lives outside "church" that were little different from those of everyone else in the surrounding communities. Too often, instead of transforming the local culture through Christ's call to radical discipleship and love, the Christianity of the missionaries was transformed by the culture into just another expression of fallen humanity. It continued to attract new adherents because mission Christianity meant access to stuff and was perceived as a way out of poverty and into opportunity. But this meant that, increasingly, many churches were full of people who might be "saved" but were there for other reasons than responding to the call of Christ.

For some churches, national events overwhelmed local experience and forced change in a destructive way. Sometimes armed conflict, or a change in government policy or regimes, forced the removal of foreign missionaries with little notice or time to prepare local congregations for the shock. These local Christians were left on their own, as happened in Ethiopia, for example, after the Marxist Derg took over following the removal from power and subsequent murder of the Christian Emperor Haile Selassie in 1974. Some of the Christians who had been drawn to Protestant Christianity by their association with the missionaries and what they provided did not endure the transition and quietly followed the opportunities into a new Marxist identity. Others persevered, sometimes suffering imprisonment or other forms of persecution, to the extent that when Ethiopia emerged from seventeen years of Marxist domination in 1991 there were not only Protestant Christians who had survived, but there were many more than there had been before the Marxists took over and sought to undo the influence of Christianity.

Kenyan Christianity never experienced this sort of persecution, but the transition out of missionary patronage was nonetheless challenging, if in a more subtle way. A significant part of the problem had to do with the nature of the gospel that was preached, first by missionaries and then by national evangelists and pastors. Too often, the gospel was reduced to resolving one's legal problem before God:

> Because we have broken God's commandments and sinned, we are now liable to God's judgment and would go to hell if left to our own devices. But God in his mercy sent his Son to be our Savior. Jesus took our sin upon himself when he died upon the cross. By receiving the punishment we deserved, Jesus opened the way for us to be forgiven if we respond to this gospel opportunity to turn back to God. By accepting Christ as our Savior and Lord, and receiving forgiveness, we are "saved" and will therefore not be judged but will go to heaven when we die.

This "salvation" was accessed through responding to an "altar call," an invitation for individuals convicted by the preaching to come forward and publicly pray the "sinner's prayer" and "accept Jesus Christ as my Lord and Savior."

People who did this were understood to be "saved." They would usually go on to be baptized and then they would take their place as members of the church. This version of the gospel succeeded in winning many converts across Kenya, and indeed all of Africa. It was rightly viewed as a "good deal" because it essentially made few if any demands other than those of association on the part of the "believer." Moreover, with salvation viewed in terms of forgiveness and the resolution of our legal problem before God the Judge, there was no incentive to be concerned about the corresponding New Testament teaching concerning becoming more and more like Christ in our character and relationships. As a consequence, many Christians believed a gospel that resolved their impending crisis before the judgment seat of Christ, but which left untouched their characters and lives today. The result has been a parade of church leaders who could most charitably be described as unsanctified afflicting many churches in every denomination, not to mention many churches full of the so-called "saved" who have no sense of responsibility to live in a way that Jesus might recognize as that of one of his disciples, or to give sacrificially in order to provide for the needs of their pastor or church, much less the poor around them. And why should they if "Christianity" and "church" mean that these things have always been done for them by their missionary or denominational patron?

In all fairness, it must be said that there have been missionaries who recognized the dangers of the patronage strategy of church planting and sought to rectify their mistakes. They realized that their churches must learn to stand on their own two feet and walk without support from the mission. This meant that pastors would no longer be supported with foreign money, nor would projects be undertaken with mission support. This change was very hard for the local churches who had been used to receiving everything from the mission. A few churches responded well and were able to devise a way toward self-sufficiency. But many if not most churches were and are mired in poverty that is fed by the impoverished thinking of its members that they can do nothing because they have nothing. Other churches are filled with members who actually are not poor, but who have never been acquainted with what the New Testament teaches about the gospel, discipleship, and stewardship. Christianity is instead about meeting *their* needs, and about them getting into heaven when the time for that comes. But when it comes to their money and their resources, these members have instead learned not to trust their church leadership, perhaps because of unfortunate experiences in the past, and choose instead to do other things with their relative wealth.

As if this were not enough of a challenge, Pentecostal and charismatic preachers arrived on the scene and began to have an impact in Kenya in the 1960s and 1970s. These preachers often criticized mission churches for not telling their members about the "full gospel." Specifically, God had more on offer than just "salvation" for his people: he promised to send his Holy Spirit and to grant baptism in the Holy Spirit to every believer. This was so that all Christians could be empowered for ministry. And for many Pentecostals, the sign that one had been "baptized in the Spirit" was the gift of speaking in tongues.[14] Resulting Pentecostal services tended to be raucous affairs, with drums (and later electric guitars and keyboards) replacing the rather dire Western hymns sung to Western tunes that characterized the very Western worship services of many mission churches.

---

14. I am making a distinction between "Pentecostals" and "charismatics" here. Pentecostals are those who teach the baptism of the Holy Spirit as a second experience of grace. Most Pentecostals insist that the "sign gift" of speaking in tongues is different from the "spiritual gift" of tongues described by Paul in 1 Cor 12–14. The sign gift of tongues is given by the Holy Spirit to everyone who is baptized in the Spirit. This is also understood by many Pentecostals as their "prayer language." Charismatic Christians, on the other hand, do not accept that there is a mandatory second experience of grace known as the baptism of the Spirit. Instead, there may be one or a number of experiences of the Spirit's filling. The Spirit indeed empowers individual Christians for ministry by giving spiritual gifts. The gift of tongues is one among many gifts that one may receive, but it is neither the most important of the spiritual gifts, nor is it mandatory that Spirit-filled Christians exhibit it as proof of their baptism in the Spirit. Many of the Protestant missionaries in Kenya came from theological traditions that believed that the supernatural gifts of the Spirit, including the gift of tongues, ceased with the apostles. The implication was often given that these new teachings and experiences must therefore have Satan as their origin.

It is not surprising that many people in mission and their subsequent denominational churches found the Pentecostal message and worship style to be compelling. Since then, while the initial explanation of Pentecostal gifting placed the focus on empowering Christians to be the ministers Christ was calling them to be, subsequent developments have demonstrated Pentecostal churches to be not that different in kind from the denominational Christianity they were often reacting against, at least in terms of attitudes toward stewardship and personal responsibility. First of all, spiritual gifts have in practice been viewed hierarchically, with some viewed as definitely more important than others, the most important being given to those who have faith and being a sign of God's blessing and favor. So speaking in tongues, for example, is very high on the list, as is prophecy or ecstatic utterance, or miracles and healing. People who can do these are viewed as being particularly blessed by God. People without these upper-echelon spiritual gifts tend to be viewed as deficient in faith, for whatever reason.

The important point to note is that Pentecostalism in its manifold expressions has become increasingly self-consumed and all about the receiving of spiritual blessings and power and authority. For many Pentecostal Christians, the posture is more about what I can get, not about what I can give, and not just in terms of spiritual blessings. Indeed the "miracle" so many are seeking on any given Sunday at any given service is a financial one, or maybe a healing. It would seem that the Holy Spirit has simply replaced the mission-station *bwana* as the dispenser of good things. And a case could be made that many Pentecostal churches in Kenya are simply, in terms of their fundamental attitude, the old mission churches on steroids.[15]

This mix of spiritual power and lack of any corresponding concept of discipleship, stewardship, or controlling authority has proven dangerously flammable, and has opened the door for the influence of Western health and prosperity preachers to take root in Kenyan soil. These teachers are shameless in their promotion of their version of *me*-centered "Christianity." And everyone but their followers can see that they are using the people around them as

---

15. See Paul Gifford, *Christianity, Politics and Public Life in Kenya* (London: Hurst, 2009). Gifford contends that neither the Protestant nor Catholic churches are interested in countering the corrupt political culture that has characterized Kenyan society, but instead are focused on facilitating development through a continued dependence on foreign missionaries and resources. Moreover, the rapidly expanding Pentecostal movement, by its strategic deployment of media and the attention-grabbing use of "crusades," as well as its idiosyncratic use of Scripture and theology, has placed the emphasis on power, success, achievement, and prosperity. As such, Pentecostal churches as a rule do not so much critique the current political and societal trends in Kenya as reflect them.

the primary source for their own income stream. In the West, schemes to defraud investors usually promise some financial return for those who buy into their conspiracy, and there are a whole range of such plots, known as Ponzi schemes.[16] But prosperity preachers make no pretense of promising any return on their contribution – they just want one's money, and claim that such donations to their "ministry" are a demonstration of one's faith. They "promise" that God will bless such giving, but they themselves seem much more interested in getting access to one's wallet or pocketbook than in giving any assistance to the many people in desperate need who flock around them hoping that the "prophet's" promise of a miracle is for them and their situation. The preachers claim that it isn't just spiritual gifting that God has for every Christian; he desires every believer to experience his healing power and his blessing, understood as the wealth and prosperity of this world. And all that is required is faith. And of course, you can demonstrate your faith by contributing to this ministry, and God will "bless" your "seed" of faith and grow it into what you are asking him to do.

This message of God's blessing of health and prosperity is actually the patronage of the missionaries' Christianity come back to haunt the land with a vengeance – even though Kenya and the rest of Africa have suffered through a previous version of this variant of Christianity and continue to suffer the consequences thereof. It is ironic that no connection is being made between mission Christianity and the prosperity preachers, and the kind of Christianity at the grassroots level that both encourage, and that people are running to these new churches and their leaders as if they are God's miracle potion to what ails them. Casino Christianity may inspire wild hopes and dreams that God will somehow come through and give me what I need and want, but, as practiced by the TV preaching gods and goddesses, it is little more than a scam. The health and prosperity "gospel has more in common with African Traditional Religion than its current practitioners would be comfortable admitting, which is probably why there is such a deep resonance with the message of the prosperity gospellers among their many followers. Wanting to secure the good things of life and to avoid the bad things is at the core of both and of all the religious things they do. But neither of these popular options is Christianity, at least, not as Jesus understood it.

---

16. Named after Charles Ponzi, who in 1920 devised a fraudulent investment program whereby the investor gives the operator capital and is repaid dividends, not from any monies earned by the investment but from new capital paid by new investors. These new investors are attracted to participate by the promise of unrealistically high short-term returns on their investment. A Ponzi scheme is also known as a pyramid scheme.

Statistics hail Kenya as a majority Christian nation, with more than 80 percent of its people professing to be members of one church or another. If only these statistics reflected the number of people who understood the gospel and were disciples of Christ. Kenya would be a very different place socially, politically, and economically if such statistics accurately reflected actual understanding and behavior. But they don't, and so the statistics, as such, are misleading. As we have seen, the history and subsequent reality of Christianity in Kenya are much more complicated.

To sum up, the version of Christianity assumed by the early missionaries is part of the problem that has led Kenyan Christianity to the fractured, compromised place it is in today. The early missionaries practiced a form of patronage church planting that seemed to be met with success, at least in terms of attracting numbers of adherents. But, as we have seen, this method of doing missions had unintended consequences that began to have an immediate impact in terms of what new "Christians" understood Christianity to be about. With an emphasis on getting numbers of converts to the gospel and getting people "saved" so that they "went to heaven" when they died, the resulting model of Christian church and discipleship became increasingly skewed away from discipleship and personal responsibility, and bent toward dependence upon the missionary and the resources the mission could provide. This posture made the transition from Western mission to Kenyan leadership fraught with challenges, as Christians and their churches had to find their way without the lifeline of outside support. The advent of Pentecostal teaching found many Christians eager to be the recipient once again of God's blessing, with a corresponding lack of any meaningful concept of discipleship in the preaching of most preachers. With the way already paved by the rapid expansion of Pentecostalism in the 1980s and 1990s, the prosperity preachers found a ready audience for their "faith"-based message of God's desire to bless each believer with health and riches.[17] Once again, a message pretending to be Christian that

---

17. Ironically, many of these "prosperity" preachers had ties to the "Faith" or "Word" movement that emerged from the ministries of American prosperity gospel proponents Kenneth Hagin, Kenneth Copeland, and others. Paul Gifford has suggested that these Kenyan wannabee prosperity ministers are actually dependent upon American patronage for their model of ministry and their growth. As such, this form of Prosperity Pentecostalism is simply another kind of neo-colonialism creating its own form of dependence. See Paul Gifford, *Christianity and Politics in Doe's Liberia* (Cambridge: Cambridge University Press, 1993), 196–199, 294, 314–315. See also Gifford, *African Christianity*, 236–244. As Allan Anderson observes, "Gifford's analysis . . . seems to ignore some fundamental features of Pentecostalism, now predominantly a Third World phenomenon, where experience and practice are more important than formal ideology or even theology. As Obgu Kalu points out, the relationship between the African Pentecostal pastor and his or her 'western patron' is entirely eclectic, and the 'dependency' in

twists the gospel into a strategy that provides a way up and out of my current situation is substituting itself for the actual Christian gospel of transforming love, self-denying discipleship, and generous stewardship of one's resources.[18] With so many seductive, false versions of Christianity everywhere we go, each one promising an easy way "by faith" to attain my life goals, it is not surprising that the way of the cross we discover in the Gospels and in the rest of the New Testament is struggling to gain a hearing in twenty-first-century Kenya.

But this way of the cross is the way that Christ calls us to live, first as disciples and then as his people in his church. Every other way, even if it is intended as a short cut, will not end well and ultimately takes everyone on it further and further from Christ. The old missionary strategies and the subsequent patronage systems, the Pentecostal distractions, and the false promises of the prosperity preachers have all given an impression of success, if the ability to attract large numbers of people is "success." But Jesus himself says, "You will know the tree by its fruit" (Matt 7:16). In a similar way, the apostle Paul reminds the Galatians that the fruit of the Spirit is not the ability to speak in tongues, work miracles, perform healings, or have ecstatic worship experiences; rather "The fruit of the Spirit is love, joy, peace, patience, kindness, goodness, gentleness, faithfulness, and self-control" (Gal 5:22). Find these things and one will find the presence and power of God.

The above-mentioned distractions have hobbled many Kenyan churches to this day. Again, not every church has lost its way, and not every Christian has missed Jesus's call to discipleship, but the trend is clear and disturbing. Mission churches bequeathed to Kenya an uneven legacy. And the shortcomings of the parents have been passed down to the children, to subsequent generations of Christian churches and their members. The challenges facing Christians who have grown up knowing only the present "way things are done" as their reality

---

fact has been mutual. The western supporter often needs the African pastor to bolster his own international image and increase his own financial resources." Moreover, "Identifying these churches with the American 'prosperity gospel' is a generalization which particularly fails to appreciate the reconstructions and innovations made by the new African movement in adapting to a radically different context, just as the older AICs [African Initiated Churches] did some years before." Allan Anderson, "Evangelism and the Growth of Pentecostalism in Africa," paper (Center for Missiology and World Christianity, University of Birmingham, 2000), http://www.artsweb.bham.ac.uk/aanderson/publications/evangelism_and_the_growth_of_pen.htm#_edn42.

18. See Douglas John Hall's discussion of stewardship as a metaphor for the whole of Christian discipleship: Douglas John Hall, *The Steward: A Biblical Symbol Come of Age* (Grand Rapids, MI: Eerdmans, 1990), 5–24.

remain daunting. But it should come as very good news that it doesn't have to be this way, and that there is a way out.[19]

Bibliography

Anderson, Allan. "Evangelism and the Growth of Pentecostalism in Africa." Paper, Centre for Missiology and World Christianity, University of Birmingham, 2000.

Black, Joseph W. "Offended Christians, Anti-Mission Churches and Colonial Politics: One Man's Story of the Messy Birth of the African Orthodox Church of Kenya." *Journal of Religion in Africa*, 43 (2013): 261–296.

Gifford, Paul. *African Christianity: Its Public Role*. Bloomington, IN: Indiana University Press, 1998.

———. *Christianity, Politics and Public Life in Kenya*. London: Hurst Publishers, 2009.

———. *Christianity and Politics in Doe's Liberia*. Cambridge: Cambridge University Press, 1993.

Hall, Douglas John. *The Steward: A Biblical Symbol Come of Age*. Grand Rapids, MI: Eerdmans, 1990.

Kalu, Ogbu U. *African Christianity: An African Story*. Pretoria, SA: University of Pretoria, 2005.

Karanja, James. *The Missionary Movement in Colonial Kenya: The Foundation of Africa Inland Church*. Göttingen, Germany: Cuvillier Verlag, 2009.

Njoku, Chukwudi A. "The Missionary Factor." In *African Christianity: An African Story*, edited by Ogbu Kalu. Pretoria, SA: University of Pretoria, 2005.

Thomas, Nganda. "How the Orthodox Church Started in Kenya." In *Yearbook and Review 2009*. Edited by Makarios Tillyrides, translated by Eliud Ng'ang'a Mwaura. Nairobi: Greek Orthodox Archbishopric of Kenya, 2009.

---

19. See my forthcoming book, *Stewardship in the African Christian Context* by Oasis International, estimated date of publication: 2018/2019.

7

The Impact of an Essential African Christian Theological Reconciliation Schema in Peace-Building in Africa

Fredrick Amolo
Lecturer, Africa Nazarene University, Nairobi, Kenya

Abstract

The contemporary world epoch has been exemplified by the upsurge of conflict, hostility, and the deepening of ethno-political schism. In the last few years, increasing violence in sub-Saharan governments has been seen. The conflict phenomena experienced in the world today continues to devastate and disintegrate the web of societal co-existence including death, destruction of properties and displacement of people. Reconciliation therefore stands at the heart of contemporary African Christian Theology (ACT) in light of peace-building. In healing the African continent against the threats of war, a critical change on character, attitude and social structure, and obligations is necessary. The African Christian Theological Reconciliation Scheme can be considered a peace-building design critical in African socio-political society. ACTRS is idealized as a tool that (1) promotes a deeper appreciation of the meaning of life in Christ, (2) strengthens personal identity and (3) reinforces community solidarity. Is also promotes key principles regarding life, value for creation, integrity and community. It challenges the culture of egoism, destructive competition, self-righteousness and unconcern. It is therefore critical that individual members' characters must be transformed, ethnic communities of Africa must engage their attitude, and African societies must embrace social transformation.

Key words: peacebuilding, reconciliation, transformation, community solidarity, African Christian Theology, attitude change, ethnic conflict.

Introduction

The modern era is characterized by the extraordinary rise in conflict, hostility, terrorism, and humanitarian disaster, and by the deepening of ethno-political schism across the globe.[1] In the last decade there has been increasingly violent engagement by governments in sub-Saharan Africa, including in Democratic Republic of Congo, Rwanda, Uganda, Namibia, Zimbabwe, Somalia, Sierra Leone, South Africa, and Kenya.[2] The conflict phenomena experienced in the world today devastate and disintegrate the webs of societal coexistence through death, destruction of property, and displacement of people.[3] Several works indicate that in Africa, death, destruction of property, and displacement of people are evidence of violence and conflict.[4]

Given these circumstances, communities all over the world are seeking for ways to reconcile and to build peace among warring people groups. In this respect, peace-building in theological circles incorporates the extensive sense of peace and reconciliation found in the Bible.[5] In line with this, African Christianity has embraced the work of Christ in reconciliation as the authentic hope that transforms destructive conflict.[6] This work of Christ as a heart-

---

1. Peter Wanyagi Mbaro, *Makers of Peace* (Nairobi: Finese, 2010), 1.

2. See Fredrick Wanyama, "The Role of the Presidency in African Conflicts," in *Conflict in Contemporary Africa*, eds. Godfrey Okoth and Bethwell Ogot (Nairobi: Jomo Kenyatta Foundation, 2000), 30–32.

3. Acquiline Tarimo and Pauline Manwelo, *African Peacemaking and Governance* (Nairobi: Acton Publishers, 2008), 11–22. See also TJRC report, volume 1, p. x, available: https://digitalcommons.law.seattleu.edu/cgi/viewcontent.cgi?article.

4. See Joshia Osamba, "Violence and Dynamics of Transition: State, Ethnicity and Governance," *Africa Development* 26, no. 1–2 (2001): 47–48.

5. Cletus Chukwu, "Peace Building: From Concept to Strategy," in *Peace Building in East Africa: Exploring the Role of the Churches*, ed. Paddy Musana (Nairobi: Paulines Publications Africa, 2013), 34.

6. Loise Kriesberg, "Comparing Reconciliation Action Within and Between Countries," in *From Conflict Resolution to Reconciliation*, ed. Yakov Bar-Siman-Tov (Oxford: Oxford University Press, 2008), 82.

changing agent can result in renewal of interpersonal relations through healing and restoration of community – that is, reconciliation.[7] Reconciliation therefore stands at the heart of contemporary African Christian Theology (ACT) approaches to peace-building. The paradigm of reconciliation embodies the transformation of individual hearts and the restoration of interpersonal relationships, and ensures harmonious community coexistence.[8]

The growth of Christianity on the African continent has generated the quest and revitalized the longing for a more African Christian reconciliation schema in peace-building. This schema is embedded in the concept of transformation which deals with social, behavioral, and attitudinal aspects of conflict. The African Christian Theological Reconciliation Schema (ACTRS) is based around change of heart and life, and renewed interpersonal relations through healing, restoration of community, and social transformation. This paper will advance the view that character transformation based on Christian morals, attitude change based on Christian values of harmony and coexistence, and social transformation based on the Christian principles of community are fundamental to building peace among African communities.

Fundamental ACT Reconciliation Schema in Peace-Building in Africa

Reconciliation Paradigm from an African Christian Theological Perspective

Reconciliation has been conceptualized from the original Latin root word *reconcilio* to include the ideas of restoration, unity, and the bringing back into harmony of conflicting humanity.[9] Increasingly, reconciliation is understood as a multidimensional phenomenon covering several processes that address conflict and relationships. Kriesberg considers reconciliation as actions that transform destructive relationships.[10] Thus reconciliation ends conflict, reinstates peace, and produces a fresh peaceful and interpersonal shared life.

The theology of reconciliation (*katallassoo*) as advocated by the apostle Paul is grounded on the Old Testament (OT) concept of covenant and atonement. The shedding of the covenant blood and the reconciliatory sacrificial rituals of the OT are embodied in the life, work, and death of Christ for the reconciliation

---

7. See John Rucyahana, *The Bishop of Rwanda* (Nashville: Thomas Nelson, 2003).

8. See Joseph O. Omolo, *Reconciliation in African Context* (Nairobi: Uzima Publishing, 2008), 1–2.

9. See Omolo, *Reconciliation in African Context*, 1.

10. Louis Kriesberg, "External Contributions to Post-Mass-Crime Rehabilitation," in *After Mass Crime: Rebuilding States and Communities*, eds. B. Pouligny, S. Chesterman, and A. Schnabel (Tokyo: United Nations University Press, 2007), 243–270.

of sinful humanity.[11] Reconciliation therefore has both vertical and horizontal dimensions in human society. Omolo affirms that "The Old Testament has two underlying concepts of reconciliation – vertical and horizontal. In the vertical aspect of reconciliation, the common term is atonement (*Kippur*), in which God reconciles his people to himself . . . [In] the horizontal aspect of reconciliation the people knew . . . they were to reconcile themselves to their fellow citizens."[12]

Within African societies, the purpose of reconciliation in peace-building is to restore harmony and reconcile the parties at war.[13] Scholars have noted the importance for reconciliation founded in African society's fundamental tenets of community governance, coexistence, and relationship management embedded in basic principles of belief, norms, and legal procedures.[14] Tom noted that the principles and practices of African societies in relation to conflict support reconciliation, as demonstrated in several African traditional models of reconciliation.[15] Reconciliation therefore constitutes restoration of harmony by removing existing obstacles to peace and creating change from enmity to friendship.

In the African Christian context, therefore, reconciliation is generally considered to be a central process for a society after conflict. It must address structural injustices, social-economic concerns, and personal character, as well as attitude problems. This inter/intra-personal dimension of reconciliation enables the establishment of a new peace and the taking of responsibility for the offense and consequences of conflict.[16] Drawing from the Old Testament concept of atonement, the New Testament idea of reconciliation is about establishing a shared relationship of mutual obligation in accordance with the stipulations of that relationship.[17] The concept of reconciliation in both the Old and New Testaments underscores that humanity has been alienated from God

---

11. Omolo, *Reconciliation in African Context*, 8–11.

12. Omolo, 11–12.

13. Don John Omale, "Justice in History: An Examination of the African Restorative Traditions and the Emerging Restorative Justice Paradigm," *African Journal of Criminology and Justice Studies* 2, no. 2 (2006): 45–46.

14. See Jeffrey A. Fadiman, "Mountain Witchcraft: Supernatural Practices and Practitioners among the Meru of Mount Kenya," *African Studies Review* 20, no. 1 (April 1977): 87–101.

15. See Patrick Tom, "The Acholi Traditional Approach to Justice and the War in Northern Uganda," *Beyond Intractabilty* (blog), August 2006, https://www.beyondintractability.org/casestudy/tom-acholi.

16. John Blad, "More Conciliation and Less Punishment: Demanding a Public Choice," *Journal of Law and Conflict Resolution* 2, no. 5 (May 2010): 82.

17. See Robert J. Schreiter, "Reconciliation," in *Dictionary of Mission: Theology, History, Perspectives*, eds. Karl Müller et al. (Maryknoll, NY: Orbis, 1997).

by sin, which has ruined our relationships.[18] The stories in Genesis chapters 3, 4, 6, and 11 demonstrate how the human problem of sin ruined relationships both with God and with humanity. Sin created animosity, conflict, and rivalry that spread down through biblical history. Reconciliation therefore is the means by which God has established everlasting peace with humanity and the universe (2 Cor 5:18–19). In this respect, the church has been commissioned by Jesus to be the reconciling agent in society.

Conflicts have both life-affirming and life-destroying aspects that are manifested in attitudes, community affairs, and behavior. Reconciliation is about building trust and confidence as individuals abide by the basic norms and values of the community. It is a process of addressing fractured relationships and restoring community to the right understanding of humanity made in the relational image of God. In this respect, standing in a right relationship with God and with fellow human beings is one aspect constituting the *Imago Dei*.[19]

Critical to the reconciliation perspective of African Christianity are character transformation, changes in attitude, and social transformation. Reconciliation sets aside past animosities and promises regeneration and transformation.[20] Thus reconciliation includes critical change in character, attitudes, social structure, and obligations.

Character Transformation

The biblical predicament of sin resulting in the separation between humanity and God is exemplified in the hostility among humanity. This conversion of human behavior into bad character, animosity, and conflict is deeply rooted in the sinfulness of humanity, noted as early as the book of Genesis.[21] It is evidenced by the concern with human conduct demonstrated in the Pauline letters of Romans and Galatians.[22] Sin has therefore considerably altered, enslaved, and controlled human character, resulting in personal and societal conflict.

---

18. Richard D. Phillips. *What Is the Atonement?* (Phillipsburg, NJ: P&R, 2010), 21.

19. See H. Ray Dunning, *Reflecting the Divine Image: Christian Ethics in Wesleyan Perspective* (Downers Grove, IL: InterVarsity, 1998).

20. Sarah Maddison, *Conflict Transformation and Reconciliation: Multi-Level Challenges in Deeply Divided Societies* (New York: Routledge, 2016), 46.

21. See Genesis chapters 3–4. This shows that the sin problem of chapter 3 resulted in the conflict and death in chapter 4.

22. Charles B. Cousar, *The Letters of Paul* (Nashville: Abingdon, 1996), 120–122.

Character is a group of behavior traits within our conduct that expose who we are. It is usually evident in our attitudes, ethical fiber, and behavior.[23] Character transformation, therefore, is a process by which God develops Christ's character in believers through the ministry of the Holy Spirit in the context of community. As demonstrated in the biblical concept of salvation, the work of God in Christ transforms human behavior and life toward love for God and neighbor. It involves change in human thoughts, behavior, and relationships.[24] Willard and Simpson agree that a constant personal relationship God establishes character transformation in human relationships. It changes people's notions, principles, approaches, practices, and social relations.[25] It results in a life of service to others and witness for Christ.

In light of the above, reconciliation is understood as central to the biblical paradigm for peace, as exemplified in Jesus's restoration of human relationships.[26] The concept of biblical reconciliation, as argued by several scholars, illuminates a new imagination of a shared relational vision of transformation of individual hearts, rehabilitation of interpersonal relationships, and restoration of community neighborhood.[27] It is specifically about God making restoration with and between human beings, as indicated in Romans 5:1–12 and Colossians 1:18–23.

Attitude Change

Attitude, whether positive or negative, has a critical and direct influence on peace-building in African societies. Attitude can be considered as a feeling or opinion held about somebody or something, often in a rude or unpleasant way.[28] A bad attitude generally hinders relationships among people within a

---

23. Richard J. Krejcir argues in his paper, "What Is Christian Character," that character is shown in attitudes, ethics and behavior. Available online: http://www.discipleshiptools.org/apps/articles/default.asp?articleid=37081&columnid=4166.

24. This definition is adopted from Center for Christian Leadership at Dallas Theological Seminary, *Integrity: Examining How I Live* (Richardson, TX: Biblical Studies Press, 2004), 3, https://bible.org/series/integrity-examining-how-i-live.

25. Dallas Willard and Don Simpson, *Revolution of Character: Discovering Christ's Pattern for Spiritual Transformation* (Colorado: NavPress, 2005), 12–14.

26. Ross Langmead, "Transformed Relationships: Reconciliation as the Central Model for Mission," *Mission Studies* 25, no. 1 (2008): 5–20.

27. See Desmond Tutu, *No Future Without Forgiveness* (New York: Doubleday, 1999); and Tristan Anne Borer, "Reconciling South Africa or South Africans? Cautionary Notes from the TRC," *African Studies Quarterly* 8, no. 1 (Fall 2004): 19–38.

28. See *Cambridge Advanced Learners Dictionary* (Cambridge: Cambridge University Press, 2003).

community. Post-conflict African societies, for example, have been fractured by feelings of hatred, prejudice, negative stereotypes of ethnicity, and religio-cultural and political divisions.[29] Herrera affirms that conflict dynamics include attitudes that dehumanize others in order to justify inappropriate behavior.[30]

Tarimo and Manwelo agree that, in resolving conflict, it is vital that attitudes are transformed and that disputants renounce their claims and accommodate the interests of others for the sake of the common good.[31] Cole argues that attitude informs interpretation of events, situations, and relationships, as well as determining behavior.[32] Attitude change, therefore, is about human beings changing their perspectives and feelings about each other for the good of society. The apostle Paul advocates attitude change, pointing to the example of Jesus's life and relationships (Phil 2:5–8).

The process of reconciliation involves the pursuit of the values of mutuality, respect, and honor. Such a process calls for transformation of attitudes. The dynamics of reconciliation require an appreciation of other human beings to prepare the way for healing. The process entails transformation of the emotional and psychological aspects of conflict toward inner understandings, perceptions, memories, and restoration of community bonding.[33] Reconciliation presupposes forgiveness, justice, and the abandonment of revenge, which in turn comes from a change in attitude toward a desire to build a new relationship between the offender and the offended. This is founded on the principle of love that transcends enmity and is expressed in kindness, compassion, and mercy.[34]

Social Transformation

Social transformation is a community change aimed at creating a humane, equal, and just community order. It is a process of rebuilding broken relationships and establishing a community of peaceful coexistence. The purpose of social transformation is to reinforce mutual care, establish justice,

---

29. From reading through various authors, these seem to be the general causes of conflict in Africa. Several authors in *Conflict in Contemporary Africa*, eds., Godfrey Okoth and Bethwell Ogot (Nairobi: Jomo Kenyatta Foundation, 2000).

30. Fernando A. Herrera, *Pastoralist Conflict in the Horn of Africa* (Nairobi: Paulines Publications Africa, 2013), 56.

31. Tarimo and Manwelo, *African Peacemaking and Governance*, 66.

32. Dorian Scott Cole, "Meaning Transformation: Creating Characters with Attitude," *Visual Writer*, 1998, http://www.visualwriter.com/HumanCond/Transformation.htm.

33. Tarimo and Manwelo, *African Peacemaking and Governance*, 75.

34. See Ada María Isasi-Díaz, "Reconciliation: A Religious, Social, and Civic Virtue," *Journal of Latino Theology* 8, no. 4 (2001): 17.

and seek to improve and defend the welfare of others.[35] This social revolution is a biblical and theological agenda that eliminates discrimination on the basis of class, race, ethnicity, and gender, as exemplified in the Christian images of salt and light.[36] Tarimo and Manwelo contend that this transformation underlines the defense of the principles of community and the common good.[37]

Conflict cannot be resolved until the demands for equality, social justice, and human rights are respected. These demands require social transformation for the good of the community. Crucial to social change is the establishment of social structures conducive to peace-building. These structures should be founded on the principles of mediation, negotiation, and reconciliation.[38]

The vital components of social transformation include proper appreciation of the value of community and church elders, women, values systems, and reconciliatory religious rituals in peace-building. In theological circles, scholars reiterate the vital contribution toward peace of these community-rich human and value resources.

The ideas of love, unity, and moral societal reconstruction promote the communal neighborhood and holistic relationships for peace. These concepts constitute the function of reconciliation in social transformation. Scholars thus agree that religious virtues and values inspired by God transcend the horizons of self-interest and generate commitment to a sense of obligation.[39] The major purpose of reconciliation is to eradicate the social evils of hatred, animosity, and violence. As scholars have noted, reconciliation is concerned with human relationships.[40]

The Impact of the ACT Reconciliation Agenda on Peace-Building in Africa

Christianity has widely been accepted as part of the African heritage in this century. It is considered to be a unifying factor in community well-being on the

---

35. See Isa 1:12–17; Amos 4:4; Jer 7:1–14; and Matt 23:23.

36. T. M. Hinga, "The Biblical Mandate for Social Transformation: A Feminist Perspective," in *Moral and Ethical Issues in African Christianity: A Challenge for African Christianity*, eds. J. N. K. Mugambi and A. J. Nasimiyu-Wasike (Nairobi: Acton, 2003), 38–41.

37. Tarimo and Manwelo, *African Peacemaking and Governance*, 66.

38. Several peace scholars have reiterated the importance of third-party mechanisms of mediation, negotiation, and reconciliation in conflict resolution. For example, see David Augsburger, *Conflict and Mediation across Cultures* (Louisville: Westminster Press, 1992).

39. Tarimo and Manwelo, *African Peacemaking and Governance*, 119.

40. John Paul Lederach, *Building Peace: Sustainable Reconciliation in Divided Societies* (Washington, DC: Institute of Peace Press, 1997), 30.

African continent.[41] Christianity has therefore been regarded as a custodian of moral values and lifestyle critical to character transformation, attitude change, and social redress. This Christian lifestyle promotes peace that is founded on Christ the Prince of peace (Eph 2:13–18). This peace in Christ is conceptualized as a state in which human beings love each other, seek others' interests, and meet each other with respect and patience. It implies accountability and the defense of freedom that necessitates forgiveness, reconciliation, and community unity.[42] This peace is a fundamental divine attribute that empowers human existence. It emanates from a deep relationship and fellowship with the Holy Spirit, as seen in John 14:27.[43]

The African Christian Theological Reconciliation Schema (ACTRS) can be considered a peace-building design critical for African socio-political society. ACTRS, as demonstrated in the above discussion, is designed to be a tool that (1) promotes a deeper appreciation of the meaning of life in Christ, (2) strengthens personal identity, and (3) reinforces community solidarity. It also promotes key principles regarding life and the valuing of creation, integrity, and community. It challenges the culture of egoism, destructive competition, self-righteousness, and unconcern.

Authentic peace-building is a peace process that averts the degeneration of social wellbeing into conflict and hostilities. Authentic peace in Africa can be realized as it emanates from God to his people and among his people. In that respect, reconciliation with God is the recipe for human reconciliation.[44] Following Jesus demands that we seek the good and tranquility of the wider community, regardless of tribe, culture, and ideologies.

Reconciliation, then, is focused on building relationships between antagonists. It creates a space for encounter. It reframes the conflict so that there is a creative way to address, integrate, and embrace the painful past and share the future as a means of dealing with the past. The story of Jacob and Esau in Genesis 32–33 validates the radical call to forgive and reconcile when we have wronged each other. Consequently, the New Testament urges real love for our enemies, saying that such an attitude is synonymous to "[being]

---

41. Tarimo and Manwelo, *African Peacemaking and Governance*, 117–120.

42. Theresa Tinkasiimire, "Women, Peacebuilding and Reconciliation in East Africa: A Case of Uganda," in *Peace Building in East Africa: Exploring the Role of the Churches*, ed. Paddy Musana (Nairobi: Paulines Publications Africa, 2013), 75.

43. Chukwu, "Peacebuilding: From Concept to Strategy," 28.

44. Peter Mageto, "The Shalom Church in East Africa: Challenges in Peace Building and Reconciliation," in *Peace Building in East Africa*, ed. Paddy Musana (Nairobi: Paulines Publications Africa, 2013), 95.

perfect, as your heavenly Father is perfect" (Matt 5:48). Jesus's teaching shows what constitutes unconditional love.

The process of reconciliation transforms conflict by creating a situation of objectivity in the problem and not in the people. It is about working together on a common problem. It enables seeing the issue as an opportunity to explore, understand, and change the deeper patterns that cause conflict.

Change in individuals, in intergroup relations, and in social structures is vital for peace in Africa. Changed individuals engage with schemes that alter attitudes and perceptions, behavior, and the social fiber of society. The aim is to transform antagonistic or damaging attitudes and to provide new, hopeful possibilities for peace. Behavioral change strategies aim to advance communication, integrate arbitration and problem-solving skills, promote interpersonal support, and reduce the use of hostile language, physical violence, and discrimination.

Conclusion and Recommendations

Conclusion

Conflict is inevitable in all human interactions, including on the African continent. With the upsurge in violence across Africa, conflict interventions often try to improve intergroup relations by establishing conditions for supportive and significant relations between members of opposing groups. Reconciliation has been supported as a critical pillar in peace-building in Africa. African Christian spirituality therefore encourages a move to a level of transformation of character, attitude, and society.

For there to be peace within a society, humanity must be renewed in the depths of the inner being, in attitudes, and in social structures. It is from the content of our human heart that we interpret reality and react decisively, whether toward peace or conflict. The reconciliation scheme advocated in this paper suggests that meeting basic human spiritual needs changes the underlying conditions that foster violence. In addition, it is guided by the assumption that changing social structures can shift the behaviors and attitudes of people.

Recommendations

For sustainable peace to be built in African society, the reconciliation scheme must be considered carefully. The African Christian community must endeavor to work on the following:

1. The characters of individual members must be transformed if peace is to be attained in conflict-ridden Africa. The church needs to move tirelessly in its mission to evangelize Africa for Christ in order to nurture character. In evangelistic campaigns and discipleship programs, the church must endeavor to inculcate biblical moral values through activities such as Bible studies, prayer meetings, purposeful church services, cell-group meetings, and strategic social activities. The activities of the church must lead people into a personal encounter with God, leading to a fully restored relationship with God and neighbor. This is the newness in Christ Jesus described by Paul in 2 Corinthians 5:17–19.

2. Ethnic communities in Africa must change their attitudes toward each other for the sake of community integration and coexistence. Wrong attitudes can block human interactions, fellowship, and engagement for the common good. Prejudices, stereotypes, and negative and dehumanizing opinions of others must be eliminated for peaceful coexistence. Negative attitudes are among the major triggers of persistent conflict between bordering communities in Africa. We must be willing to accept and live in harmony with each other, regardless of our cultural differences. Ethnic communities in Africa must emphasize moral values on issues to do with love and community, rather than ethnic differences.

3. African societies must embrace social transformation to eliminate discrimination and social evils. Love, trust, harmony, and community must be the principles that govern African human interactions. We must engage in mediation and arbitration with a humane council of elders, women, and youth as we employ Christian values. These values are a precondition for lasting peace in Africa. There are various social transformative activities that African societies must embrace to deal with ethnic differences, including sport, common trade, and intermarriages. There are diverse social problems in African societies, such as cattle rustling, land and boundary disputes, animosity, and hatred among communities, but propagating social engagement with the help of community elders, women, and youth will advance the cause of peace and harmony.

Bibliography

Augsburger, David. *Conflict and Mediation across Cultures*. Louisville: Westminster Press, 1992.

Blad, John. "More Conciliation and Less Punishment: Demanding a Public Choice." *Journal of Law and Conflict Resolution* 2, no. 5 (May 2010): 80–90.

Borer, Tristan A. "Reconciling South Africa or South Africans: Cautionary Notes from TRC." *African Studies Quarterly* 8, no. 1 (Fall 2004): 19–38.

Cambridge Advanced Learners Dictionary, Cambridge University Press, 2003.

Centre for Christian Leadership. *Integrity: Examining How I Live*. Richardson, TX: Biblical Studies Press, 2004. Available at https://bible.org/series/integrity-examining-how-i-live.

Chukwu, Cletus. "Peacebuilding: From Concept to Strategy." In *Peacebuilding in East Africa: Exploring the Role of the Churches*, edited by Paddy Musana, 26–40. Nairobi: Paulines Publications Africa, 2013.

Cole, Dorian Scott. "Creating character with Attitude." Available online: http://www.visualwriter.com/HumanCond/Transformation.htm.

Cousar, Charles B. *The Letters of Paul*. Nashville: Abingdon, 1996.

Dunning, H. Ray. *Reflecting the Divine Image: Christian Ethics in Wesleyan Perspective*. Downers Grove, IL: InterVarsity, 1998.

Fadiman, Jeffery A. "Mountain Witchcraft: Supernatural Practices and Practitioners among the Meru of Mount Kenya." *African Studies Review* 20, no. 1 (April 1997): 87–101.

Herrera, Fernando A. *Pastoralist Conflict in the Horn of Africa*. Nairobi: Paulines Publications Africa, 2013.

Hinga, T. M. "The Biblical Mandate for Social Transformation: A Feminist Perspective." In *Moral and Ethical Issues in African Christianity: A Challenge for African Christianity*, edited by J. N. K. Mugambi and A. J. Nasimiyu-Wasike, 38–41. Nairobi: Acton Publishers, 2003.

Isasi-Diaz, Ada Maria. "Reconciliation: A Religious, Social, and Civic Virtue." *Journal of Latino Theology* 8 (May 2001): 5–28.

Krejcir, Richard J. "What Is Christian Character?" Available online: http://www.discipleshiptools.org/apps/articles/default.asp?articleid=37081&columnid=4166.

Kriesberg, Loise. "Comparing Reconciliation Action Within and Between Countries." In *From Conflict Resolution to Reconciliation*, edited by Yakov Bar-Siman-Tov, 81–110. Oxford: Oxford University Press, 2008.

———. "External Contributions of Post-Mass-Crime Rehabilitation." In *After Mass Crime Rebuilding States and Communities*, edited by B. Poulgny, S. Chesterman, and A. Schnabel, 243–270. Tokyo: United Nations University Press, 2007.

Langmead, Ross. "Transformed Relationship: Reconciliation as the Central Model for Mission." *Mission Studies* 25, no. 1 (2008): 5–20.

Lederach, John Paul. *Building Peace: Sustainable Reconciliation in Divided Societies*. Washington, DC: Institute of Peace Press, 1997.

Maddison, Sarah. *Conflict Transformation and Reconciliation: Multi-level Challenges in Deeply Divided Societies*. New York: Routledge, 2016.

Mageto, Peter. "The Shalom Church in East Africa: Challenges in Peacebuilding and Reconciliation." In *Peacebuilding in East Africa: Exploring the Role of the Churches*, edited by Paddy Musana, 92–110. Nairobi: Paulines Publications Africa, 2013.

Okoth, Godfrey, and Bethwel Ogot, eds. *Conflict in Contemporary Africa*. Nairobi: Jomo Kenyatta Foundation, 2000.

Omale, Don John. "Justice in History: An Examination of the African Restorative Traditions and the Emerging Restorative Justice Paradigm." *African Journal of Criminology and Justice Studies* 2, no. 2 (2006): 33–63.

Omolo, Joseph O. *Reconciliation in African Context*. Nairobi: Uzima Publishing, 2008.

Osamba, Joshia. "Violence and Dynamics of Transition: State, Ethnicity and Governance." *Africa Development* 26, no. 1 (2001): 37–54.

Phillips, Richard D. *What Is the Atonement?* Phillipsburg, NJ: P&R, 2010.

Rucyahana, John. *The Bishop of Rwanda*. Nashville: Thomas Nelson, 2003.

Schreiter, Robert J. "Reconciliation." In *Dictionary of Mission: Theology, History and Perspective*, edited by Karl Muller et al., 379–381. Maryknoll: Orbis Books, 1997.

Tarimo, Acquiline, and Pauline Manwelo. *African Peacemaking and Governance*. Nairobi: Acton Publishers, 2008.

Tinkasiimire, Theresa. "Women, Peacebuilding and Reconciliation in East Africa: A Case Study of Uganda." In *Peace Building in East Africa: Exploring the Role of the Churches*, edited by Paddy Musana, 67–69. Nairobi: Paulines Publications Africa, 2013.

TJRC Report, Volume 1, x. Available online: https://digitalcommons.law.seattleu.edu/cgi/viewcontent.cgi?article.

Tom, Patrick. "The Acholi Traditional Approach to Justice and the War in Northern Uganda." *Beyond Intractabilty* (blog), August 2006. https://www.beyondintractability.org/casestudy/tom-acholi.

Tutu, Desmond. *No Future without Forgiveness*. New York: Doubleday, 1999.

Wanyagi Mbaro, Peter. *Makers of Peace*. Nairobi: Finese Publishing, 2010.

Wanyama, Fredrick. "The Role of the Presidency in African Conflicts." In *Conflict in Contemporary Africa*, edited by Godfrey Okoth and Bethwell Ogot, 30–43. Nairobi: Jomo Kenyatta Foundation, 2000.

Willard, Dallas, and Don Simpson. *Revolution of Character: Discovering Christ's Pattern for Spiritual Transformation*. Colorado: NavPress, 2005.

8

Widow Cleansing in Rural Kenya: Toward a Critically Contextualized Theological Response

Mary Thamari Odhiambo
Country Director, Life in Abundance-Kenya, Nairobi, Kenya

Abstract

The phenomenon of widow cleansing has received considerable attention in relation to livelihood concerns and HIV/AIDS among women in Kenya. Using ethnographic methods, an investigation into the lived experiences of widows was conducted as part of a larger study on women's negotiations of gender relations in southwestern Kenya. This paper illustrates the intricate interplay between the practice of widow cleansing, livelihoods, and health in the context of strained social and economic realities in this region. While development actors have engaged various forms of mitigation efforts to address problems associated with widow cleansing, some significant gaps persist. By highlighting the gaps in structural and behavioral approaches to the "problem of widow cleansing," the need for a holistic and contextualized theological response becomes obvious, a thought which this paper advances. A holistic strategy which recognizes and appreciates the multifaceted contextual realities and that addresses the widow's spiritual, social, and economic needs is proposed.

Key words: widow inheritance, widow cleansing, livelihoods, customary and statutory land laws, HIV/AIDS, structural interventions, behavioral interventions, critical contextualization, Luo.

Introduction

> Because of my church rules, I stayed for two years before I got cleansed. It was hard, and after that my brother-in-law took me. I think I got HIV from him.[1]
>
> *Ne ongiewi gi dhiang. Koro gima dwawach onge* (We were bought with cows. So we cannot say anything).[2]

As part of an ongoing research project on gender relations and women's access to and participation in income labor in rural Kenya, the issue of widow cleansing has come to the fore in regard to dilemmas widows face in pursuit of their livelihood and social inclusion. This paper follows the African Society for Evangelical Theology consortium (ASET) theme on "African Contextual Realities" by drawing attention to the reality of widow cleansing and exposing gaps and limitations in behavioral and some structural interventions to the "problems of widow cleansing." A phenomenological description of widow cleansing is given, followed by a biblical and theological reflection on how the Christian community might fill the intervention gaps in regard to widow cleansing and its ensuing predicaments.

Widow Cleansing: Phenomenological Analysis

Widow cleansing has received considerable attention in relation to livelihood options and HIV/AIDS among women in Kenya. The term "widow cleansing" has been used interchangeably with "widow inheritance," "widow guardianship," and "levirate union." Though these expressions are related, with overlapping goals and rituals, it is useful to distinguish them. "Widow inheritance" and "widow guardianship" are loosely used to refer to the taking ownership of a deceased brother's or cousin's widow. "Taking ownership" connotes taking the roles and obligations of a husband, including perpetuating the lineage through childbearing and management of resources, and ensuring that the livelihood

---

1. Atieno, "Story of My Life," face to face interview, November 2015.
2. This was a statement made by one of the widows during a focus-group discussion on issues of land access and customary law.

of the widow is taken care of. "Widow inheritance" or "widow guardianship" may or may not be preceded by widow cleansing rituals.

"Levirate union" refers to an arrangement in which a brother is obligated to perpetuate a deceased brother's name or lineage after his death.[3] Levirate union was key in ancient Judaism, as it has been and still is among some African ethnic groups, such as the Luo, Teso, Mijikenda, Pokot, and Abaluhya,[4] Hausa of West Africa, Dinka and Nuer of South Sudan,[5] and also among the Kurds in the Middle East.[6] Although the intention of levirate union does not always work as intended, as seen in the case of Tamar and Onan in the Genesis 38 account, it has also been abused in African communities which practice it.[7]

"Widow cleansing" refers to a sexual ritual performed between a widow and her deceased husband's brother or other male relative after the death of a husband.

Atieno's Story[8]

I met Atieno at her home in Mbita in November 2015. She lost her husband nine years ago and according to Luo custom she needed to be cleansed; but since she belonged to the "power of Jesus around the world church," she did not heed this ritual. Her church forbids widow cleansing for its members. For two years Atieno stayed "uncleansed." Due to her uncleansed state she was regarded as having *chola* (impurity) and as being a danger to others, and a number of restrictions were placed upon her. To ensure the danger of *chola* was not transmitted to others she was restricted from attending public functions, greeting people with her hands, participating in community gatherings, selling in the market, or tilling her land. These restrictions were difficult to bear. Her only source of livelihood was the fish trade. However, she couldn't engage in this as her state of *chola* did not allow trading. In addition, other people did not respect her. They did not want to associate with her. Atieno gave up on

---

3. Stephanie Beswick, "We Were Bought Like Clothes: The War over Polygyny and Levirate Marriage in South Sudan," *Northeast African Studies* 8, no. 2 (2001): 35–61; Dvora E. Weisberg, *Levirate Marriage and the Family in Ancient Judaism* (Waltham, MA: Brandeis University Press, 2009), xvii.

4. C. R. Ambasa-Shisanya, "Widowhood in the Era of HIV/AIDS: A Case Study of Siaya District, Kenya," *Journal of Social Aspects of HIV/AIDS* 4, no. 2 (2007): 606–615.

5. Beswick, "We Were Bought Like Clothes."

6. James J. Ponzetti, ed., *International Encyclopedia of Marriage and Family*, 2nd ed. (New York: Macmillan Reference USA, 2003).

7. Beswick, "We Were Bought Like Clothes."

8. Atieno, "Story of My Life."

the church regulations and decided to be cleansed according to custom. Her brother in-law, who has also since died, cleansed her and later inherited her.

According to a 2009 demographic survey, Atieno's story echoes the stories of about 27,744 widows in Homabay County where this study was carried out.[9] Homabay County has drawn attention due to the high prevalence of HIV/AIDS, which now stands at 27 percent.[10]

The Luo people are patrilineal – their descent is reckoned through the father – and it is organized in clans made of a number of lineages that trace their descent to a common ancestor.[11] The nature of the Luo patrilineal descent determines significant social organization features, such as postmarital residence, when a newly married couple adopt a patrilocal residence, living near the husband's family. The woman is required to relocate from her natal home to her husband's clan's territory. In patrilineal communities, bride wealth is given to the wife's clan by the man's clan. The bride wealth paid by the clan to obtain a wife symbolizes the transfer of a woman's rights from one clan to the other; the receivers of the bride wealth know that the children that are produced by the woman will belong to the clan that paid the bride wealth.[12] In essence, "bride-wealth ensures that a woman becomes part of the lineage, and if widowed, she would be cared for by a brother-in-law."[13]

Luo marriages are considered permanent, as has been observed by Ogutu,[14] Potash,[15] and Nwoye.[16] Its permanency is symbolized by the exchange of

---

9. Kenya National Bureau of Statistics, "Population and Household Characteristics of Kenya, 2009," *Knoema*, 2009, http://knoema.com/KEPHC2009/population-and-household-characteristics-of-kenya-2009?location=1000900-homa-bay. The 2006 data shows that 42.3% of households in Homabay were headed by women and 57.7% headed by men out of the 206,255 total number of households. Of the female heads of households, 31.8% were widows.

10. National Aids Control Council, "Kenya AIDS Response Progress Report 2014," March 2014.

11. Ruth Prince and Wenzel P. Geissler, "Becoming 'One Who Treats': A Case Study of a Luo Healer and Her Grandson in Western Kenya," *American Anthropological Association* 32, no. 4 (December 2001): 447–471; Gilbert E. M. Ogutu, "Marriage Rights and Privileges: Luo Levirate Marriage Revisited," in *Emerging Issues on Population and Development in Africa*, 5th Africa Population Conference (Arusha, Tanzania: EQUAL TIME, 2007).

12. Angela Reynar, "Fertility Decision Making by Couples amongst the Luo of Kenya," (Diss., University of Pennsylvania, 2000), 31.

13. Patricia Achieng Opondo, "Dodo Performance in the Context of Women's Associations amongst the Luo of Kenya," (PhD Diss., University of Pittsburgh, 1996), 82–83.

14. Ogutu, "Marriage Rights and Privileges."

15. Betty Potash, "Some Aspects of Marital Stability in a Rural Luo Community," Cambridge University Press, *International Africa Institute* 48, no. 4 (1978): 380–397.

16. Augustine Nwoye, "The Practice of Interventive Polygamy in Two Regions of Africa: Background, Theory and Techniques," Springer, *Dialectical Anthropology* 31, no. 4 (2007): 383–421.

animals and a series of ceremonies which bind the two families together, a practice which Shipton relates to the exchange of "entrustment and obligation" between families and communities.[17] At marriage, a woman is entrusted by her natal family to her husband's family with expectations of a consequent good relationship. Such a marriage relationship whose formation involves the wider family and not just the couple cannot, according to the Luo, be annulled, not even in the event of death. This, Ogutu explains, is the reason behind levirate marriages. Luo people value marriage and lineage propagation as well as family solidarity. It is for this reason that when death occurs in a home, a state of disharmony ensues.[18] Death is believed to cause some psychic pressure and dissonance which must be restored. Part of this dissonance is due to the impurity that the widow acquires upon the death of her husband.[19] This impurity necessitates purification, which is achieved through sexual union with the deceased husband's brother or relative.[20] The choice of who cleanses and takes the widow is limited to the husband's kin, although current practice shows that some men have taken up the role of being "professional cleansers." It is believed that failure to comply with this obligation of cleansing can bring negative consequences upon the family, including death.[21] Ogutu, writing about widow cleansing and inheritance, states, "A Luo who lost a spouse had Tora (a load of psychic pressure that often leads to bad omen and fatal ailments). This remained traumatizing until purification rituals were performed and the household or homestead restored to normality, that is, the wife or husband was cleansed and cleared to mix freely with people and to perform his/her normal duties without undue pressures."[22]

Restoration of normalcy takes two stages: widow cleansing and eventual taking over of the widow – that is, widow inheritance or guardianship. These two practices serve different purposes. According to the Luo, cleansing is aimed at dealing with the impurity that is believed to befall a woman once

---

17. Parker MacDonald Shipton, *The Nature of Entrustment: Intimacy, Exchange, and the Sacred in Africa*, Yale Agrarian Studies Series (New Haven: Yale University Press, 2007), 13.

18. Ogutu, "Marriage Rights and Privileges."

19. Ogutu.

20. Rose Ayikukwei et al., "HIV/AIDS and Cultural Practices in Western Kenya: The Impact of Sexual Cleansing Rituals on Sexual Behaviours," *Culture, Health and Sexuality* 10, no. 6 (August 2008): 587–599; T. M. Okeyo and A. K. Allen, "Influence of Widow Inheritance in the Epidemiology of AIDS in Africa," *African Journal of Medical Practice* 1, no. 1 (1994): 20–25.

21. Michael C. Kirwen, *African Widows* (New York: Orbis, 1979); Ogutu, "Marriage Rights and Privileges"; M. A. Sossou, "Widowhood Practices in West Africa: Silent Victims," *International Journal of Social Welfare* 11 (2002): 201–209.

22. Ogutu, "Marriage Rights and Privileges," 5.

her husband dies. Widow cleansing is therefore regarded as a mandatory ritual after the death of a husband. Widow inheritance or levirate union, on the other hand, is aimed at giving support and a sense of belonging to a brother's widow as well as propagating his progeny. The Luo's original intention for widow inheritance can be paralleled with Ruth and Boaz's story in the Old Testament. Although the phrases "widow cleansing" and "widow inheritance" are used interchangeably, it is important to note their salient differences and their changing expressions among the Luo. These days, as noted above, a group of people referred to as commercial *joter* or paid widow cleansers has emerged.[23] This new practice has arisen with the advent of HIV/AIDS, as Ambasa-Shisanya notes: "If the family suspects that the death was related to HIV/AIDS, it hires a professional cleanser, and gives him alcohol. Thereafter, he is taken to the widow's house to perform a sex ritual on her. Family members sometimes supervise the ritual, to ensure that actual sexual intercourse takes place, thereby effecting the cultural cleansing."[24]

Various forms of change and continuity are seen in regard to widow cleansing and widow inheritance. Ambasa-Shisanya noted that educated widows are more likely to resist widow inheritance as they are not entirely dependent on family for their livelihoods.[25] "There are also known cases where the widows (mostly Christian and affluent) have gone through less elaborate rituals secretly or avoided the rituals altogether."[26] Some widows also resist and migrate to live in a setting where they are not known and where expectation of that ritual is minimal. Some widows migrate to beach villages or to city slums, like Joyce and Janifa:

> I refused to be cleansed and ran away to a beach village where no one knew me. When I went back home to till my land, they refused. Now I live here at the beach village with my children.[27]

> Life was hard in the village when my husband died. They wanted me to get a cleanser but I did not want [to]. I ran away to Nairobi slum. Here no one cares about *chola* [impurity], no one knows me.[28]

Some widows accept cleansing but resist inheritance. Ambasa-Shisanya argues that "the fact that widows require cleansing as a pre-requisite for

---

23. Ogutu, 5.
24. Ambasa-Shisanya, "Widowhood in the Era of HIV/AIDS."
25. Ambasa-Shisanya.
26. Ogutu, "Marriage Rights and Privileges," 9.
27. Joyce, "Story of My Life," face to face interview, 26 November 2015.
28. Janifa, "Why I Came to Kibera," face to face interview, 28 October 2014.

incorporation into their society and as a means of neutralising the assumed cultural impurity means that their decision is culturally compelled rather than self-willed."[29] In some cases, when the widow resists, a *joter* (cleanser) is brought by force.

Although the essence or intention of leviratic union or widow inheritance has some pragmatic basis – offering the widow a sense of belonging and livelihood support – it is fair to say that this intention has often been abused. Instead of offering the widow livelihood support, the cleanser and inheritor may grab or misuse her resources, or bar her from using her land. Instead of being offered a sense of belonging and identity, the widow is isolated and barred from interaction with other members. Instead of protecting her from abuse, a paid cleanser is called to sexually "cleanse her" from perceived impurity. Fear is inflicted in place of the needed consolation! One widow had this to say: "After the death of my husband, they came and took away even the grains that were in the store; they do not care about me or their brother's children, even if I know they should."[30]

The practice of widow inheritance has been turned upside down!

Current Interventions and Their Limitations

The reason why widow cleansing has received considerable attention in the recent past is its association with the spread of HIV/AIDS. With the ritual of cleansing requiring sexual intercourse without condom use, it is expected that HIV/AIDS will be linked to cleansing. Meanwhile, other emotional, social, spiritual and livelihood needs are overlooked or given minimal attention. Attempts to mitigate the "problem" of widow cleansing have followed two key strategies. First, due to the association of widow cleansing with HIV/AIDS, attention has been tilted toward behavioral models which focus on "health promotion and health outcomes."[31]

Creation of awareness of risky behavior constitutes the main behavioral intervention.[32] In this case, widow cleansing is regarded as high-risk behavior which ought to be changed. Although this intervention may reduce the

---

29. Ambasa-Shisanya, "Widowhood in the Era of HIV/AIDS," 613.

30. Auma, "Story of My Life," face to face interview, 25 November 2015.

31. Justin O. Parkhurst, "HIV Prevention, Structural Change and Social Values: The Need for an Explicit Normative Approach," *Journal of the International AIDS Society* 15, no. 1 (2012): 2.

32. Avert, "HIV Prevention Programmes Overview," Global Information and Advice on HIV and AIDS, 25 January 2015, http://www.avert.org/professionals/hiv-prevention-programming/overview.

incidences of widow cleansing, its effectiveness is limited because behavior is a superficial aspect of reality and is merely what is observed as a result of certain deep-seated tenets of worldview. From the phenomenological analysis of widow cleansing it is clear that the act of engaging in sexual cleansing (the behavior in this case) is compelled by certain beliefs and ensuing consequences that make it worthwhile for a widow to concede. There exists a deeper belief which is entrenched in the normative values of widow cleansing. Since behavioral intervention strategies tend to focus on shallow, observable actions, the ingrained motivations remain untouched and therefore unchanged. In the case of widow cleansing, behavioral strategies urge the widows to resist widow cleansing by dangling threats of HIV/AIDS infection. However, for a widow, the consequences of engaging in widow cleansing with the risk of HIV/AIDS and of not engaging in it are the same. One widow had this to say: "If I do not get cleansed I die of *chola*. This *chola* will kill me as no one will talk to me. I will be lonely, then I will die. If I get cleansed I may die of AIDS but I will be accepted and no one will look down upon me."[33]

Clearly this presents some dilemmas which the behavioral strategists do not address. The behavioral strategy ignores the deep-seated belief systems. The strategists also implore widows to use condoms in a matter over which they have very limited control and, besides, sexual cleansing using a condom is not considered complete. They ignore the salient normative values embedded in patterns of behavior.

The second strategy that has dominated the mitigation of the problems of widow cleansing is structural models. "Structural interventions seek to address underlying factors that make individuals or groups vulnerable."[34] In this case, the issue of widow cleansing is seen as a significant factor in vulnerability to HIV/AIDs.[35] Studies have shown that "the Nyanza province has a high prevalence of HIV infection among widows, at 63 percent, and that widows who are inherited for the purpose of performing sexual rituals have increased odds of being infected with HIV when compared with widows who are not inherited or are inherited for the purpose of companionship."[36] For

---

33. Magda, "Story of My Life," face to face interview, November 2015.

34. Avert, "HIV Prevention Programmes."

35. Lennah Oluoch et al., "Widow Cleansing and Inheritance among the Luo in Kenya: The Need for Additional Women-Centred HIV Prevention Options," *Journal of International AIDS Society* 17, no. 1 (2014): 2.

36. Brian Perry et al., "Widow Cleansing and Inheritance among the Luo in Kenya: The Need for Additional Women-Centred HIV Prevention Options," *Journal of International AIDS Society* 17 (2014): 2.

this reason, emphasis is given to dealing with legal and economic structural factors. For instance, widows are provided with micro-credit and business skills, as it is believed that lack of an alternative livelihood encourages widow cleansing as widows ally with men for support. While provision of micro-credit and business skills is useful and helps buffer the difficulties of a widow's livelihood, it appears that this intervention alone does not necessarily mitigate the "problems" of widow cleansing. Other interventions include enactment of laws to protect women's access to land and property.

In Kenya, the Land Registration Act,[37] Matrimonial Property Act,[38] and Articles 60a, f, and g of the Constitution[39] seek to address land-access issues promoting non-discriminative ownership of land. Closer observation, however, reveals that women in rural Kenya, particularly widows, are still faced with difficulties regarding access to land due to entrenched customary norms on land access, use, and control. Although these laws are aimed at minimizing problems such as those widows encounter, including the sexual cleansing that is linked to tenure security on the land of the deceased husband, a contrary picture is seen in rural Kenya. Responding to Article 60a of Kenya's constitution which upholds equitable access to land devoid of discrimination on gender lines, a group of young adults in rural Kenya said, "That law is on paper; there is another powerful law here, which is the customary law. That law is impractical here. Girls cannot own land and should not own land."[40] Awino, a widow who had been ejected from her land, said: "My in-law sold my land, and when I asked, he said I should shut up. One day I realized he was also selling the piece where my house was. I was very scared and did not talk, but when he sold a lot of land I decided to go to the chief, who asked me for a bribe. I had nowhere to go. Now I rent a room in the shopping center."[41]

Seemingly, the statutory laws have not sufficiently dealt with issues of land access for widows. Even after adhering to widow cleansing the rights of widows, as in the case of Awino, are abused, rendering them liable to deeper vulnerabilities such as migration to rural trading centers or to urban slums. Unequal gender relations which are embedded in patriarchal family arrangements ensure that women do not dare approach law courts when their

---

37. The Republic of Kenya, *Land Registration Act, 2012*, vol. 3 of 2012.
38. The Republic of Kenya, *Matrimonial Property Act, 2013*, vol. 49 of 2013.
39. Republic of Kenya, *The Constitution of Kenya* (Nairobi: Government Printer, 2010).
40. Badilisha young adults, Focus group discussion on women and land access, face to face correspondence, July 2013.
41. Awino, "Story of My Life," face to face interview, July 2016.

property or land is threatened. Those who do manage to seek legal redress are socially isolated, even by other women.

Some interventions promote economic empowerment of widows to offer alternative livelihoods in the hope that widows can refrain from widow cleansing. Widow cleansing, however, is not a factor of economic needs only, as Awour's story indicates: "They said I could get a loan to start a business, but look, who will buy my goods when I have *chola*? When people learn I have not been cleansed, they will not buy my goods."[42]

At the core of any Luo wife is the identity that is embedded in her relationship with her husband. Often women introduce themselves by making reference to their husbands as their "address," indicating a self-identity which is rooted in their husbands. It is no wonder that the pressure to be cleansed upon the death of a husband is also driven by the widows, who do not want to risk the loss of identity and isolation that may ensue. Although this may be subtle, it constitutes a key felt need of widows which structural interventions such as access to credit may not meet.

The case of Awour shows that the presence of *chola* (impurity) prohibits women from participating in trade and other social interactions, hence rendering this intervention impractical in the circumstances. Presenting a merely economic solution or legislation does not sufficiently address the question of widow cleansing and its dilemmas. Offering access to credit facilities that offer livelihood options to widows is intended to reduce vulnerability brought about by their dependence on men, but their needs go beyond that. The social isolation and fear presented by *chola* are significant factors that should not be ignored or trivialized.

From the above analysis we see that the current structural interventions such as law reform, access to credit and provision of public health services are insufficient in dealing with the underlying needs and realities around widow cleansing. Both the behavioral and the structural interventions being implemented assume a value-neutral stance and ignore the normative values and social goals that widow cleansing presents. No wonder widow cleansing continues unabated, driving widows into deeply vulnerable situations.

Due to the scourge of HIV/AIDS, widow cleansing has also largely been seen as an epidemiological problem. Actually, looking at widow cleansing through an epidemiological lens raises the question of whether widow cleansing would have been a "problem" if HIV/AIDS was not in the picture. Would there be any interest in widows? What vulnerabilities besides health does widow

---

42. Awour, "Story of My Life," face to face interview, November 2015.

cleansing present that would offer a justification for such attention? A holistic approach should see widow cleansing as a matter which encompasses other social goals beyond health outcomes.[43] Although health promotion, enactment of protective laws, livelihood support, and access to credit constitute significant key factors that improve a widow's wellbeing, there are other critical social goals that require attention. A sense of belonging, security, and identity are also key to people's quality of life and they determine the uptake of any social transformation efforts. While a widow needs to have a sense of belonging and identity, behavioral interventions emphasize some forms of isolation – the opposite of what widows need. Parkhurst has noted that "many behaviour change campaigns strive to achieve some form of self-imposed isolation."[44] Writing on "the Politics of Widowhood and Re-Marriage among the Luo of Kenya," Gunga notes that the "resolutions of the problems posed require a multi-dimensional approach that must improve psycho-social, educational, cultural, spiritual and emotional development."[45] Recognizing these gaps in the behavioral and ongoing structural interventions promotes a deeper reflection. Can biblical dogma and theological tradition fill these gaps?

Bridging the Gap: Theological and Biblical Reflection

Hiebert, writing on critical contextualization, noted that "social systems and cultures are human creations marked with sin and there is need to take a stand against corporate as well as individual sin."[46] Critical contextualization seeks to subject social arrangements and systems to investigative judgment through the lens of Scripture or other pragmatic values. The core of critical contextualization is understanding the phenomenon in context through the lens of insiders. Further, the problems are looked at with a wider scope, not just in regard to individual expressions of them. For instance, although widows are collateral participants in the ritual of widow cleansing, their actions should not be judged only on the basis of what they do or do not do. Doing this is a dishonest way of understanding human realities. Instead, familial arrangements, the whole community, and other contributing factors need

---

43. Parkhurst, "HIV Prevention."
44. Parkhurst, 3.
45. Samson O. Gunga, "The Politics of Widowhood and Re-Marriage among the Luo in Kenya," *Thought and Practice: A Journal of the Philosophical Association of Kenya (PAK)* 1, no. 1 (June 2009): 161–174.
46. Paul Hiebert, "Critical Contextualization," *International Bulletin of Missionary Research* 11, no. 3 (1987): 5.

closer examination. In this way, if sin is ascribed to "widow cleansing," it will be sin on the part not only of the widow but also of the man who cleanses and the community that endorses it, including those who fail to question norms that violate human dignity.

This is where the church or Christian religious movements come in. Will the church watch in silence and feign ignorance or innocence, and fail to question structures that entrench widow cleansing? Will the church vilify the "cleanser" and still not offer any solutions to the needs presented by this phenomenon? Fortunately, the Bible, from which the Christian agency draw their ethics, is filled with significant instructions and responses in regard to matters of cleansing and widows' support.

The term "cleansing" implies prior uncleanliness, impurity, or pollution. Impurity may be observable, as in dirt, stains, or a stench, but it may also connote unseen danger or hidden contamination. In the case of widow cleansing among the Luo, cleansing connotes unseen danger or pollution brought about by the death of a husband. This state of "impurity," with its resultant consequences, draws attention to various significant needs of widows. Besides the economic insecurity and health threats, social isolation and emotional vulnerability are also encountered. As Mary Douglas argues, "anyone approaching rituals of pollution nowadays would seek to treat a people's ideas of purity as part of a larger whole."[47] Therefore, a holistic view of a human's impure nature in a complex social setting needs close attention.

In connection with the fears resulting from impurity (*chola*) among the Luo widows, the Bible outlines ways in which Christians ought to look at impurity. Leviticus[48] is packed with detailed instructions on ritual impurity and the process of cleansing or purification. Theologically, Leviticus shows the relationship between "Yahweh (theology) and Israel (Israeology)," showing the obligations or standards of operation of humanity before Yahweh.[49] In Leviticus we see God's intervention through the provision of various purification rites, despite any form of human impurity.[50] God's intervention as seen in Leviticus can therefore act as a springboard to point Luo widows to the ultimate "cleanser," who is Jesus Christ. The message of Christ's complete "cleansing" should be amplified, a task that only the local Christian church can meet. As

---

47. Mary Douglas, *Purity and Danger: An Analysis of the Concepts of Pollution and Taboo* (London/New York: Routledge, 1991).

48. Leviticus 12 and 15.

49. Joe M. Sprinkle, "Clean, Unclean," in *Baker's Evangelical Dictionary of Biblical Theology*, ed. Walter A. Elwell (Grand Rapids, MI: Baker, 1996).

50. Sprinkle, "Clean, Unclean."

well, the message of the limitations and incapability of human cleansers (*joter*) must resound!

The Bible is also a rich reservoir of instruction in regard to *livelihood support* for widows. Deuteronomy 24:19 states, "When you reap your harvest in your field and have forgotten a sheaf in the field, you shall not go back to get it; it shall be for the alien, for the orphan, and for the widow, in order that the LORD your God may bless you in all the work of your hands" (NASB). Further Deuteronomy 14:28–29 says, "At the end of every third year you shall bring out all the tithe of your produce in that year, and shall deposit it in your town. The Levite, because he has no portion or inheritance among you, and the alien, the orphan and the widow who are in your town, shall come and eat and be satisfied, in order that the LORD your God may bless you in all the work of your hand which you do" (NASB). The case studies in Deuteronomy demonstrate a setting of standards for God's people. As one significant standard, God expected his people to remember the widows in their midst and provide for their livelihood.

Given the potential for widows to be abused due to their vulnerable status, particularly in regard to customary laws regarding the land, a call to *defend and protect* them is made in Isaiah 1:17: "Learn to do good; seek justice, reprove the ruthless, defend the orphan, plead for the widow" (NASB). Defending widows can take different approaches, including directly speaking out against abuses meted out on them. Defending may also take the form of symbolic "cleansing." In Luo, there are a few reported cases of symbolic cleansing which involves a man hanging his coat in a widow's house.[51] Hanging his coat symbolizes that a man has taken guardianship of that home and no other man can lay claim to it. Coat-hanging may be used by Christian men as a way of warding off exploitative men, especially the "professional *joter* (cleansers)" who intrude into widows' homes disguised as well-meaning supporters. How about using the "coat-hanging" symbolism to protect widows? How many Christian men would offer their coats for this?

The need for *social inclusion and identity* of the widow is seen in the act of Boaz in regard to Ruth, the widow of Mahlon (Ruth 4:10). Boaz legitimately took Ruth and swore before witnesses that he would take on the obligatory role of ensuring that his deceased relative's widow was included in the family. This was critical for Ruth's adaptation and reintegration into the community, and the same support is essential for widows even today. How can Christian fellowship in a local church address this critical need?

---

51. Atieno, "Story of My Life."

Conclusion

This paper has explored the phenomenon of widow cleansing in wider Luo family arrangements. An analysis of the current behavioral and structural mitigation strategies and their limitations in addressing the problems in connection with widow cleansing has been offered. Potential lessons from a biblical and theological viewpoint have been suggested, raising questions about the place of the Christian community in addressing the gaps which the behavioral and structural models fail to address. It is hoped that this discussion will stimulate further reflection and academic engagement on African contextual realities.

Bibliography

Ambasa-Shisanya, C. R. "Widowhood in the Era of HIV/AIDS: A Case Study of Siaya District, Kenya." *Journal of Social Aspects of HIV/AIDS* 4, no. 2 (2007): 606–615.

Atieno. "Story of My Life." Face to Face Interview, November 2015.

Auma. "Story of My Life." Face to Face Interview, 25 November 2015.

Avert. "HIV Prevention Programmes Overview." Global Information and Advice on HIV and AIDS, 25 January 2015. http://www.avert.org/professionals/hiv-prevention-programming/overview.

Awino. "Story of My Life." Face to Face Interview, July 2016.

Awour. "Story of My Life." Face to Face Interview, November 2015.

Ayikukwei, Rose, Duncan Ngare, John Sidle, Joyce Baliddawa, and James Greene. "HIV/AIDS and Cultural Practices in Western Kenya: The Impact of Sexual Cleansing Rituals on Sexual Behaviours." *Culture, Health and Sexuality* 10, no. 6 (August 2008): 587–599.

Badilisha Young Adults. Focus group discussion on women and land access. Face to Face Correspondence, July 2013.

Beswick, Stephanie. "We Were Bought Like Clothes: The War over Polygyny and Levirate Marriage in South Sudan." *Northeast African Studies* 8, no. 2 (2001): 35–61.

Douglas, Mary. *Purity and Danger: An Analysis of the Concepts of Pollution and Taboo.* London; New York: Routledge, 1991.

Gunga, Samson O. "The Politics of Widowhood and Re-Marriage among the Luo in Kenya." *Thought and Practice: A Journal of the Philosophical Association of Kenya (PAK)* 1, no. 1 (June 2009): 161–174.

Hiebert, Paul. "Critical Contextualization." *International Bulletin of Missionary Research* 11, no. 3 (July 1987): 104–112.

Janifa. "Why I Came to Kibera." Face to Face Interview, 28 October 2014.

Joyce. "Story of My Life." Face to Face Interview, 26 November 2015.

Kenya National Bureau of Statistics. "Population and Household Characteristics of Kenya, 2009." *Knoema*, 2009. http://knoema.com/KEPHC2009/population-and-household-characteristics-of-kenya-2009?location=1000900-homa-bay.

Kirwen, Michael. *African Widows*. New York: Orbis, 1979.

Magda. "Story of My Life." Face to Face Interview, November 2015.

National Aids Control Council. "Kenya AIDS Response Progress Report 2014," March 2014.

Nwoye, Augustine. "The Practice of Interventive Polygamy in Two Regions of Africa: Background, Theory and Techniques." *Springer*, Dialectical Anthropology 31, no. 4 (2007): 383–421.

Ogutu, Gilbert E. M. "Marriage Rights and Privileges: Luo Levirate Marriage Revisited." Paper presented at the Emerging Issues on Population and Development in Africa Conference. Arusha, Tanzania, 10–14 December 2007.

Okeyo, T. M., and A. K. Allen. "Influence of Widow Inheritance in the Epidemiology of AIDS in Africa." *African Journal of Medical Practice* 1, no. 1 (1994): 20–25.

Oluoch, Lennah, Brian Perry, Kawango Agot, Jamilah Taylor, Jacob Onyango, Lilian Ouma, Caroline Otieno, and Corneli Amy. "Widow Cleansing and Inheritance among the Luo in Kenya: The Need for Additional Women-Centred HIV Prevention Options." *Journal of International AIDS Society* 17 (26 June 2014).

Opondo, Patricia Achieng. "Dodo Performance in the Context of Women's Associations amongst the Luo of Kenya." PhD Dissertation, University of Pittsburgh, 1996.

Parkhurst, Justin O. "HIV Prevention, Structural Change and Social Values: The Need for an Explicit Normative Approach." *Journal of the International AIDS Society* 15, no. 1 (2012).

Perry, Brian et al., "Widow Cleansing and Inheritance among the Luo in Kenya: The Need for Additional Women Centred HIV Prevention Options." *Journal of International AIDS Society* 17 (2014): 2.

Ponzetti, James J., ed. *International Encyclopedia of Marriage and Family*. 2nd edition. New York: Macmillan Reference USA, 2003.

Potash, Betty. "Some Aspects of Marital Stability in a Rural Luo Community." Cambridge University Press, *International Africa Institute* 48, no. 4 (1978): 380–397.

Prince, Ruth, and Wenzel P. Geissler. "Becoming 'One Who Treats': A Case Study of a Luo Healer and Her Grandson in Western Kenya." *American Anthropological Association* 32, no. 4 (December 2001): 447–471.

Reynar, Angela. "Fertility Decision Making by Couples amongst the Luo of Kenya." Dissertation, University of Pennsylvania, 2000.

Shipton, Parker MacDonald. *The Nature of Entrustment: Intimacy, Exchange, and the Sacred in Africa*. Yale Agrarian Studies Series. New Haven: Yale University Press, 2007.

Sossou, M. A. "Widowhood Practices in West Africa: Silent Victims." *International Journal of Social Welfare* 11 (2002): 201–209.

Sprinkle, Joe M. "Clean, Unclean." In *Baker's Evangelical Dictionary of Biblical Theology*, edited by Walter A. Elwell. Grand Rapids, MI: Baker Books, 1996.

The Republic of Kenya. *The Constitution of Kenya*. Nairobi: Government Printer, 2010.

———. *Land Registration Act. 2012*. Vol. 3 of 2012.

———. *Matrimonial Property Act, 2013*. Vol. 49 of 2013.

Weisberg, Dvora E. *Levirate Marriage and the Family in Ancient Judaism*. Waltham, MA: Brandeis University Press, 2009.

9

Religion, a Means to Disobedience: A Reflective Analysis of the Story of the Golden Calf in Exodus 32

Hermann Mvula
Lecturer, Chancellor College, University of Malawi, Zomba, Malawi

Abstract

The Bible calls for singleness of mind in worship. It portrays the worship of Yahweh as the only true worship. The overarching theme of the Pentateuch is how people are to relate to God in their manner of worship and how they should relate to each other as well. This is why in Hebrew, this fivefold corpus is known as the Torah, meaning instructions or guidance: it gave instructions and guidance on how Israel was to relate to God. This chapter argues that if religion involves human inventions when it comes to worshiping God, it can actually be a means to disobedience. The arguments are drawn from an exegetical analysis of the story of the golden calf in Exodus 32. Among other pertinent theological motifs, this passage exposes syncretistic tendencies, impatience, blasphemy, deification of persons, and the divine grace operative among the people. This chapter challenges Christians in Africa today to make every effort not to add anything to what God requires when it comes to worshiping him. It cautions us that in our worship of God, adding anything to what he has prescribed in his Word becomes a misinterpretation of his grace and is blasphemous of his person and character.

Key words: golden calf, syncretism, disobedience, grace, forgiveness, impatience, blasphemy, deification.

Introduction

"Africans are *notoriously* religious, and each people has its own religious system with a set of beliefs and practices. Religion permeates into all the faculties of life so it is not easy or possible to isolate it [from other aspects of African culture]. A study of these religious systems is, therefore, a study of the peoples themselves in all the complexities of traditional and modern life."[1] So said Kenyan-born Professor John Mbiti, one of Africa's most renowned theologians of the twentieth and twenty-first centuries. According to Mbiti, religion is the heartbeat of Africans in their day-to-day affairs, such as naming children, raising them, working in their gardens, planting seeds, conducting weddings and passing all the rites of passage: all are religious activities for Africans.[2]

Critical reflection shows that this adherence to religious activities among Africans may to some extent hinder their acceptance of the gospel of salvation as they continue to cherish the spirits of their deceased ancestors in their day-to-day affairs. It is this very religiousness in Africa that may keep us away from perceiving what God has done in Jesus Christ and what he is doing in our communities. It is this same religiosity that may become a means to disobedience, especially when we close ourselves to the gospel of Jesus Christ and faith in him.[3]

This is the problem that the author herein contends with: that religion can be a means to disobedience – a fact that this chapter demonstrates through a

---

1. John S. Mbiti, *Introduction to African Religion* (Oxford: Heinemann Educational Books, 1991), 1. According to Professor Mbiti, all African cultures and societies, traditional (pre-colonial) and contemporary, across the continent and regardless of differences in national origin, language, or ethnicity, are deeply religious.

2. The assertion by Mbiti that all Africans – and perhaps all human beings in general – are notoriously religious has profound implications for what humans do and how they do what they do in regard to their religiosity. It means that there is an innate element within humans that makes them always want to be connected to the supernatural world. This is very evident in the African worldview and way of life.

3. Like the Athenians during Paul's time, Africans may already be in a situation where receiving the gospel of Jesus is not a problem as they already have a belief in the Supreme Being. Following Paul's example, the starting point to avert a seemingly disobedient attitude to the gospel is to tell them that knowing the one they already believe in – that is, the Supreme Being – comes not through the spirit world, but through faith in Jesus Christ.

reflective analysis of the story of the golden calf in the book of Exodus alongside the parallel story in 1 Kings 11:26–40; 12:26–33; and 13:33.

Clearly, the beginning point for evangelicals could be the description of religion – that is, Christianity – itself. John W. Ritenbaugh argues that the Bible reveals Christianity to be a comprehensive way of life. Nine times in the book of Acts it is referred to as "the way," "this way," "that way," "the way of God," "the way of the Lord," or "the way of salvation."[4] Ritenbaugh notes, "A way can be a path, course or road upon which one travels. It can also be a manner, method or system to achieve a desired goal. Being comprehensive, the Christian way touches on every element of life, but it focuses on the worship of God the Creator."[5]

Methodologically, this paper takes a narrative theology approach as it relates the story of the golden calf from the book of Exodus. Procedurally, it begins by discussing how religion can be a means to disobedience through a reflective analysis of Exodus 32 in which the threefold process of Israel's blasphemy and fall into idolatry is demonstrated. This is followed by a discussion of three pertinent theological motifs from the passage. Embedded in the three theological motifs are other equally pertinent motifs of blasphemy and deification. Finally, the conclusion provides application especially for evangelical Christians in Africa, cautioning against falling away from worshiping Yahweh.

A Reflective Analysis of Exodus 32:[6] How Religion Can Be a Means to Disobedience

The background to the golden calf incident is the important story of the exodus. As Carver, relying on Childs, writes, "after Moses had shared with the people the Book of the Covenant and led them in the covenant confirmation ceremony, he 'entered the cloud as he went on up the mountain' to receive the instructions for the tabernacle. After he disappeared from their sight, the people soon fell

---

4. John W. Ritenbaugh, "Why Worship God?," Church of the Great God, 2000, accessed 21 August 2015, https://www.cgg.org/index.cfm/fuseaction/Library.sr/CT/personal/k/64/Why-Worship-God.htm.

5. Ritenbaugh, "Why Worship God?"

6. This section critically discusses the issues at stake in this passage relating to the sin of Israel. The discussion focuses on critical themes that arise in the passage after analyzing the text. The thematic narrative approach will help us arrive at the great truths that the passage is speaking to us now just as it spoke to the nation of Israel then. In what ensues, I loosely follow David Guzik's outline at https://enduringword.com/bible-commentary/exodus-32/, accessed 16 August 2014.

into flagrant idolatry – the story of the golden calf whose 'cutting edge is its penetrating insight that religion itself can be the means to disobedience.'"[7]

Moses, the Israelites' leader and authority figure, with mesmeric charisma, was absent from them for forty days when he was on the mountain with God.[8] When the people saw that Moses was taking a long time to come back down from the mountain, they confronted Aaron with the cry, "Come, make us gods who will go before us. As for this fellow Moses who brought us out of Egypt, we don't know what has happened to him" (Exod 32:1).[9]

Then Aaron, whom God had appointed to speak for Moses due to the latter's reluctance to obey God's call, made them a god, the golden calf, in place of God. Carver argues that what is fascinating in this story is that the Israelites had deified "the now absent" Moses so he had to be replaced immediately. The result was a religious orgy, a worship that was highly sensual, for after they "sacrificed burnt offerings and presented fellowship offerings . . . they sat down to eat and drink and got up to indulge in revelry" (32:6).[10]

Critical analysis of the passage shows that after Aaron had made the golden calf blasphemously, the children of Israel effectively broke the first and second commandments.[11] Israel's breaking of the second command was a slap in God's face. The Israelites quickly forgot that it was God who had brought them out of the bondage of slavery in Egypt. They proclaimed, "These are your gods, O Israel, who brought you up out of Egypt" (Exod 32:4). This was a direct affront to Yahweh their God.

It can be argued that this story contains the cutting-edge truth that most of the world's religions could actually be a means to disobedience. A number of the world's religions and cults owe their allegiance to their founders whose teachings the people are to follow. People often deify such figures and delegate their responsibilities before God, and eventually their spiritual freedom, to these people. They ardently "listen" to them and see them as a means to relate

---

7. Frank G. Carver, "The Quest for the Holy: The Darkness of God," *Wesleyan Theological Journal* 23, nos. 1 and 2 (Spring-Fall 1988): 15.

8. The story of Israel has eternal truths. The Israelites' faith was such that the only way the law could work was for it to be personified in a charismatic authoritative figure. Africans, Christians included, have fallen into this same trap, even deifying some religious founders, especially in the contemporary trend of "Prophetism."

9. See Carver, "Quest for the Holy," 16.

10. See Carver, 15.

11. The first command: "You shall have no other gods before me." The second command: "You shall not make for yourself an image in the form of anything in heaven above . . . You shall not bow down to them or worship them" (Exod 20:3-4).

to God. Hence, Frank Carver argues, "they obey a god-substitute."[12] This is the reason why some people strongly argue that Christianity is not a religion but a relationship: a person's relationship with God through the Son, characterized by worshiping him in spirit and in truth (John 4:24).

As the foregoing discussion demonstrates, the problem with human beings is that they always want to worship something they can see or touch. And this is what God forbids. He is above all and anything human beings can imagine. Therefore, he is beyond representation by anything that human beings can make. That is the whole essence of the first and second commandments: "You shall have no other gods before me." Why? Because any other god(s) will result in a different way of worship and will require different ethical and moral conduct. The second commandment states: "You shall not make for yourself an image [or idol]." Christopher Wright argues:

> The prohibition of idols in Israel was not because they were material whereas God is spiritual, or because they were visible whereas God is invisible. It was primarily because they were lifeless, impotent and (especially) dumb, whereas the God of Israel was living, active and one who speaks. That is why the only image that was "allowed" was the one God had designed and created himself – the image of God, man himself. It is this kind of thinking, living, choosing, and speaking, moral agent, who alone reflects the living God of the Old Testament.[13]

This therefore means that any attempt to represent God by a static or lifeless object, including the golden calf but also even a human statue, reduces him and denies the most fundamental thing about him. This is not only a theological or religious issue. It is a deep ethical command, for a false view of God destroys the central foundation of ethics as well, and people will not worship God in the splendor of holiness. The implication is that only the living God of history, who acted in the history of the nation of Israel, can initiate, shape, and motivate the true worship of any people; anything else becomes blasphemy and idolatry.

A similar story to the incident of the golden calf is found in 1 Kings 11:26–40; 12:26–33; 13:33. Apparently, one of Jeroboam's sins here is subordinating religious observance and traditions to political ends. A critical reading of Scripture shows that the northern kingdom began and ended with a word of prophecy from Abijah: first, predicting Jeroboam's successful revolt

---

12. Carver, "Quest for the Holy," 15.
13. Christopher J. H. Wright, *Living as the People of God: The Relevance of Old Testament Ethics* (Leicester: IVP, 1983), 31.

against Rehoboam; second, promising an enduring dynasty on condition of his obedience; and finally, pronouncing his doom as punishment for his policy of religious pragmatism. Religious pragmatism is indeed the very essence of religion as a means to disobedience.

Jeroboam erected golden calves at the northern and southern ends of his kingdom – Dan and Bethel – and appointed shrines and priests (not from the tribe of Levi) and surrogate festivals – a mixture of original and innovative actions. It all began thus:

> Jeroboam thought to himself, "The kingdom will now likely revert to the house of David. If these people go up to offer sacrifice at the temple of the LORD in Jerusalem, they will again give their allegiance to their lord, Rehoboam king of Judah. They will kill me and return to King Rehoboam." After seeking advice, the king made two golden calves. He said to the people, "It is too much for you to go up to Jerusalem. Here are your gods, Israel, who brought you up out of Egypt." (1 Kgs 12:26–28)

First, Jeroboam thought to himself. It all began with his rationalization of the unestablished or unfounded problem. Who told him that God was not able to make the people of the north loyal to his kingdom? Who told him that the people would kill him? Jeroboam did not have confidence in the divine promise given to him through the prophet Abijah, and thus took actions that forfeited the theocratic basis for his kingship. Consequently, Jeroboam was led to the same old Aaronic sin of the golden calf.

Therefore, what Jeroboam did was to harness the existing religious traditions to his political ambition, and to create new ones wherever the interests of his new independent kingdom required it. Consequently, he turned the faith of Israel into a tool of royal policy, and thereby rendered it idolatrous.

The two stories of Jeroboam and Aaron show that imaging God in the golden calf was the sin of the children of Israel. In the worship of the golden calf, according to Carver, "Israel was defying the only security they had, their covenant relationship with God."[14] They had forgotten that to maintain their relationship with God they had been given the Torah. They were to live their lives by the covenant stipulations which revealed the will of God, his justice and his righteousness. In so doing, they would be drawn closer to and rely on Yahweh, the gracious God of the exodus. They would know that his grace was the ultimate foundation for their ethical existence, true worship in spirit and

---

14. Carver, "Quest for the Holy," 15.

in truth. As Walter Martin wrote, "It has been wisely observed that 'a man who will not stand for something is quite likely to fall for almost anything.' So I have elected to stand on the ramparts of biblical Christianity as taught by the apostles, defended by the church fathers, rediscovered by the reformers . . ."[15]

The point is that any kind of worship of God other than the revealed will of God in the Scriptures and through his Son Jesus could be a false religion.[16] John warns us, "This is how you can recognize the Spirit of God: Every spirit that acknowledges that Jesus Christ has come in the flesh is from God, but every spirit that does not acknowledge Jesus is not from God" (1 John 4:2–3).

From an evangelical theological perspective, Walter Martin states that "the cults contain many major deviations from historical Christianity or biblical faith."[17] He argues, "While I am in agreement that 'in general the cults represent the earnest attempt of millions of people to find the fulfilment of deep legitimate needs of the human spirit, which most of them seem not to have found in the established churches,' I feel there is still much more to be said."[18] Many in Africa fall into the same trap of idolatry these days, as is evidenced by the mushrooming of so many "prophetic ministries and churches."

Israel stepped into idolatry in a process that happened very quickly. The threefold process intrinsically comprised blasphemy, misuse, and misinterpretation of the divine grace, as follows:

The People's Need

There is an irony regarding what the people needed. Evidently, they needed Moses and at the same time they needed God. When the people saw that Moses was taking a long time to come down from the mountain, they went to Aaron and said to him, "Come, make us gods that shall go before us. As for

---

15. Walter Martin, *The Kingdom of the Cults*, ed. Ravi Zacharias (Minneapolis: Bethany House, 2003), 18.

16. From an evangelical perspective, one cannot but see the Jehovah's Witnesses (Watchtower Bible Tract Society), Christian Science, Mormonism, Spiritism, Buddhism, the Baha'i faith, Unitarians, Scientology, the Unification Church, Eastern religions (Confucianism, Taoism, etc.), Voodooism, the New Age, and Olumba religion as religious cults. For instance, the Jehovah's Witnesses are, for the most part, followers of the interpretations of Charles T. Russell and J. F. Rutherford. The Christian Scientist of today is a disciple of Mary Baker Eddy. Mormonism traces its origins in the writings of Joseph Smith and Brigham Young. See Justo L. González, *The Story of Christianity: The Early Church to the Present Day* (Peabody, MA: Prince Press, 2004), 258–261. See also http://northcountrychapel.com/wp-content/uploads/2015/04/The-gospel-the-cults-the-occult_Mormonism.pdf (accessed 13 April 2018).

17. Martin, *Kingdom of the Cults*, 18.

18. Martin, 18.

this fellow Moses who brought us up out of Egypt, we do not know what has happened to him" (Exod 32:1).

Moses was gone for forty days (Exod 24:18), and that period was a long time to the Israelites, though it was a short time related to God's gracious plan for Israel.[19] *But* if Moses was their main *problem*, why did they go and replace God?

In our own everyday undertaking, "how we handle God's ordained delays is a good measure of our spiritual maturity. If we allow such delays to make us drift off into sin or lapse into resignation to fate, then we react poorly to His ordained delays. If we allow such times to deepen our perseverance in following God, then they are of good use."[20]

We read in the passage that the Israelites went to Aaron, and said to him, "make us gods." "This sinful impulse came first from the people, not Aaron."[21] It is clear that the sin described in this chapter started with popular opinion and this is a vivid example of how the will of the people is not always the will of God. This is the great danger with some of the popular religious beliefs flourishing in Africa, for example, where the will of the people revolves especially around their founders. This is true in society in general, but it is also true among God's people. This cautions us that when it comes to representing God and serving others there is danger in starting with what people want or what they feel they need.[22]

"Come, make us gods who will go before us." The Israelites wanted gods to go before them, leading them to the Promised Land. They obviously had just experienced God's power in delivering from out of Egypt and they knew the Lord God had revealed himself on Mount Sinai. Yet, foolishly, they were willing to trust a god they had made with their hands. Just as Israel later wanted a human king, not the invisible divine king (1 Sam 8:4–8), so now they wanted a god with a face, like everybody else. They wanted a god they could see and possibly touch.[23]

The implication for evangelical Christians in Africa is that "it is possible to begin the Christian life trusting Jesus, and then at a later time trust one's own

---

19. See Dick Lockhart, "Exodus 32: The Golden Calf," *Look at the Book* (blog), 1 September 2013, accessed 26 February 2018, https://dicklockhart.wordpress.com/2013/09/01/exodus-32-the-golden-calf/.

20. Lockhart, "Exodus 32."

21. Lockhart, "Exodus 32."

22. Lockhart, "Exodus 32."

23. Centuries later, the apostle Paul "dealt with the same error with the Galatians: 'Are you so foolish? Having begun in the Spirit, are you now being made perfect by the flesh?'" (Gal 3:3). Lockhart, "Exodus 32."

spirituality forgetting that true Christian life is life through the spirit."[24] As it was a blasphemous misuse and misinterpretation of God's grace for Israel then, so it is for us as believers today in twenty-first-century Africa. God cannot be served and worshiped in a manner dictated by our whims.

Aaron's Response to the Israelites' Request and Need

> Aaron answered them, "Take off the gold earrings that your wives, your sons and your daughters are wearing, and bring them to me." So all the people took off their earrings and brought them to Aaron. He took what they handed him and made it into an idol cast in the shape of a calf, fashioning it with a tool. Then they said, "These are your gods, Israel, who brought you up out of Egypt." (Exod 32:2–4)

One cannot but perceive the foolishness of idolatry here. "This statue of a calf did not exist the day before, and now they worship it as the god that brought them out of Egypt."[25]

"Aaron did not anoint this thing as their god. He simply went along with the people as they proclaimed it as their god. He was probably flattered at their admiration of his creation."[26] Indeed, "true leadership would have cried out, 'This is idolatry! We must destroy this golden calf. You people are wrong in calling this creation of man your god!'"[27] – exactly as Moses did immediately he came down from the mountain. "But Aaron wasn't a true leader. He is an example of the one who leads by following popular opinion . . . It was the flesh-inspired work of Aaron. He thought it out, melted the gold, molded it, and fashioned it carefully with an engraving tool."[28] Kenneth Harris states that "the plural 'these' and 'gods' may indicate that Israel considered the calf to be another god alongside the LORD. Whatever the people may have thought, their words and actions are clearly out of accord with both the first

---

24. See Galatians 3:1–5; see also Romans 8, which depicts life through the Spirit.

25. Lockhart, "Exodus 32." It should be noted that a molded calf was an ominous worship symbol. Not only were the cow and bull worshiped in Egypt, but the bull was a familiar embodiment of Baal seen in Canaan. See *The Nelson Study Bible*, ed. Ronald B. Allen (Nashville: Thomas Nelson, 1997), 156–157.

26. Lockhart, "Exodus 32."

27. Lockhart, "Exodus 32."

28. Lockhart, "Exodus 32."

and second commandments (Exodus 20:4–6)."[29] This kind of proclamation was blasphemous of God's character and his holy name. Coincidently, it became a misuse and misinterpretation of his grace.

Israel's Ungodly and Immoral Worship before the Golden Calf[30]

After the golden calf had been made, Aaron "built an altar in front of the calf." Then he made a proclamation: "Tomorrow there will be a festival to the LORD." "So the next day the people rose early and sacrificed burnt offerings and presented fellowship offerings. Afterward they sat down to eat and drink and got up to indulge in revelry" (Exod 32:5–6).[31] "Aaron honored and sanctified the idol with animal sacrifice. He made the calf, and then he made the altar to worship it."[32]

In summary, Aaron and the Israelites thought they could give honor to the LORD *through* the golden calf. Evidently, "Aaron was not crass enough to say, 'Let's do away with the LORD God' . . . Aaron didn't take away the LORD God, he simply added the golden calf."[33] But that action was contrary to the very first and second commandments of God. And this is the epitome of religiosity: "the urge to add." It must be reckoned that God is enough in himself.[34] The whole process is summed up in six words: disobedience in the name of religion. Such a process to sinfulness – idolatry – constitutes blasphemy, misuse and misinterpretation of the divine grace.

---

29. Kenneth Laing Harris, "Exodus," in ESV Study Bible, ed. Lane Dennis, Wayne Grudem, et al. (Wheaton, IL: Crossway, 2008), 197.

30. What follows is from Lockhart, "Exodus 32."

31. According to Lockhart, "when Aaron saw [the calf he] was flattered by the enthusiastic response of the people. When he saw their devotion to this idol, he built an altar before it. He began to organize the worship of the idol he just made. It was bad enough to have a golden calf the people praised for their escape from Egypt . . . They served their idol with great energy and personal sacrifice. People usually find a way to rise early for the things that are really important to them. This shows that Israel was willing to give their time, their sleep, and their money in the service of this idol."

32. Lockhart, "Exodus 32."

33. Lockhart, "Exodus 32."

34. For a thorough discussion on the sufficiency of God, see John MacArthur, *Our Sufficiency in Christ* (Wheaton, IL: Crossway, 1998).

Pertinent Theological Motifs from the Golden Calf Narrative

The theological motifs from the story are very pertinent to African evangelical religiosity. In their religiosity, Africans may become sidetracked by other religious beliefs and practices.

Evidently, the multitudes were led into idolatry by agitators. But if the Israelites thought of replacing Moses, why did they actually replace God? And why did Aaron join the multitudes in sinning, instead of advising them to exercise a little patience, reminding them of God's grace in delivering them? Harris points out that "In the New Testament, Stephen's response before the high priest recounts aspects of Israel's history and says of this event that Israel thrust [Moses] aside, and in their hearts they turned to Egypt."[35]

The following are pertinent theological themes from the story.[36]

Impatience

As noted above, it was because their leader Moses was with the LORD on the mountain and taking a long time to return (Exod 24:18) that the Israelites grew impatient and turned to Aaron, who had been left in charge while Moses was absent (24:14), and demanded, "Make gods [Hebrew *elohim*] for us" (32:1). Kenneth Laing Harris notes that, "After hearing the LORD speak from Mount Sinai (20:22) and agreeing to keep the covenant (24:3, 7), the people of Israel became impatient with the length of time Moses was up on the mountain and broke the covenant by making an idol and worshiping it with offering and feast (32:1–6)."[37]

The Israelites had deified Moses such that they could not live without him. This is the problem of looking up to people for our security. When they are not there, we think life will be unbearable. The people of Israel had access to Yahweh only through Moses. Without Moses, it seemed that there was no God for them. Therefore, impatience gripped them and forced them to find a replacement for Moses. However, such thinking was foolish because the golden calf was static and lifeless, unlike Moses. This is the folly of trusting in religions and religious founders – which is precisely what African Traditional Religions (ATR) do, deifying dead ancestors who, to the ATR adherents, still exist and do things for them. Someone once said, "Africans have no time to

---

35. Harris, "Exodus," 197.

36. Intrinsic to the three themes discussed here are issues of blasphemy, deification of persons and objects, and misinterpretation of divine grace.

37. Harris, "Exodus," 197.

rest – even after dying they have to work as ancestors." This kind of thinking and belief among some ATR adherents, and even some Christians, must be corrected by biblical truth among evangelicals.

Just as with the Israelites, weariness in waiting can lead many into temptation today. Reflecting on impatience reminds us of the impatient attitude of our first parents, Adam and Eve. I believe that such an attitude is one of the reasons why Adam and Eve sinned and their posterity today continues drifting away from the divine will.[38] No wonder, if we are to be right with God, we need to be filled by the Holy Spirit, who produces patience as part of his fruit (Gal 5:22). Christians are being led astray today and among the reasons for this is that they are impatient in waiting upon the LORD. Yet God's word tells us, "But they that wait upon the LORD shall renew their strength; they shall mount up with wings as eagles; they shall run, and not be weary; and they shall walk, and not faint" (Isa 40:31 KJV).[39]

In summary, imbedded within the larger theme of impatience is deification as one of the main issues in the story of the golden calf. Because the Israelites could not wait for Moses to come, they sought to replace him. And that was because the Israelites had *deified* Moses to the extent that they thought they could not live without him. This *deification* was pervasive in the minds of the people and became a misrepresentation of God's commands. That is blasphemy at its worst. It is such blasphemous attitudes and actions that some in African Traditional Religions practice – deifying their dead ancestors and believing that they work for them in whatever they do.

Syncretism

As noted above, there is a strong relationship between the narrative of the golden calf in Exodus 32 and that of the erection of the two golden calves in the shrines of Bethel and Dan by Jeroboam the first king of Israel (1 Kgs 12:26–33). Lane Dennis and Wayne Grudem state that "scholars are divided on the question of the chronological relationship of the two accounts. The traditional view is that the Jeroboam incident is dependent on the Exodus

---

38. We are told in the Bible that God used to come in the cool of the day to be with his creation. The serpent came and posed a question: "Did God really say . . .?", initiating doubt in Eve. The best response would have been: "All right, you say so, but that is not what God told us" – and then, when God next appeared "in the cool of the day" they could have asked him for clarification. But impatience caused them not to wait for God's word, and the result was catastrophic – the fall, as recorded in Genesis 3.

39. The Scriptures implicitly and explicitly convey the message that the Lord must be waited for till he comes, even though he tarries (see Hab 2:3).

story. Other scholars, however, hold the view that Exodus 32 presupposes 1 Kings 12."[40]

David Guzik argues that it is possible, perhaps even likely, that, just like Aaron many years before, "Jeroboam intended the golden calves to represent the God of Israel. This was not the introduction of a new god, but a perversion of the proper worship of the true God."[41] Regardless, down through the ages and in cultures around the world, humans have been adept at finding ways to pervert or corrupt the true worship of God or replacing it altogether with something else. In some instances, some Africans, as discussed above, worship ancestors – people whom they deify after they are dead.

The people of the Ancient Near Eastern nations were very religious – just as Mbiti claimed is the case for Africans today in the quote at the start of this paper. The Ancient Near Eastern peoples also worshiped many gods. For instance, God brought judgment on the Egyptians by defeating their gods. In so doing Yahweh demonstrated that he alone is the living and powerful God and was greater than Egypt's gods. Moses's father-in-law, Jethro in Midian, was a priest and a worshiper of the true God. He was aware of the religious pluralism pervasive in Midian and Egypt. This is evidenced in his response to hearing about God's works: "Now I know that the LORD is greater than all other gods, for he did this to those who had treated Israel arrogantly" (Exod 18:11).

Therefore, Christopher Wright argues, "When God gave his laws to the Israelites he began by addressing this religious pluralism."[42] Yahweh stated,

> I am the LORD your God, who brought you out of the land of Egypt, out of the house of slavery.
>> You shall have no other gods before me.
>> You shall not make for yourself a carved image, or any likeness of anything that is in heaven above, or that is in the earth beneath, or that is in the water under the earth. You shall not bow down to

---

40. Ian Provan argues that "the bull had an important role in the art and religious texts of the Ancient Near East. It is said that the storm-god Hadad is frequently represented standing on a bull. Taking these facts into account it is generally assumed that Jeroboam's calves corresponded to the cherubim of Solomon's Temple, i.e., they were regarded as seats or pedestals upon which the LORD was thought to stand invisible to human eyes. This use of statues of calves or bulls in worship in ancient times has a ring of authenticity to it. Archaeologists have uncovered images or statues of calves or bulls that were used in worship in many ancient religious sites from biblical times, both within Israel and in surrounding cultures." See Ian Provan, "1 and 2 Kings," ESV Study Bible, eds. Lane Dennis, Wayne Grudem, et al. (Wheaton, IL: Crossway, 2008), 624.

41. David Guzik, https://enduringword.com/bible-commentary/1-kings-12/, accessed 28 January 2016.

42. Wright, *Living as the People of God*, 85.

them or serve them, for I the LORD your God am a jealous God, visiting the iniquity of the fathers on the children to the third and the fourth generation of those who hate me. (Exod 20:2–5 ESV)[43]

Wright describes the comprehensiveness of the Decalogue by arguing that "The first 'word' [commandment] takes aim at atheism (we must have a God), idolatry (we must have Yahweh as our God), polytheism (we must have the LORD God alone), [and] formalism (we must love, fear, and serve the LORD God with all our heart, soul, strength, and mind)."[44]

Therefore, as we deal with the issue of syncretism, it must be clear to us that "at first glance it may be contrary to the issue of the golden calf."[45] This means that in our own time, the issue might not be like that of the golden calf, as was the case with the Israelites. Kenneth Harris comments on Exodus 32:6 ("the people sat down to eat and drink and rose up to play") that "in 1 Cor 10:7 Paul cites this to show that simply being a part of God's people is not enough; God's own people must show faithful loyalty to him, and avoid thinking that mixing pagan practices into their lives is harmless."[46] The warning in this is that Christians in Africa must be very discerning to avoid falling into the trap as did the Israelites.

This is the very heart of syncretism: mixing things together. And the problem of syncretism is that one fails to pinpoint what is what, or which is which! Eventually, the whole enterprise becomes an affront to Yahweh, the true God. God abhors being mixed together with other things in worship of him. He requires singleness of mind: "You shall love the LORD your God with all your heart, with all your spirit, with all your might and with all your mind."[47] God requires this singleness of attitude of all people everywhere, in

---

43. Scripture quotations marked ESV throughout this book are from The Holy Bible, English Standard Version® (ESV®), copyright © 2001 by Crossway, a publishing ministry of Good News Publishers. Used by permission. All rights reserved.

44. See Wright, 85. The story of Jeroboam has the same issues at stake as the Exodus narrative. "Jeroboam's initiative must have had some basis in an old tradition; otherwise he could not have succeeded in his enterprise. Jeroboam's bulls, contrary to the Ark symbolism, were meant to be accessible to worshipers in the temples (cf. 1 Kings 12:27); and thus they developed from symbols of the Lord to fetishes in their own right (cf. e.g., 2 Kings 17:16; Hos. 8:5–6; 10:5; 13:2)" ("Encyclopedia Judaica: The Golden Calf," Jewish Virtual Library, http://www.jewishvirtuallibrary.org/golden-calf). Jeroboam established a priesthood of his own to further his religion in service of his political ends.

45. Harris, "Exodus," 197.

46. Harris, 197.

47. See http://ccbiblestudy.net/Old%20Testament/05Deut/05CE06.htm (accessed online 26 February 2018). See also the biblical admonitions on this: Deut 6:4–5; 11:1, 13, 22; 19:9; Mark 12:29–30.

all generations, and it is what the first three commandments were intended to inculcate in people then and now. Some Africans, especially those who adhere to ATR traditions, fall into this problem of syncretism.

God's Gracious Offer of Forgiveness

The theme of God's offer of grace underscores Israel's sin and God's willingness to forgive.[48] The narrative in Exodus shows that God was angry with the people's idolatry so soon after their deliverance from Egypt and following their agreement to the covenant and its stipulations. Consequently, God commanded Moses to "Go down, because *your* people, whom *you* brought up out of Egypt, have become corrupt" (Exod 32:7, emphasis added). Previously, God had referred to Israel as "my people"[49] whom "I brought out of the land of Egypt."[50] But after their fall into idolatry by worshiping the golden calf, God rejected them and declared that the Israelites were *Moses's* people whom Moses had brought out of Egypt. The separation between God and Israel seemed mutual and a shift of responsibilities between God and Moses ensued.[51]

After denying ownership of the people, God's statement to Moses is startling and terrifying: "Now therefore let me alone, that . . . I may consume them" (32:10 ESV). Here, God resolved to destroy all the Israelites and raise another people through Moses: ". . . in order that I may make a great nation of you" (32:10 ESV). Apparently, Dennis Olson argues, "the LORD offers to Moses the chance to become a new Abraham, the sole originator of a whole new people who will be a substitute for the destroyed Israelites."[52] However, despite the offer,

> Moses denies himself the opportunity to become a new Abraham. Instead, Moses prays and intercedes for Israel with three strong reasons why the LORD should not carry out the planned destruction of Israelites.

---

48. For more information on this, see Randy Maddox, *Responsible Grace: John Wesley's Practical Theology* (Nashville, TN: Kingswood Books, 1994). See also Michael Lodahl, *The Story of God: Wesleyan Theology and Biblical Narrative* (Kansas City, MO: Beacon Hill Press, 1994).

49. Exod 3:7, 10; 5:1; 6:7; 7:4, 16; 8:1, 8, 20–23; 9:1, 13, 17; 10:3; 12:31; 19:5–6; 22:25.

50. Exod 3:17; 6:6–7; 20:2; 29:46.

51. Michael Lodahl suggests that this is a consequence of sin or the fall – a shift of responsibilities. This could yet be one of the key theological motifs derived from this story. See, for example, Lodahl, *The Story of God*, 76–79.

52. Dennis Olson, "Exodus 32:1–14 Commentary," *Biblia.Work*, 4 October 2016, accessed 26 February 2018, http://www.biblia.work/sermons/exodus-321-14-commentary-by-dennis-olson/.

1. Remember, these are not my people. They are "your people," LORD, whom "you brought out . . . of Egypt" (32:11).

2. Destroying your own people, Israel, in the wilderness would be bad for your international reputation. What would the Egyptians say? (32:12).

3. Remember the promises of land and descendants that you made to Abraham, Isaac and Israel/Jacob long ago. You always keep your promises! (32:13).[53]

Kenneth Harris notes that "Moses responds to the Lord's statement about destroying the people and making a nation out of *him* (v. 10) appealing to God's own reputation among the Gentiles (whom God intends to bless through Israel, cf. Gen. 12:2–3) and his promises to Abraham (Ex. 32:11–13)."[54] Here Moses's intercession focuses on the LORD's words "when he refers to Israel as 'your people, whom you have brought out of the land of Egypt.'"[55]

It is interesting to note that in the past, Moses was not successful in changing God's mind, as shown during his own call (Exod 3:7 – 4:17). However, when advocating for others and therefore denying his own interests in becoming the head of a new nation through his descendants, and appealing to the grace and mercy of God, Moses caused God to relent. It is remarkable that in response to Moses's prayer, "the LORD relented and did not bring on his people the disaster he had threatened" (32:14). This is grace – God reaching out to redeem and forgive his people. In fact, intrinsic to the grace and forgiveness motifs is the theme of intercession. Moses interceded just as Abraham had done for Sodom and Gomorrah in the past. God's people must exercise a priestly role, interceding for others.

In summary, despite Israel's sin of idolatry, God's grace covered them and he forgave them. Grace is the inspiring and eternal theme in the story of the golden calf – and it is the theme of God's salvation. By extension, Kenneth Harris points to another important trajectory of the story: "While illustrating the unfaithfulness of many people, the account highlights the faithful maturing of Moses as a leader and shows him bearing aspects of God's character."[56] Moses had been transformed by the grace of God throughout the time he had been with the LORD since Exodus 3.

---

53. Olson, "Exodus 32:1–14 Commentary."
54. Harris, "Exodus," 197.
55. Harris, 197.
56. Harris, 197.

Conclusion

The story of the golden calf has been described as "the greatest scandal of the wilderness period."[57] In Egypt, and during their sojourn in the wilderness as well as in their life in Canaan, the Israelites lived in environments where cultures related only to corporeal forms of deity. The other peoples believed that they must pay homage to God and win his grace, but they could not relate to an intangible deity. They must therefore deify objects of their choosing and make them represent their lofty idea of the world.[58] And, according to John Oswalt, "Israelites schooled in the Abrahamic belief in one omnipresent, incorporeal God, were nevertheless influenced by surrounding cultures. Contrary to the other peoples, they did believe that man could relate to an incorporeal God, but they clung to the notion that a concrete, tangible link is required, hence, the visible Golden Calf."[59]

The evidence demonstrates that after their Sinai experience, the Israelites viewed Moses as the primary intermediary between themselves and God. When God spoke the commandments, the experience overwhelmed the Israelites and they requested that Moses be their mediator and convey God's message to them. Consequently, they might have thought that Moses was endowed with some properties of deity and powers to link them to the true God; "their mistake was that they saw their 'intermediary,' rather than God, as the initiative for revelation. For them, it was not God who had brought them out of Egypt by means of Moses, but Moses who had influenced God to redeem them."[60] Consequently, "without [Moses] there would be no further access to God and no method of securing his grace. But this time they sought a physical object rather than a living human. Physical objects, they reasoned, can be safely preserved; they don't walk away and disappear as Moses did."[61]

In an era of rapid growth in cults, interest in the occult, and religious pluralism throughout the world, men and women are prone to demonic

---

57. See Dr Jeffrey Tigay, "The Golden Calf," *My Jewish Learning*, accessed 26 February 2018, https://www.myjewishlearning.com/article/the-golden-calf/. See also Dr Jeffrey Tigay, "The Story of the Golden Calf," 19 August 2014, Friends of Sion, accessed 26 February 2018, https://friendsofsion.org/index.php/2014/08/19/the-story-of-golden-calf/.

58. See John Oswalt's interesting discussion in his *Called to Be Holy: A Biblical Perspective* (Nappanee, IN: Evangel, 1999), 10–16.

59. Oswalt, *Called to Be Holy*, 10–15.

60. Yaakov ben Chaim Tzvi, "Why the Israelites Made a Golden Calf," *On Faith*, 25 September 2015, accessed 25 September 2015, https://www.onfaith.co/dvartorah/why-the-israelites-made-a-golden-calf.

61. Tzvi, "Why the Israelites." See also https://www.onfaith.co/bible/kjv/exodus/32, accessed 26 February 2018.

compromise of the holiness and true worship of God, by, among other things, personifying their religiosity in human figures. Thus, they become vulnerable to a form of "golden calf" religion which can appear among us in various forms, especially among Africans in ways that manifest some demonic impulse. Frank Carver says, "When ethics run to legalism, we have a pagan rather than a Biblical spirituality."[62]

Consequently, evangelical theologians and Christians in Africa should be careful because, "where we find truth, often in close proximity we also find a way of thinking that distorts and faults that truth."[63] As a matter of fact, Carver argues, the religious pluralism exemplified by the cults and their central figures holds on to some "partial truth – such as a verse used as a proof-text – and blends it with an untruth so that the mix has the appearance of truth but in reality it is systematically false."[64] That is syncretism – the mixing up of things. Such is the lesson of the incident of the golden calf: if we are not careful, religion can *indeed* be a means to disobedience!

The story of the golden calf is our story today in contemporary Africa and world religions: the very way of trying to find fulfillment of our own legitimate deep spiritual needs by our own standards – religiosity. Religion itself can become idolatrous if it allows a perversion of total devotion to Yahweh, the only true God. Distorted religion can corrupt the fruit of the Spirit as quickly as outright sin. Idols, even idols of the mind, lead to ungodly actions. This is the heart of the story of the golden calf which evangelical theologians must articulate to the popular Christian understanding in Africa.

The Scriptures tell us that God cannot be mocked (Gal 6:7). This includes the fact that God will never tolerate any representation of himself, as he is above all things. He will never tolerate any intermediaries such as in ATR, where ancestors are venerated and even worshiped. He created everything and cannot be reduced by our way of thinking and worshiping that is not according to the ways he has prescribed. From an evangelical perspective, this may be exactly what some religions do.[65] How we should approach and worship God

---

62. Carver, "Quest for the Holy," 16.

63. Carver, 16.

64. Carver, 16.

65. I am aware of the issues surrounding religious pluralism in theological scholarship. Theologians wrestling with the question of "salvation outside the church" have formulated five main views: Absolute Exclusivism, Absolute Relativism, Hegemonistic Inclusivism, Realistic Pluralism, and Regulative Pluralism. For a detailed discussion on this, see Ninian Smart, "Pluralism," in *A New Handbook of Christian Theology*, ed. Donald W. Musser and Joseph L. Price (Nashville: Abingdon, 1992), 360–364. See also Hendrix Kraemer, *The Christian Message in a Non-Christian World* (Bangalore: Centre for Contemporary Christianity, 2009); Ninian Smart,

has been revealed by him and is contained in the Bible. We do not need to add anything else to this holy book.

Exodus 34:5–8 recounts the dialogue between God and Moses after the golden calf scandal. Moses sought assurance from God and requested him to show him his glory. God graciously allowed Moses to see his back and went further, pronouncing his holy character: "The LORD, the LORD God, merciful and gracious, longsuffering, and abounding in goodness and truth, keeping mercy for thousands, forgiving iniquity and transgression and sin, and that will by no means clear the guilty; visiting the iniquity of the fathers upon the children, and upon the children's children, unto the third and to the fourth generation" (34:6–7 KJV). "Moses bowed to the ground at once and worshiped" (34:8). Moses's response is what we are all urged to do as believers in Africa: reverently worship and serve Yahweh, for he alone is worthy of worship.

Therefore, Moses's honoring and worship of God shows us how we should live our lives. Through his experience with God since his call in Exodus 3, Moses had come to understand that Yahweh, the God of Israel's forefather Abraham, was a holy God and that idolatry could not coexist with him because he cannot be identified with the material world. Biblical faith is uniquely dependent on the truth that God transcends this world.[66] Consequently, God cannot be likened to anything under the sun, beneath the earth, or in the waters (Exod 20:4–5).

Finally, the following questions suggested by Frank Carver[67] could form a basis of lessons from this rich narrative of the golden calf for both adherents of ATR and African evangelical theologians and believers:

1. Which golden calves in our culture today draw our loyalty and love away from God when we get impatient with waiting for God's timetable?

2. Have we made the God whom we worship into an idol, a small fixed statue that we try to control and manipulate as a substitute for the free, untamed, mysterious, and surprising God of the universe who will not be tied down to small and humanly constructed images, ideologies, institutions, and idols?

Beyond Ideology (London: Collins, 1981); Ninian Smart and Steven Konstantine, *A Christian Systematic Theology in World Context* (Minneapolis, MN: Fortress, 1991); Wilfred Cantwell Smith, *Towards a World Theology* (London: Macmillan, 1981); and R. C. Zaehner, *Concordant Discord* (Oxford: Clarendon, 1970).

66. See Oswalt, *Called to Be Holy*.
67. Carver, "Quest for the Holy." The first three questions are adapted from Carver.

3. How do we maintain this story's delicate balance between divine judgment with consequences for disobedience and God's dominant leaning toward mercy, forgiveness, and faithfulness to the promises he has made (see Exod 34:6–7)?

4. Are we, as Christians in Africa, maturing in our faith so that we will not be easily swayed by every wind that comes?

5. Do we in Africa act as Moses did, selflessly interceding for those who go astray or those who have not yet known Yahweh, the true God of the universe? Or what do we do with adherents of African Traditional Religions in Africa?

Contextually, as Africans, with our intrinsic nature of being religious, our worship must be to God alone. We must not disobey God's Word, as that is blasphemous. We must not misinterpret God's grace. We must be patient enough to wait on the Lord alone. We must not mix our worship of him with our reverence for and veneration of our ancestors, for that is tantamount to idolatry – making any form of image or likeness in our worship of God. Such tendencies amount to disobedience, syncretism, blasphemy, and deification of persons (our ancestors) and, ultimately, are a misuse of God's name and a misinterpretation of the divine grace in our midst.

Bibliography

Allen, Ronald B., ed. *The Nelson Study Bible*. Nashville: Thomas Nelson, 1997.

Cantwell Smith, Wilfred. *Towards a World Theology*. London: Macmillan, 1981.

Carver, Frank G. "The Quest for the Holy: The Darkness of God." *Wesleyan Theological Journal* 23, nos. 1 and 2 (Spring–Fall, 1988).

González, Justo L. *The Story of Christianity: The Early Church to the Present*. Peabody, MA: Prince Press, 2004.

Gurkow, Lazar. "Why the Israelites Made a Calf." *Chabad.org*. http://www.chabad.org/parshah/article_cdo/aid/259461/jewish/Why-the-Israelites-Made-a-Calf.htm.

Guzik, David. https://enduringword.com/bible-commentary/exodus-32/. Accessed 16 August 2014.

———. https://enduringword.com/bible-commentary/1-kings-12/. Accessed 28 January 2016.

———. *Commentaries on the Bible – Deuteronomy*. http://ccbiblestudy.net/Old%20Testament/05Deut/05CE06.htm. Accessed 26 February 2018.

Harris, Kenneth L. "Exodus." In *ESV Study Bible*, edited by Lane Dennis, Wayne Grudem, et al. Wheaton, IL.: Crossway, 2008.

Kraemer, Hendrix. *The Christian Message in a Non-Christian World*. Bangalore: Centre for Contemporary Christianity, 2009.

Lockhart, Dick. "Exodus 32: The Golden Calf." *Look at the Book* (blog), 1 September 2013. https://dicklockhart.wordpress.com/2013/09/01/exodus-32-the-golden-calf/.

Lodahl, Michael. *The Story of God: Wesleyan Theology and Biblical Narrative*. Kansas City, MO: Beacon Hill Press, 1994.

MacArthur, John. *Our Sufficiency in Christ*. Wheaton, IL: Crossway, 1998.

Maddox, Randy. *Responsible Grace: John Wesley's Practical Theology*. Nashville, TN: Kingswood Books, 1994.

Martin, Walter. *The Kingdom of the Cults*, edited by Ravi Zacharias. Minneapolis: Bethany House, 2003.

Mbiti, John S. *Introduction to African Religion*. Oxford: Heinemann Educational Books, 1991.

Olson, Dennis, "Exodus 32:1–14 Commentary." *Biblia.Work*, 4 October 2016. http://www.biblia.work/sermons/exodus-321-14-commentary-by-dennis-olson/.

Oswalt, John. *Called to Be Holy: A Biblical Perspective*. Nappanee, IN: Evangel, 1999.

Provan, Ian. "1 and 2 Kings." In *ESV Study Bible*, edited by Lane Dennis, Wayne Grudem, et al. Wheaton, IL: Crossway, 2008.

Ritenbaugh, John W. "Why Worship God?" *Church of the Great God, 2000*. https://www.cgg.org/index.cfm/fuseaction/Library.sr/CT/personal/k/64/Why-Worship-God.htm. Accessed 21 August 2015.

Smart, Ninian. *Beyond Ideology*. London: Collins, 1981.

———. "Pluralism." In *A New Handbook of Christian Theology*, edited by Donald W. Musser and Joseph L. Price, 360–364. Nashville: Abingdon, 1992.

Smart, Ninian, and Steven Konstantine. *Christian Systematic Theology in World Context*. Minneapolis, MN: Fortress, 1991.

Tigay, Jeffrey. "The Golden Calf." *My Jewish Learning*. https://www.myjewishlearning.com/article/the-golden-calf/.

———. "The Story of the Golden Calf." *Friends of Sion*, 19 August 2014. https://friendsofsion.org/index.php/2014/08/19/the-story-of-golden-calf/.

Tzvi, Yaakov ben Chaim. "Why the Israelites Made a Golden Calf." *On Faith*, 25 September 2015. https://www.onfaith.co/dvartorah/why-the-israelites-made-a-golden-calf.

———. "Why the Israelites Made a Golden Calf." https://www.onfaith.co/bible/kjv/exodus/32. Accessed 26 February 2018.

Wright, Christopher J. H. *Living as the People of God: The Relevance of Old Testament Ethics*. Leicester: IVP, 1983.

Zaehener, R. C. *Concordant Discord*. Oxford: Clarendon, 1970.

10

Interfaith Dialogue between Christians and Muslims as a Response to Religious Radicalization in Kenya

Patrick Mburu Kamau
Lecturer, Africa Nazarene University, Nairobi, Kenya

Abstract

Interfaith dialogue is indispensable to peace and tranquility globally within the context of religious pluralism. Christians and Muslims worldwide stand in need of greater intercommunication, collaboration, and interfaith dialogue for harmonious living. Leaders of these faiths concur that Christian-Muslim dialogue is imperative. However, the interaction between Christians and Muslims has generally been characterized by distrust, apprehension, and mutual rivalry, sometimes resulting in loss of life and destruction of property. In Kenya, mistrust, disharmony, and intolerance of mosque adherents have been witnessed in churches. This calls for a fresh look at the relationship between Christians and Muslims in a spirit of interfaith dialogue. The chapter explores the possibility of interfaith dialogue between Christians and Muslims as a response to religious radicalization in Kenya. The methodology used in this paper includes examining the basis of interfaith dialogue with a focus on Islamic radicalism in Africa and Islamic radicalizing terror activities in Kenya. In addition, it assesses interfaith dialogue principles found in Christian and Muslim theology, including the Prophet Muhammad's attitude toward Jesus Christ; divergent issues for interfaith dialogue in biblical and Qur'anic teachings; and Christian and Muslim views of each other. The paper seeks to underscore some cross-cutting issues in biblical and Qur'anic teachings and the challenges to constructive Christian-Muslim dialogue in Kenya. Finally, the paper promotes interfaith dialogue as a response to radicalization through recommendations and strategies for overcoming radicalism in Kenya.

Key words: interfaith dialogue, interfaith relation, religious radicalization, Christian-Muslim dialogue, *salafi*.

Introduction

Interfaith dialogue is indispensable to peace and tranquility globally within the context of religious plurality. In order to live harmoniously, and as a response to Islamic radicalism, Christians and Muslims worldwide stand in need of greater interfaith dialogue, interfaith relations, and particularly Christian-Muslim dialogue. Christian-Muslim interactions as well as their relations have an intricate history, sometimes marked by rivalry or war and sometimes by constructive, harmonious living. This is evidenced by the early jihads against Christians and the retaliatory medieval crusades. Over the years, Islamic radicalism has raised great concern among Kenyans and for world peace generally through terrorist activities and radicalizing ideologies. This paper looks first at interfaith dialogue and the general basis for Christian-Muslim dialogue.

"Interfaith dialogue" is defined as a constructive, honest, objective, and sincere conversation between Christians and Muslims. It encompasses harmonious relations, religious freedom, and interfaith relations. "Interfaith relations" refers to the relationships established and nurtured among peoples of different faiths. "Religious radicalization" in this paper refers in general to an attempt to revive and restate Islamic exclusivism teaching in the contemporary world, regardless of the religiously pluralistic state of global society. "Christian-Muslim dialogue" is the building up of relationships between Christians and Muslims in an attempt to overcome doctrinal and mutual prejudices in order to enhance tolerance and de-radicalization. "De-radicalization" can be understood as a religious process to overcome violent ideologies, religious extremism, and terrorism through positive teaching on the need to embrace religious plurality and tolerance. This, for example, can be done through a hermeneutical process and approach that seeks to tone down violent texts in the Qur'an.[1]

Basis for Christian-Muslim Dialogue

"Interfaith dialogue" and "Christian-Muslim dialogue" are used interchangeably in this paper. In line with the definition given above, the former is a constructive, honest, objective, and sincere conversation between Christians and Muslims, while the latter is the building up of a relationship. The basis for Christian-Muslim dialogue is that Christianity and Islam are geographically the most widespread world religions. Christianity has approximately 2.3 billion adherents and Islam approximately 1.2 billion followers, making a total of 50 percent of the world population. Christianity and Islam are the major faiths in Kenya, though Christianity is the predominant faith.[2] Kenyan Muslims stand at roughly 10–20 percent, while Christians constitute 60–70 percent, notwithstanding the lack of precise authentic data on actual percentages of Christians and Muslims in Kenya.[3] It matters, then, not only to Christians and Muslims, but also to the rest of the world population, how the followers of these two religions relate to each other and how they envision their relationship in a pluralistic society.

In the decades since the 1960s, concerted efforts have been made between Christians and Muslims toward a new religious understanding in scholarship and dialogue. Contemporary developments, political and otherwise, may be threatening to build up new attitudes of distrust and hostility. Certain religious differences between Christians and Muslims create a need among the adherents of both faiths to learn more about each other's faith and to continue to improve their relationship. Such an endeavor would reduce terrorist attacks and religious brainwashing into radicalism.

---

1. Muhammad Taqi-ud-Din al-Hilali and Muhammad Muhsin Khan, *Translation of the Meaning of the Noble Qur'an in the English Language* (Madinah, KSA: King Fahd Complex for the Printing of the Holy Qur'an, 2006). This is the version of Qur'an used in this chapter.

2. Pew Research Center: Religion & Public Life, "Global Christianity: A Report on the Size and Distribution of the World's Christian Population," PewForum, 19 December 2011, accessed 11 June 2013, http://www.pewforum.org/2011/12/19/global-christianity-exec/.

3. Patrick Mburu Kamau, "Christian-Muslim Dialogue with Particular Reference to Pentecostals and Muslims in Nairobi North District, Nairobi County, Kenya," (PhD diss., Kenyatta University, 2013), 15.

Islamic Radicalism in Africa

Since the rise of Islam in contemporary Africa, various Islamic activities have overshadowed interest in interfaith dialogue. For instance, the rise of Islamic radicalism in Africa in the twentieth and twenty-first centuries and its role in terrorism has been a setback to Christian-Muslim dialogue. Proponents of radicalism emphasize a literal interpretation of the Qur'an and the Hadith, through jihadist violence and terrorism.[4] To achieve this goal, several Islamic extremists work through al-Qaeda to incorporate local radical jihadist groups, such as the *al-Shabaab* working in East Africa and other parts of the continent. Apparently, Islamic radicals are linked to al-Qaeda, Hezbollah, *al-Shabaab*, and other terrorist groups working across global society.

The Kenya National Muslim Advisory Council (KENMAC) has accused some Muslim religious leaders of promoting violence through training youths to fight in the Kenya *al-Shabaab* war in Somalia.[5] Ooko adds that, "The ungoverned space in Somalia has on its part enabled the recruitment and training of the terrorists who find their way unhindered into Kenya due to the porosity of the border."[6] Regardless of such claims, insecurity and jihadist hardliners' beliefs continue to fuel religious extremism. The Islamic concept of *Salafi* (stricter observance of Islam and the Prophet's model) has presented to the public a more conflict-minded than a peaceful Islam. Islamic radicals lack the spirit of interfaith dialogue embedded in the Qur'an, rendering attempts to theologize on Christian-Muslim dialogue a challenge.

Islamic Radicalism and Terror Activities in Kenya

Islamic radicalism vis-à-vis Christian-Muslim dialogue in Kenya demonstrates a level of mistrust between these Abrahamic faiths. Islamic radicalism in Kenya has its basis in the 1979 Islamic Revolution in Iran. In 1998, terrorist attacks on US embassies in Kenya and Tanzania were alarming signs of the activities of fundamentalist Muslims in Kenya. Subsequent attacks propagated by jihadist Muslims have been felt in Nairobi and other parts of the country. Islamic jihadists have used grenades or shot civilians, sometimes in bus stations, shopping malls, churches, or educational institutions. Such terrorist attacks

---

4. A. Rabasa, et al., *Beyond Al-Qaeda: Part 1, The Global Jihadist Movement* (Santa Monica, CA: Rand Corporation, 2006).

5. NTV Media, 25 December 2011.

6. Otieno Samuel Ooko, *The Global Terrorism Threat: Youth Radicalization in Kenya* (Bachelor of Arts in International Studies paper, University of Nairobi, 2014), 61.

weaken the already fragile relationship between Christians and Muslims in Kenya. This calls for a new consideration of Christian-Muslim dialogue as an urgent priority for coexistence and cooperation, as well as an endeavor to de-radicalize already intoxicated minds. The sense of urgency for Christian-Muslim dialogue should incorporate the long-term necessity of continuing to deepen mutual understanding and trust, as indicated in biblical and Qur'anic teachings.

Interfaith Dialogue Found in Christian and Muslim Theology

Interfaith dialogue is evident in Christian and Muslim theology. The Bible, particularly the Old Testament, tells stories of key persons to whom God communicated regardless of their religious orientation. They include the Egyptian Pharaoh, Nebuchadnezzar, Balaam, and King Cyrus (the king of Persia – today's Iran), who were non-worshipers of Yahweh. When God interacted with them he did not give the prerequisite that they must change their religion, but he used them anyway; and this may provide an avenue to interfaith dialogue. In the book of Jonah, God required of the Ninevites not a change of their religious background but an act of repentance.

The New Testament is not short of interfaith notions. Jesus's birth narrative recorded in the Gospel of Matthew (2:1–12) tells of the arrival of magi (wise men) from the East who came to Jerusalem looking for the newborn King of the Jews. They were not Jews or adherents of Judaism. Yet they were guided by a star to where Jesus was.

Jesus's new command is love for each other which may be called "religious love," as shown in John 13:34. Religious love incorporates compassion, tolerance, and forgiveness. Furthermore, 1 Corinthians 13 teaches about love. Love can be seen as that indispensable constituent of every being, which when allowed to operate in an individual life, will become a radiating light to resist and overcome evil forces. In any situation, love wants to promote the interests of the recipient and prepares the journey to interfaith dialogue with people perceived as "other."

Mark (9:39–40) and Luke (9:50) record an incident when one of Jesus's disciples tried to stop someone casting out demons in Jesus's name. Jesus responded, "Do not stop him . . ." Jesus was open to dialogue, or was at least tolerant. The implication of this verse is that, as we share the gospel with other people, it should not be a source of religious intolerance and conflict; instead, it should demonstrate religious love to all human beings.

Similarly, the Qur'an and the Hadith support human self-worth and embolden people to live positive lives colored with humane values for the betterment of humanity (Qur'an 4:36). Submission to Allah should lead to developing good relationships with others. Christians and Jews are regarded as "People of the Book" in the Qur'an:

> O People of the Book! Come to common terms as between us and you: that we worship none but God; that we associate no partners with Him; that we take not, from among ourselves lords and patrons other than God. (Qur'an 2:136, 253, 285; 3:3, 64–65, 84, 111–115; 61:6)

The Prophet Muhammad's Attitude toward Jesus Christ

In the Qur'an Jesus is called the Christ six times (3:45; 4:157, 171, 172; 5:75; 9:31); Son of Mary (ibn-Maryam) twenty-three times; Jesus, son of Mary sixteen times; and son of Mary or with other titles seven times. In the Bible Jesus is called the son of Mary only once.[7] Mary's consecration is extensively shown in Qur'an 19 and in part of Qur'an 3. Mary dedicated what was in her womb, according to Qur'an 3:44–45. Furthermore, Qur'an 3:47 and 19:2 say that Jesus was born of the Virgin Mary. Jesus was supported by the Holy Spirit of God not only at his birth, according to the Qur'an, but in the cradle, in his youth, and as a grown man (Qur'an 2:87, 253; 16:2, 102; 26:193; 40:15; 58:22).

Muhammad thought of himself as a prophet but he called Jesus the "Christ" (Qur'an 3:45–46) and admitted that Jesus was "strengthened with Holy Inspiration" (2:87; 5:110) and given revelation from God (3:45–49; 5:110). As noted above, the Qur'an teaches that Jesus was born of a virgin (3:47–49), possibly the work of God. Muhammad taught that Jesus was a person of great honor, righteous, a prophet (43:59), and God's apostle (4:157). Jesus was one to whom God imparted his revelation (3:47–49; 5:110). Moreover, the Prophet Muhammad taught that Jesus healed the blind, healed lepers, and even raised the dead (5:110). The idea that Jesus was much more than just a great prophet is also clear from Muhammad's own teachings. For example, to Muslims, Muhammad was a prophet, but Muhammad taught that Jesus was a "Word" or "Spirit" coming from Allah himself (2:87; 4:17).

The Prophet Mohammed taught about the second coming of Jesus, the doctrine of eschatology (the parousia):

---

7. Mohmoud Ayoub, *Toward an Islamic Christology: An Image of Jesus in Early Shiite Muslim Literature* (New York: Muslim World, 1976), 165–166.

> And (Jesus) shall be a Sign (for the coming of) the Hour (of Judgment): therefore have no doubt about the (Hour), but follow ye Me: this is a Straight Way. By him in whose hands my soul is, Son of Mary (Jesus) will shortly descend amongst you people (Muslims) as a just ruler . . . (43:61)

He further says,

> And there is none of the people of the Scriptures (Jews and Christians) But must believe in him (i.e. Jesus as an Apostle of Allah and a human being) before his death. And on the Day of Judgment He will be a witness against them. (4:159)

The Prophet felt that his heart was with Jesus, saying:

> Whosoever from amongst you lives to see Jesus, son of Mary, he should convey my greetings to him. By him in whose hand is my life, *Ibn Maryam* (Jesus Christ) would certainly pronounce Talbiyah for Hajj or for Umrah or for both (simultaneously as a Qarin) in the valley of Rawha. (Sahih Muslim, Book 7, No. 2877)

The day the Prophet ascended to heaven, he had the following to report:

> I saw myself (in a dream) near the *Ka'ba* last night, and I saw a man with whitish red complexion, the best you may see amongst men of that complexion having long hair reaching his earlobes which was the best hair of its sort, and he had combed his hair and water was dropping from it, and he was performing the *Tawaf* around the *Ka'ba* while he was leaning on two men or on the shoulders of two men. I asked, "Who is this man?" Somebody replied, "(He is) Messiah, Son of Mary." Then I saw another man with very curly hair, blind in the right eye which looked like a protruding out grape. I asked, "Who is this?" Somebody replied, "(He is) Messiah, *Ad-Dajjal*." (Sahih Bukhari, Vol. 9, Book 87, No. 128; Malik's Muwatta, Book 49, No. 49.2.2)

It can be concluded that the Prophet did not bear any ill-will toward Jesus. Muhammad thought of Jesus as the Christ, both in his teaching and in his convictions. Such should be taught in madrasas and be heavily emphasized in the mosque as a means of de-radicalization by imams, sheikhs, and madrasa teachers.

Divergent Issues for Interfaith Dialogue in Biblical Teachings

Several theological understandings of the Christian and Muslim faiths are quite distinct. This paper does not try to delve into the question of whether the Yahweh of Judaism, the God of Christians, and Allah are the same. Instead, we will look at biblical and Islamic teachings on certain doctrinal matters and their application.

The doctrine of the Trinity serves as a dividing line between Christianity and Islam. God, in Christian doctrine, is viewed as a Trinity: the Father, Son, and Holy Spirit. Furthermore, the Bible attributes deity to the Holy Spirit (Isa 6:8–9; Jer 31:31–34; Acts 28:25–26; Heb 10:15–17). The deity of the Holy Spirit is confirmed by the fact that he is said to have the attributes of God (Gen 1:2; Job 26:13; 1 Cor 2:9–11; Heb 9:14) and he performs the works of God (Job 33:4; Ps 104:30; Luke 12:11–12; Acts 1:5; 20:28; 1 Cor 6:11; 2:8–11; 2 Pet 1:21). The Bible's affirmation of the existence of God in three persons is an anathema to Qur'anic teaching.

Another Christian doctrine is found in John 14:6: "I am the way and the truth and the life. No-one comes to the Father, except through me." The passage argues that Christianity is superior to all other religions. It is only through Christ that we can have salvation. Christians affirm that the personal experience of salvation and eternal life hangs on this passage and through the substitutionary death of Christ.

Divergent Issues for Interfaith Dialogue in Qur'anic Teachings

The death of the Qur'anic Messiah is a controversial teaching. One text affirms Jesus's death while another denies it:

> And there is none of the people of the Scriptures (Jews and Christians) But must believe in him (i.e. Jesus as an Apostle of Allah and a human being) before his death. And on the Day of Judgment he will be a witness against them. (4:159)

> And their [Jews] boasting: "We killed Messiah Jesus, son of Mary, the apostle of Allah," but they [Jews] killed him not, nor crucified him, but the resemblance of Jesus was put over another man (and they killed that man). (4:157–158)

This type of teaching falsifies the teaching of the four Gospels that Jesus was indeed crucified, rendering their crucifixion account inaccurate. Dialogue between Christians and Muslims will be incomplete if such a discrepancy is not rectified. Furthermore, Qur'an 2:62 (cf. 5:69) reads as if Christians will go to heaven, but 3:85 and 5:72–73 are pretty clear that Christians will go to hell.

Some of the Qur'an's depictions of violence sometimes deter viable interfaith dialogue. For example, the following verse calls for the destruction of non-Muslims:

> This is the recompense of those who fight against God and his Messenger, and hasten about the earth, to do corruption there: they shall be slaughtered, or crucified, or their hands and feet shall alternately be struck off; or they shall be banished from the land. That is degradation for them in this world; and in the world to come awaits them a mighty chastisement. (5:33)

Lewis and Churchill state that, according to the Qur'an, paradise is in the shadow of the sword, as stipulated by Muhammad.[8] The desires of some to attain paradise lead them to adopt a radicalized ideology and to propagate terror attacks based on some Qur'anic teaching. Concerning jihad, Muslims have a duty under any ruler, whether devout or tyrannical. They are told that a day and a week at war are better than a month of fasting and prayer. A Muslim who dies without having taken part in such campaigns dies in a kind of unbelief. Muslims may wage war against four types of enemy: infidels, apostates, rebels, and bandits. The first two call for jihad, while the rest do not. Notice the following verses which support terror attacks:

> Then, when the sacred months have passed, slay the pagans wherever you find them – take them [captive], besiege them, and prepare for them each ambush. But if they repent and establish worship and pay the poor-due [i.e. submit to Islam], then leave their way free. Lo! Allah is Forgiving, Merciful. (9:59)

> Fight those who believe not in Allah nor the Last Day, nor hold that forbidden which hath been forbidden by Allah and his Messenger [i.e. do not adhere to Islamic law], nor acknowledge the religion of Truth [i.e. Islam], from the people of the book [i.e. Jews and Christians], until they pay tribute with willing submission, and feel themselves utterly subdued. (9:29)

Radicalized ideologies teach that non-Muslims are required by Islamic law either to convert to Islam or to be killed. For instance, Qur'an 9:29 teaches intolerance of Christians and Jews. The pillaging and plundering of infidels,

---

8. Bernard Lewis and Buntzie Ellis Churchill, *Islam: The Religion and the People* (Upper Saddle River, NJ: Wharton School Publishing, 2009), 145–155.

enslaving of their children, and placing their women as concubines are well supported in the Qur'an and Muhammad's Sunna (4:24, 92; 8:69; 24:33; 33:50). The question is, how can interfaith dialogue move beyond these texts to become constructive? There is a need for Islamic jurists and teachers of hermeneutics to reinterpret the above texts in light of the current global order and religious freedom, which was absent when the theocratic concept was established during the early years of the formation of Islam. A new hermeneutical understanding of tyrannical qur'anic verses will provide a new outlook on those verses for a pluralist society, and will avert further conflict.

Christians' Views on Interfaith Dialogue in Kenya

Some Christians view interfaith dialogue as a mode of evangelism. Muslims are to be won to Christ by highlighting the obstacles which prevent them from converting to Christianity. The gospel is God's final self-disclosure and other religions are a reflection of a fallen humanity. This argument implies that, with appropriate methodology and a firm dependence upon the Holy Spirit, Muslims can be saved. The study of Islam and a zeal to win Muslims to faith in Christ should strengthen effective mission to Muslims. Such Christians contend that Christian-Muslim dialogue should be apologetic and polemic. The call of Jesus is to reach out, to influence people, and to receive them into Christian faith, including Muslims. These Christians feel that they should press on with propagating the gospel among those who have been blinded to the truth of God. Muslims should be approached with the claims of Christ through prayer, friendship, listening, and the proclamation of Christ.

How dialogue should progress beyond negating the misconceptions of the others' beliefs and praxis has to be addressed for harmonious interfaith living. Christian "missionary" efforts using the gospel in a "frontal attack" against Muslims have ended in disaster. There is a need to evaluate the possibilities for enriching religious education and existing church and mosque policies with the values of harmonious interfaith relations. The process of Christian-Muslim dialogue involves a thorough understanding of the fundamental elements embedded in Christian and Muslim teaching on interfaith dialogue. An adequate theological framework, therefore, needs to provide an evaluation procedure whereby the areas of contact between Christians and Muslims can be strengthened to foster mutual concord.

Muslim Attitudes toward Christians

Historically, Muslims have held Christianity in high esteem. Male Muslims were encouraged to marry Christians as long as their offspring would be brought up under Islamic teaching. In our contemporary society we see, for instance, Christians flourishing in some Muslim-dominated countries. Combined with the ecumenical principles of *ah al-kitab* (people of the book) is the tolerance principle of *IaIkraha fid-din* (there is no compulsion in religion), an idea of religious tolerance that is widely held in Arab countries.[9] Mazrui affirms that the Muslim worldview is divided between the *dar-la-islam* (house of Islam), where Muslim rule and sharia are enforced, and *dar-al-harb* (house of war), the rest of the world where infidels rule.[10] According to traditional concepts and teaching, jihad is to continue until all come to adopt Islam or submit to sharia.

The Qur'an portrays a mixed attitude toward Christians. On the one hand is the teaching of Qur'an 2:256 which, as mentioned above, says "there is no compulsion in religion." On the other hand, there are calls to wage war against non-Muslims (8:38–39). Radicalized Muslims seek to use the ideologies in the Qur'an accompanied by sharia to overthrow secularist governments and institutions foreign to a true Muslim *ummah*. Islamists believe that Islamic teaching should be applied as a complete code that encompasses all areas of life, whether spiritual, intellectual, political, social, or economic. When comparing 2:256 and 8:38–39, it is clear that one passage supports such ideologies and permits violence, while the other seeks a truce. As noted earlier, it is vital to move beyond practical application of these verses, which were more appropriate for a theocratic nation in the seventh century than for today's open, pluralistic societies.

Cross-Cutting Issues for Interfaith Dialogue in Biblical and Qur'anic Teachings

Both the Muslim and Christian Scriptures claim divine origin. Qur'an 2:2 states, "This is the Book; wherein there is no doubt; guidance to the pious ones"; while the Bible says, "All Scripture is God-breathed and is useful for teaching, rebuking, correcting, and training in righteousness" (2 Tim 3:16). The degree to which God reveals himself is described in Qur'an 2:3–4: "Who believe in the Unseen, are steadfast in prayer, and spend out of what we have provided

---

9. A. A. Mazrui, *Islam between Globalization and Counterterrorism* (Trenton, NJ: Africa World Press, 2006), 81, 148.

10. Mazrui, *Islam*, 81, 148.

for them; and who believe in what is sent to you and what was sent before you, and (in their hearts) have the reassurance of the hereafter." A similar teaching in the Bible is found in 1 Timothy 3:16: "Beyond all question, the mystery of godliness is great: he appeared in the body, was vindicated by the Spirit, was seen by angels, was preached among the nations, was believed on in the world, was taken up in Glory."

The Bible and the Qur'an, despite their disparities, have areas of common ground that, when well utilized, can support interfaith dialogue. For example:

> For this cause we have prescribed to Jews "whoever kills an innocent life it's as if he has killed all of mankind. And whoever saves an innocent life it's as if he has saved all mankind." (Qur'an 5:32)

> You shall not murder. (Exod 20:13)

> You have heard that it was said to the people long ago, "Do not murder, and anyone who murders shall be subject to judgment." But I tell you that anyone who is angry with his brother will be subject to judgment. Again, anyone who says to his brother, 'Raca,' is answerable to the Sanhedrin, but anyone who says, 'You fool!' will be in danger of the fire of hell. (Matt 5:21–22)

If we compare these texts, we quickly notice the common spirit of respect for human life. On the one hand, Christians and Muslims are called to a greater awareness of the need for dialogue and that they are called to be agents of and witnesses to God's universal mercy. On the other hand, the Qur'an and the Bible invite adherents to move beyond prejudice, suspicion, and half-truths in order to arrive at an understanding with each other.

Challenges to Constructive Christian-Muslim Dialogue in Kenya

The essential component in interfaith dialogue is not doctrinal agreement but the willingness to re-examine one's faith in the light of how others relate to their tradition. This includes the ability to listen, instruct, strengthen, or adjust one's own engagement and interaction with the sacred based on the experiences of the other. Understanding the faith of others should strengthen rather than weaken a person's commitment to his or her religious tradition and free that person from prejudice and intolerance. Christian-Muslim dialogue, therefore, is the building up of relationships between Christians and Muslims in an attempt to overcome mutual doctrinal prejudices and to enlarge areas of mutual concord. However, doctrinal differences remain a challenge and cannot be ignored if fruitful interfaith dialogue is to take place.

The relationship between Christians and Muslims in Kenya is a major challenge, sometimes characterized by uninformed presumptions, stereotypes, distorted perceptions, prejudices, and discrimination. Christian-Muslim dialogue may mostly revolve around moral, socio-political, economic, and ecological issues, among others. Moreover, in most cases interfaith dialogue is usually a concern only of some mainline churches, while other denominations appear to be absent. Fundamental beliefs and the critical expression of faith is usually omitted in interfaith encounters.

Muslims' *mihadhara*, sermons preached in the open air, have contributed to marring relationships with Christians. They were introduced in Kenya around 1987.[11] *Mihadhara* in Kenya are mostly conducted in Kiswahili. The preachers normally read the Bible against the Qur'an, trying to show how erroneous the Bible is. The initial reaction of Christians to *mihadhara* is normally one of shock and surprise, as these preachers appear to be humiliating them. *Mihadhara* sometimes attack the essence of Christian doctrines in hostile and dismissive tones. Many of the Muslim speakers at *mihadhara* choose biblical texts selectively to back up their arguments and are reluctant to reason with Christian protagonists as to how the Bible should be interpreted. Most *mihadhara* generate only heated controversy between Christians and Muslims, producing little if any light. On some occasions, *mihadhara* have resulted in open physical confrontation between Muslims and Christians, leading to injury, loss of property, and even death. Nevertheless, *mihadhara* could be used to enhance Christian-Muslim dialogue through inviting seasoned preachers who are conversant with Christian doctrine.

Interfaith Dialogue in Response to Radicalization

Muslims involved in radicalism should be taught about the values of interfaith dialogue that are embedded in the Qur'an. Qur'an 2:136, 253; 3:3; and 3:64–65 demonstrate that Allah has encouraged Muslims to dialogue as a means to iron out misunderstanding with non-Muslims. These verses teach that Muslims should maintain calmness during dialogue and be sincere when giving their views. Participants in dialogue should be at liberty to discuss other issues which are not religious. Qur'an 29:49 also supports the idea that whenever

---

11. Joseph M. Mutei, "The Effectiveness of Mihadhara as Methods of Islamic Da'wah in Kenya," (unpublished MA dissertation, St Paul Theological College, 2006), 3.

there is misunderstanding between the two faiths, Muslims are to dialogue with Christians with wisdom in order to arrive at amicable solutions.

When debating issues in inter-religious dialogue, the matter in question is always much more than just theology; almost by definition, aspects of a political and economic character are involved, and conflicting claims often cause discord rather than harmony.[12] The Qur'an states that Muslims should dialogue in a peaceful, respectful, and obedient manner because as they do so, someone may be encouraged to join Islam. Muslims should dialogue in a friendly and attractive manner so that Christians or members of any other religion can know what Islam teaches (see e.g. Qur'an 5:85, 54; 15:25). For example, the Qur'an warns Muslims not to insult non-Muslims, otherwise they will insult Allah (6:108). On the same note, generally the Qur'an advises Muslims that in dialogue they should engage people of the book in a peaceful manner devoid of anger or intimidation. They should not be emotional or ask or answer questions out of disrespect (2:62; 48:29; 3:64–65; 5:82). The Qur'an (9:31; 29:49) supports some biblical books, such as the Taurat (Pentateuch-Torah), Zamburi (Psalms), and Injeel (Gospels), and this provides a good basis for interfaith dialogue. Dialogue should be a good conversation, according to Qur'an 3:64; 7:158; and 16:125; "We propagate only to those who want to listen" (112:1–4); and "yes, there is no compulsion in religion" (2:256). Dialogue, then, in spite of its many shortcomings, may be the only practical way of empathic approximation to the Truth and the way to put ourselves in somebody else's place.

People involved in dialogue should go beyond accusation and counter-accusation and major on basic principles in common and the sharing of values. Küng and Moltmann argue that Christianity and Islam have lived at close quarters and are closely related in a structural sense as religions of revelation, but sometimes tensions and petty rivalries have been common.[13] As Gülen says, Muslims accept all prophets and all books sent to different prophets throughout history, and regard belief in them as an essential principle of being Muslim.[14] In fact, so great is Jesus that, according to the Hadith, "Narrated Abu Huraira: The Apostle said, 'So they will go to Jesus and say, "O Jesus! You are Allah's

---

12. Terry Mathis, "Sacred Scriptures and Interfaith Dialogue" (paper presented at "International Conference on Peaceful Coexistence: Fethullah Gülen's Initiatives for Peace in the Contemporary World," Erasmus University of Rotterdam, 22–23 November 2007), *Fethullah Gülen*, https://fgulen.com/en/gulen-movement/conference-papers/peaceful-coexistence/25855-sacred-scriptures-and-interfaith-dialogue.

13. H. Küng and Jurgen Moltmann, eds., *Islam: A Challenge for Christianity* (London: SCM, 1994), 6.

14. M. Fethullah Gülen, *Essays, Perspectives, Opinions* (Rutherford, NJ: The Light, 2006), 4.

Apostle and *His Word*'" (6.200–201; 60.178.236)"; and "Narrated Anas: The Prophet said, 'Go to Jesus, Allah's Slave, His Apostle, and *Allah's Word and a Spirit coming from Him*'" (6.4). In other words, Muhammad called Jesus the very "Word of God." This brings closer the concept of Jesus as a unifying force in dialogue between these faiths.

It is worth noting that dialogue should not be about persuading or interfaith competition, but about accommodating each other. It is impractical and insufficient to read other religious systems in the light of the assumptions of one's own. Similarly, Muslims and Christians could expand distinctive paths toward accommodation and dialogue by drawing inspiration from their specific interests and conditions. Muslim-Christian cooperation and dialogue has been emphasized by Nursi.[15] Interfaith dialogue should reach beyond the hallways of academia and spread to the masses through education and other means. One of the Hadith says, "No one is fully a believer until he wishes for his brother what he wishes for himself."[16] And Matthew 22:39 says, "Love your neighbor as yourself." These texts invite people to move on from the past, with its misunderstandings and failures, and communicate love and concern for each other. Religious teaching can cause disharmony, and so, rather than being a hardline apologist, the theology of interfaith dialogue needs to be embraced. General revelation should be used as a starting point in any dialogue, accompanied by social ethics.

Both the Bible and the Qur'an stress the ideology of Christian community or Muslim *ummah*. Matthew 10:36 says, "A man's enemies will be the members of his own household"; and Matthew 18:20 says, "For where two or three come together in my name, there I am with them." It is erroneous to approach Christianity, with its over two billion followers, or Islam, with its over one billion adherents, from a theological perspective alone. Dialogue should be geared toward addressing sociological and theological hindrances for the community of faith. Though such may not be fully ironed out, reducing the stumbling blocks will help. Muslims should allow each individual to make his or her religious choices without interference from anyone else.

In some Muslim-dominated countries, individuals have no rights to make their own religious choices. Such lack of religious freedom contravenes some Qur'anic texts, as discussed above. A frontal attack against Muslim solidarity

---

15. Thomas Michel, "Muslim-Christian Dialogue and Cooperation in the Thought of Bediuzzaman Said Nursi," *The Muslim World* 89, no. 3–4 (Oct 1999), accessed 8 October 2011, https://onlinelibrary.wiley.com/doi/abs/10.1111/j.1478-1913.1999.tb02751.x.

16. Yahya M. A. Ondigo (compiler), *Forty Hadith on Social Poisonous Habits: With Short Commentaries* (Nairobi: Abu Aisha Stores, 2008), Hadith 13.

may produce negative results, since Muslims will use a counter-attack, possibly accompanied by violence. Muslim solidarity gets stronger when threatened. For instance, Muslims feel that if a Christian enters a mosque it actually defiles the sanctity of their house of worship. Care needs to be taken for Muslim apostates to Christianity, since immediate withdrawal from the Muslim *ummah* results in expulsion from the *ummah* and even death in some instances.[17] Within the Islamic faith 10 percent is practiced theologically by Muslims, while 90 percent is basically socio-cultural issues practiced within the *ummah*. Apostatizing from Muslim perspectives causes the individual to be excluded from the Muslim *ummah*. Freedom of worship, with no related communal religious or personal penalties, is essential for religious practice and free expression of belief. Religious freedom should serve as a social religious value to strengthen interfaith dialogue.

The Qur'anic principles of *ummah* underscore the need to develop all-inclusive social relations among all citizens. The Qur'an (2:35; 7:26) counsels Muslim believers to suppress any possible justifiable anger as the far superior course of action, and to selflessly develop relationships not only with other Muslims but also with Christians. Humankind, as taught in the Qur'an, descended from Adam and Eve, making everyone a brother or sister. Race, language, and color show the omnipotence of Allah and should never be used as a reason for discriminating against people (Qur'an 4:1). Muslims practicing radicalism should be taught and encouraged to have good relations with people of other faiths without undue favor.

Theologically, these two religions have irreconcilable differences which call for each to honor the other's religious convictions. Dorman notes, "Muslims' polemic view of Christians' missionary campaign is aimed against the solidarity of easterners, against the unit of the Islamic nations, against the purity and classic perfection of the Arabic language and against the character and person of Muhammad."[18] Christian missionaries in Islamic countries are perceived to destroy the rich heritage and lofty values of Islam, which serves as a hindrance to true dialogue. The Muslim *ummah* holds religious shared values, and common concern for all Muslims. Moreover, it is that shared and mutually compatible, complementary family of cultures belonging to Muslim people in many places. With the *ummah* concept, it is wise that radicalist ideologies and

---

17. P. Parshall, *The Dove and the Crescent* (Wheaton, IL: Tyndale, 1989), 10.

18. Harry Gaylord Dorman, Jr., *Toward Understanding Islam* (New York: Teachers College, Columbia University, 1948), 117.

teachings among some Muslims be replaced by inter-human mutual respect for Muslims and all others.

The advantage Muslims have in engaging in interfaith dialogue, says Gülen, is that they believe in the oneness and basic unity of religion, seeing it is a symphony of Allah's blessing and mercy embracing all races and beliefs, and as a road bringing everyone together in brotherhood.[19] A similar sentiment may be found in Paul's message to the Athenians, when he preached his message without interfering with the Athenians' gods or dismantling the Athenians' *ummah* (Acts 17:22).

Religious misunderstanding between Christianity and Islam has often erupted into violence. Some political systems which deny religious freedom have resulted in social instability and at times conflict among the adherents of these faiths. It is wise to overcome suspicion in dialogue since both Christian and Muslim scriptures support it, and even religious leaders like Pope Paul VI and Pope John Paul II have been in favor of it. Christian or Muslim faith in God is not a political philosophy for propagating selfishness. Dialogue should remain a life-changing spiritual force and experience which will result in compassionate and cooperative representatives of collective armistice. The teachings of the Bible and the Qur'an are the fountainhead and lay the essential groundwork for interfaith dialogue.

Recommendations and Strategies for Overcoming Radicalism

1. Muslims should be made aware of the Qur'anic teaching that diversity of culture or race is not a recipe for division but a sign of Allah's immeasurable benevolence toward humankind.

2. Children and young people should be taught the value of the Qur'anic principles of *ummah* which underscore the need to develop all-inclusive social relations among all citizens. The Qur'an (2:35; 7:26) counsels Muslim believers to suppress any justifiable anger as the far superior course of action and to selflessly develop relationships not only with Muslims but also with Christians.

3. The Qur'an teaches that humankind is descended from Adam and Eve, making everyone a brother or sister. Race, language, and color show the omnipotence of Allah and should never be used as a reason for discriminating against people (Qur'an 4.1).

---

19. Gülen, *Essays, Perspectives, Opinions*, 34–35.

4. Collectively, sharia requires Muslims to maintain good relations with neighbors, which includes up to forty houses in each direction. With that in mind, Muslims need to be reminded of the Qur'anic injunctions to collaborate harmoniously with Christians (Qur'an 2:256; 4:36).

5. Of Islamic practice, 90 percent is basically socio-cultural issues practiced within the *ummah*. Religious freedom should be taught from an early age, both in the Christian Sunday school and in the Muslim madrasa, to prevent seclusion after apostatizing. Freedom of worship, with no related communal religious or personal penalty, is essential to religious practice and the free expression of belief.

6. Christians ought to develop a social-religious peace-building (SRP) process which provides activities and mechanisms that favor interfaith dialogue and constructive means for resolving differences. Christians should use education as an approach to fostering reconciliation, conflict-resolution mechanisms, transformation, and sustainable peaceful relationships among themselves and with Muslims.

7. Christians believe in the work of Christ as exclusive and salvific, but that should not lead to discrimination and intolerance against non-Christians. Instead, Christians ought to be open to the possibility that followers of other religions may experience salvation based on a response to God's general revelation and proportional light given them by him, and that it is only God who can make such decisions.

8. The Qur'an urges Muslims toward respect as a principle which supports Christian-Muslim dialogue. This implies showing honor, kindness, and tolerance toward Christians as part of one's duty to honor and obey Allah.

9. Political leaders should promote Christian-Muslim dialogue as a key agenda and offer opportunities for bridging politics and for religious tolerance. Political leaders have a duty to heighten the visibility of and broaden commitment to a culture of peace through interfaith dialogue. Political leaders should address and denounce extremism, intolerance, religious discrimination, and terrorism perpetrated among their citizens.

10. Conferences for religious leaders are integral in fostering Christian-Muslim dialogue. Christian ministers and imams/sheikhs should organize interfaith conferences to individually champion interfaith dialogue.

11. Intellectual dialogue should move a step further into relational dialogue. Intellectual material which encourages interfaith relations should be given to people and seminars held to substantiate the need for interfaith relations. Intellectual dialogue should be simplified so that each member of these faiths can easily grasp the material.

Conclusion

This paper has shown that the unity of Muslim *ummah* – a socio-religious concept which stresses homogeneity, when Muslims' lives are patterned and regulated by sharia – is a primary goal that all must strive for; there is a serious warning from Allah in Qur'an 3:103 for those who create division. Instead, Muslims are encouraged from the Qur'an to develop constructive peaceful interfaith dialogue; this is not only permitted but commended. Peace is stipulated in the Qur'an as an indispensable means for Muslims dialoguing with the "People of the Book," the best way to avoid mistrust and overcome differences with Christians. In addition, Christians and Muslims must communally address social evils which thwart peaceful coexistence. Embracing peace will enhance tolerance, respect, and cooperation among diverse religious constituencies. Promoting spiritual values, shared religious traditions, and appreciation of religious teachings will support interfaith dialogue. Such an endeavor will limit violence perpetrated against Christians by jihadists.

Christians are urged by the Bible to live peacefully with all people, irrespective of their religious orientation. Biblical peace means soundness, health, prosperity, wellbeing, and good relations with both other human beings and God. Christians ought to practice biblical peace, which means untroubled tranquility devoid of war, schism, fear, hatred, anger, or malice toward non-Christians. They should desist from teachings which promote discord, hurt feelings, unforgiveness, selfish ambition, and acts of intolerance which disrupt social peace. Muslims and Christians should develop working relationships with each other, as explained in the Qur'an and the Bible. This could be done through offering help, visiting one another, giving invitations to eat in one's home, and sharing free time, to minimize the radicalization based on some Qur'anic teaching.

Different theological interpretations of concepts such as the Trinity and monotheism are sometimes used out of context to support religious intolerance. There is a need to establish a planned study of each other's religion to avoid the stagnation of interfaith relations at a superficial level of generalizations. Attempts should be made to respond to theological stalemates through interfaith dialogue. Christian and Muslim apologists should refrain from attacking each other's doctrines as false and unreliable. They should hold back from using time-worn, dismissive arguments against each other in dialogue. Christians should instead apply the biblical approach of leadership, which is accommodative, reflecting the prevailing cultural diversity and religious plurality of Kenyan society.

Bibliography

Ayoub, Mohmoud. *Toward an Islamic Christology: An Image of Jesus in Early Shiite Muslim Literature*. New York: The Muslim World, 1976.

Dorman, Harry Gaylord, Jr. *Toward Understanding Islam*. New York: Teachers College, Columbia University, 1948.

Gülen, M. Fethullah. *Essays, Perspectives, Opinions*. Rutherford, NJ: The Light, 2006.

al-Hilali, Muhammad Taqi-ud-Din, and Muhammad Muhsin Khan. *Translation of the Meaning of the Noble Qur'an in the English Language*. Madinah, KSA: King Fahd Complex for the Printing of the Holy Qur'an, 2006.

Kamau, Patrick Mburu. "Christian-Muslim Dialogue with Particular Reference to Pentecostals and Muslims in Nairobi North District, Nairobi County, Kenya." PhD thesis, Kenyatta University, 2013.

Küng, H., and Jürgen Moltmann, eds. *Islam: A Challenge for Christianity*. London: SCM Press, 1994.

Lewis, Bernard, and Buntzie Ellis Churchill. *Islam: The Religion and the People*. Upper Saddle River, NJ: Wharton School Publishing, 2009.

Mathis, Terry. "Sacred Scriptures and Interfaith Dialogue." Paper presented at International Conference on Peaceful Coexistence: Fethullah Gülen's Initiatives for Peace in the Contemporary World. Erasmus University of Rotterdam, 22–23 November 2007. *Fethullah Gülen*. https://fgulen.com/en/gulen-movement/conference-papers/peaceful-coexistence/25855-sacred-scriptures-and-interfaith-dialogue.

Mazrui, A. A. *Islam between Globalization and Counterterrorism*. Trenton, NJ: Africa World Press, 2006.

Michel, Thomas. "Muslim-Christian Dialogue and Cooperation in the Thought of Bediuzzaman Said Nursi." *The Muslim World* 89, no. 3–4 (Oct 1999). Accessed 8 October 2011. https://onlinelibrary.wiley.com/doi/abs/10.1111/j.1478-1913.1999.tb02751.x.

Mutei, Joseph M. "The Effectiveness of *Mihadhara* as Methods of Islamic *Da'wah* in Kenya." Unpublished MA dissertation, St Paul Theological College, 2006.

Ondigo, Yahya. M. A. (compiler). *Forty Hadith on Social Poisonous Habit: With Short Commentaries*. Nairobi: Abu Aisha Stores, 2008.

Ooko, Otieno Samuel. *The Global Terrorism Threat: Youth Radicalization in Kenya*. Bachelor of Arts in International Studies Dissertation, University of Nairobi, 2014.
Parshall, P. *The Dove and the Crescent*. Wheaton, IL: Tyndale, 1989.
Pew Research Center. "Global Christianity: A Report on the Size and Distribution of the World's Christian Population." PewForum, 19 December 2011. Accessed 11 June 2013. http://www.pewforum.org/2011/12/19/global-christianity-exec/.
Rabasa, A., et al. *Beyond Al-Qaeda: Part 1, The Global Jihadist Movement*. Santa Monica: Rand Corporation, 2006.

Part III

Christian Education in the African Context

11

African Christian Universities and the Old Testament Concept of the *Lev*

Daryll Gordon Stanton
Chair, Department of Religion, Africa Nazarene University, Nairobi, Kenya

and

Rickson Nkhata
Head of Bachelor Programs, Southern Africa Nazarene University, Manzini, Swaziland

Abstract

African Christian universities face numerous challenges, but have unique prospects. The Old Testament concept of the *lev* is applied in higher Christian education. Several challenges and prospects are unpacked. The *first* challenge looks at the "motivating spirit" in the lives of staff and students in African Christian universities that is needed to shape an African Christian "worldview" in a secular global society. A *second* challenge concerns "moral qualities" and involves Christian "formation" and "transformation," necessitating that Christian educators partner with God in his formation and transformation. This is from the standpoint of *lev* being the "seat" of a person's "moral qualities." A *third* challenge is that of "conscience." Formation of our conscience in the truth requires effort. Our Christian universities help our students acquire the moral knowledge necessary to apply ethical principles to their acts. *Fourth* is the challenge of the "intellectual function of knowing." This is related to the need to constantly form the conscience in order to help it conform ever more to what is true and good. Studying, reading, and learning from the experiences of others are pathways to gaining moral knowledge. Christian universities recognize that gaining moral knowledge cannot be left to chance. A *final* challenge is related to a "focus of life." Christian education must be seen as that ministry of the church by which it seeks to communicate its faith and nurture Christlike disciples. The prospect associated with this application of *lev* sees our African Christian universities functioning as communities of believers wherein staff and students are guided not only to come together in spiritual activities in the university setting but also to go out to reveal personal holiness in all the operations of life.

Key words: Old Testament *lev*, Christian higher education.

Introduction

Churches and other religious bodies are embracing education, building institutions of learning in order to "come out from under a pervasively secular academic shadow."[1] Catholics and Protestants alike are developing hundreds of primary and secondary schools, theological seminaries, and universities, to the extent that at least forty-six new Christian universities were founded in Africa between 1990 and 2010.[2] However, African Christian universities face numerous challenges,[3] among them the tremendous pressures in some countries "to reduce education to gaining knowledge and skills for a station in the workplace." This is especially evident in Majority World countries due to scarcity of funds and the great need for knowledgeable workers, which results in a push for business and technology education.[4] Such countries also have unique prospects when providing a holistic approach to higher education.[5] This paper applies the Old Testament concept of the *lev* to our African Christian universities, with some specific reference to Africa Nazarene University in

---

1. Joel Carpenter, Perry L. Glanzer, Nicholas S. Lantinga, eds., *Christian Higher Education: A Global Reconnaissance*, Kindle edition (Grand Rapids: Eerdmans, 2014), 17.
2. Carpenter, Glanzer, and Lantinga, *Christian Higher Education*, 16.
3. John Balema, "Christian Higher Education in Africa: Past, Present and Future," in *Africa Journal of Evangelical Theology* 24, no. 2 (2005).
4. Carpenter, Glanzer, and Lantinga, *Christian Higher Education*, 23.
5. This is the approach of universities such as Africa Nazarene University and Southern Africa Nazarene University.

Kenya and Southern Africa Nazarene University in Swaziland.[6] Psalm 51:10–13 shows a biblical connection between teaching others in God's ways and a pure *lev*. A look at the Hebrew word *lev* and its various forms, especially *levav*,[7] reveals several biblical usages relevant to this study.

What Is the לֵב (*Lev*)?

The original Hebrew masculine noun is לֵב (*lev*) which *Strong's Hebrew Dictionary*[8] lists under word number 3820 "*leb*," defining it as "inner man, mind, will and heart."[9]

In fact, the *New American Standard Exhaustive Concordance of the Bible* acknowledges that the term is translated by numerous English words.[10] The *New American Standard Bible* translates *leb* as "heart" 396 times, "hearts" forty times, "brokenhearted" three times, "heart's" twice, as well as "double heart," "merry-hearted," and "stouthearted" once each. Among the usages in the *Brown-Driver-Briggs Hebrew and English Lexicon*, *lev* is translated "for the man himself."[11]

Jeff A. Benner uses the translation "heart" for לֵב and notes, "To the ancient Hebrews the heart was the mind, the thoughts." Benner utilizes pictures for the Hebrew letter, stating: "The first picture in this Hebrew word is a shepherd staff and represents authority, as the shepherd has authority over his flock.

---

6. Daryll Stanton is a senior lecturer at Africa Nazarene University, while Rickson Nkhata is both a doctoral student at Africa Nazarene University and a lecturer at Southern Africa Nazarene University.

7. These terms are used interchangeably with *leb* and *lebab* in the literature.

8. "Leb," no. 3820 in *Strong's Hebrew Dictionary*, Power Bible CD, 2011.

9. "3820. leb," *Strong's Concordance*, Bible Hub, accessed 9 December 2015, http://biblehub.com/hebrew/3820.htm. The Bible Hub indicates that the phonetic spelling is "labe" and provides the short definition "heart."

10. Robert L. Thomas, "Leb," in *New American Standard Exhaustive Concordance of the Bible/Hebrew-Aramaic and Greek Dictionaries* (Lockman Foundation at Lockman.org), 1981. However, the NASB utilizes numerous additional translations, including accord (1), attention (5), bravest (1), care (2), celebrating (1), chests (1), completely (1), concern* (1), concerned* (1), conscience (1), consider (2), considered (2), courage (1), decided (1), determine (1), discouraged (1), discouraging (1), doing (1), encouragingly (1), Himself (1), himself (6), imagination (1), inspiration (2), intelligence (1), kindly (5), life (1), middle (2), midst (1), mind (36), minds (3), myself (6), obstinate (2), planned (1), presume (1), pride (1), recalls (1), reflected (1), regard (1), self-exaltation (1), sense (10), senseless (1), seriously (1), skill (1), skilled (1), skillful man (1), skillful men (1), skillful persons (1), skillful (3), spirits (1), stubborn-minded (1), tenderly (2), thought (3), understanding (7), undivided (1), well (2), willingly (1), wisdom (2), yourself (1), yourselves (1).

11. "Lev," *Brown-Driver-Briggs Hebrew and English Lexicon*, Unabridged Electronic Database, 2002, 2003 and 2006 by Biblesoft, Inc. (BibleSoft.com) (accessed 25 November 2015).

The second letter is the picture of the floor plan of the nomadic tent and represents the idea of being inside, as the family resides within the tent. When combined they mean 'the authority within.'"[12] Thus, when Deuteronomy 6:5 commands God's people to love him with their whole *lev*, "it is not speaking of an emotional love, but to keep our minds and our thoughts working for him."[13] Joseph Henry Thayer noted that the Greek word καρδία (*kardia*) was used to translate the Hebrew לֵב (*lev*). *Kardia* also has several meanings similar to *lev*.[14]

J. B. Payne observed that it is important to keep in mind the biblical "context" which is guiding interpretation. Payne indicates that *lev* is a "term that may stand for the whole person," but he offered several helpful insights into the use of *lev* in his discussion of "Man's Constituent Elements" that guide the following sections of this study. Among the number of possible meanings, *lev* is applied here as:

1. a "motivating spirit,"
2. the "seat" of a person's "moral qualities,"
3. one's "conscience,"
4. the head or the brain as these relate to the "intellectual function of knowing," and
5. the "focus of life."[15]

Challenges for African Christian Universities

Many challenges are faced by Christian universities in Africa and could be considered – such as the escalating cost of higher education, multifaceted infrastructure, the changing context, integrating faith and learning into

---

12. Jeff A. Benner, "Heart," "Hebrew Word Definitions," Ancient Hebrew Research Center, accessed 9 December 2015, http://www.ancient-hebrew.org/vocabulary_definitions.html#heart.

13. Benner, "Heart."

14. Note the Greek Septuagint (LXX) utilizes καρδία (*kardia*) to translate לֵב (*lev*). See Joseph Henry Thayer, "*Kardia*," in *Thayer's Greek–English Lexicon of the New Testament* (Grand Rapids, MI: Associated Publishers and Authors, 1889). Not only does *kardia* refer to the "heart" as an organ in animal bodies, it also denotes "the seat and center of all physical and spiritual life." Thus, it may refer to "the vigor and sense of physical life," as in Ps 101:2 and Luke 21:34, as well as to "the center of spiritual life, the soul or mind, as it is the fountain and seat of the thoughts, passion, desires, appetites, affections, purposes, endeavors" (the inner person), as utilized in numerous New Testament passages. It may also be used for "the middle, central or inmost part of anything, even the inanimate," as in Jonah 2:3.

15. J. Barton Payne, *The Theology of the Older Testament* (Grand Rapids: Zondervan, 1962), 223–226.

curriculum, and keeping university commitment to Christ and his truth – which contribute to the attainment of high-quality standards at the highest level possible and commitment to Christ-centered education.[16] Running a credible academic institution is extremely expensive and is demanding in many other respects, hence the need for financial and other forms of support in order to maintain intellectual rigor.[17] Another challenge faced by Christian higher education is the "anti-intellectualism" in the churches today. Many leaders in African churches do not see the need for higher education. David W. Vikner puts it like this: "Rather than seeing Christian colleges and universities as partners and settings where the Christian faith can be nurtured, these colleges and universities are considered to be uninvolved in proclaiming the faith and are often more likely considered to be antithetical to the faith."[18]

However, in this section of the paper, five challenges in relation to the biblical concept of the *lev* are unpacked.

1. Motivating Spirit

One challenge in African Christian universities relates to the "motivating spirit" in the lives of staff and students. Rodney Reeves observed that one of the reasons for the writing of the letter to the Ephesian church "was to correct their worldview." He notes, "They didn't see the world with Christian eyes."[19] What are our Christian universities doing to shape this generation's Christian worldview? Are we helping frame appropriately both the temperament and the practice of their lives? How can African Christian universities best shape an African Christian "worldview" in a secular global society? John Van Dyk spoke of one's worldview as controlling more than what one believes in "the big picture": it is also reflected in teacher–student interactions and classroom efforts, including the subject matter.[20]

---

16. Bill Brown, "Top Ten Challenges Christian Students Face in College," *Journal of the Southern Baptist Convention* (2012). Proceedings held at Cedarville University, March 21–23, 2012 in the CCCU Chief Academic Officers Conference, at the Gaylord Oryland Hotel in Nashville, USA.

17. B. J. Van der Walt, "The Challenges of Christian Higher Education on the African Continent in the Twenty-First Century," *Christian Higher Education* 1, no. 2 (2002): 195–227.

18. David W. Vikner, "Challenges to Christian Higher Education in Asia," *Christian Higher Education* 2, no. 1 (2003): 1–13.

19. Rodney Reeves, *Spirituality According to Paul: Imitating the Apostle of Christ* (Downers Grove, IL: IVP Academic, 2011), 203–204.

20. John Van Dyk, *The Craft of Christian Teaching: A Classroom Journey* (Sioux Center, IA: Dordt Press, 2000), 87.

English-speaking countries in Africa were impacted by the British system of education. Liam Gearon spoke of a "religious education of the mind," noting that while the 1870 and 1944 Education Acts in Britain distinguished religious education from the "secular" curriculum, these called for religious instruction which was "closely associated with worship within the school." Discussion for the 1944 bill called for students to "gain knowledge of the common Christian faith held by their fathers for nearly 2000 years." However, as Gearon points out, the churches were admonished to "not forget their own responsibility for the out-of-school period." The implication was that there should be shared responsibility for religious education.[21]

This shared responsibility requires cooperation in a number of areas:

1. Understanding of the mission, vision, and history of the university;
2. Understanding of the policies and procedures of the university;
3. Obtaining a basic knowledge of and appreciation for the sponsoring church and how it fits within the larger Christian community;
4. Understanding and proficiency in what it means to be a faculty member of a Christian university;
5. Integration of faith and learning in the various subject areas;
6. Facilitation of effective teaching and learning on the university's various modes of teaching and learning; and
7. Ongoing sharpening of contemporary pedagogical skills requisite for higher Christian education.[22]

2. Moral Qualities

The second challenge concerns "moral qualities" and involves Christian "formation" and "transformation." How can Christian educators partner with God in this formation and transformation to produce the moral qualities that God expects? Christian universities must do so in keeping with Ephesians 2:10: "we are God's handiwork, created in Christ Jesus to do good works." Kang

---

21. Liam Gearon, *Master Class in Religious Education: Transforming Teaching and Learning* (London: Bloomsbury, 2013), 50–59.

22. From the guidelines Africa Nazarene University (ANU) has developed for all new and part-time faculty in order to provide this kind of orientation at least three times per year. ANU has also introduced a PG diploma which requires a full-year's commitment to one's development as a Christian educational professional.

and Parrett see this kind of teaching as "creating space for obedience."[23] Such teaching must lead to setting forth "the will of God," offering God's "gracious intervention" and leading to "profession and practice."[24]

Simmons and McSwain associate spiritual formation with the development of ethical actions that reveal one as "living a Kingdom of God ethic" and "applying love and justice." The training they advocate for ethical formation requires a "study-action-reflection" methodology whereby learners first master content. Then, they do something related to that content. Finally, this needs to be followed up by reflection on the content and what was done related to it in order to better understand and contextualize it.[25]

3. Conscience

Third is the challenge of "conscience." Debeljuh describes conscience as "a judgment on the morality of particular acts"[26] and points out that "formation of our conscience in the truth" requires effort. She says, "We need to make an effort to acquire the necessary moral knowledge in order to be able to do specific things in order to apply these ethical principles to our acts."[27] Our Christian universities need to enable their staff and students to consider these in terms of timing, conforming to moral law, and type of consent. In terms of how conscience relates to timing, one must ask: "Is it antecedent or consequent?" In terms of how the judgment conforms to moral law one considers, "Is it true/right or is it erroneous/false?" Finally, in terms of the type of consent one gives to the judgment: "Is it sure or certain?" "Is it probable?" Or, "Is it doubtful?"[28]

As alternatives to public and secular universities, Christian universities must enable Christian conscience. As Osmer and Schweitzer have observed, even though "the Geneva declaration on children's rights, passed by the League of Nations in 1924, included the rights of being enabled to develop 'spiritually,'" public and secular universities tend to neglect this. Furthermore, "the United Nations' 1989 convention on children's rights includes (in article

---

23. Steve S. Kang and Gary A. Parrett, *Teaching the Faith, Forming the Faithful: A Biblical Vision for Education in the Church* (Downers Grove, IL: IVP Academic, 2009), 268.

24. Kang and Parrett, *Teaching the Faith*, 271–276.

25. Paul D. Simmons and Larry L. McSwain, "Ethical Maturity and Spiritual Formation," in *Becoming Christian: Dimensions of Spiritual Formation*, ed. Bill J. Leonard (Louisville, KY: Westminster John Knox, 1990), 66–71.

26. Patricia Debeljuh, *Ethics: Learning to Live*, trans. and adapted by Catherine Dean (Nairobi: Focus, 2006), 177.

27. Debeljuh, *Ethics*, 182.

28. Debeljuh, 178.

14) the religious freedom of the child." Nevertheless, it is not unusual for public and secular universities to disregard this in the curriculum. For, as Osmer and Schweitzer have noticed, "even these attempts to establish legal rights for the child with respect to religion fall short of establishing a right to religious education and support." Thus, they conclude, "Only if it can be shown that children need educational support in order to take advantage of their religious freedom will it become plausible that they can have a right to religious education and support."[29]

4. Intellectual Function of Knowing

The challenge of the "intellectual function of knowing" comes fourth. This is related to the need to constantly form the conscience in order to help it conform ever more to what is true and good. Christian universities must recognize that gaining moral knowledge cannot be left to chance. Debeljuh suggests at least studying, reading, and learning from the experiences of others as pathways of gaining moral knowledge.[30] Even though the moral knowledge one needs depends on a number of factors, such as personal circumstances, personal capacity, one's work, one's responsibilities, and the environment one is in, there are some specific things that need to be done to form the conscience.

The Church of the Nazarene's International Board of Education and the institutions under its umbrella are committed to educating the whole person. This requires a holistic approach to the teaching–learning process which includes content, competency, character, and context. These four Cs provide the critical areas of outcomes to evaluate teaching and learning. Faculty labor within their contexts to fulfill three familiar objectives in Christian education, producing learning change in these areas:

a. Knowledge, what one knows: the cognitive domain,

b. Attitude, what one feels: the affective domain; and

c. Behavior, what one does: the psychomotor domain.[31]

Frequently these are summarized by three words: "know," "be," and "do." These represent the kind of person the learner should be, what the learner

---

29. Richard R. Osmer and Friedrich Schweitzer, *Religious Education between Modernization and Globalization: New Perspectives on the United States and Germany* (Grand Rapids, MI: Eerdmans, 2003), 261.

30. Debeljuh, *Ethics*, 182–183.

31. Daryll Gordon Stanton, "The Importance of Regular Faculty Reviews," in *Education Leadership: Up One Level*, ed. Amy Crofford, 51. PDF online.

should know, and what the learner should be able to do. Our Christian universities must help their students develop in all these three areas. In their philosophy of education for the Church of the Nazarene in Africa, Kisoi and Stanton apply this to the African context, asking: "What are the features of an education that will help Africa?" They note that "quality is essential." Faculty must not overlook this emphasis on quality in their "haste to educate as many as possible as quickly as possible."[32]

5. Focus of Life

Finally, there is the challenge of a "focus of life." Christian education must be seen as that ministry of the church by which it seeks to communicate its faith and nurture Christlike disciples. In the Church of the Nazarene, the ministry of Christian education is expressed through local church education in numerous nursery schools, primary schools, and secondary schools, as well as higher Christian education in fifty-two colleges, universities, and seminaries. These are located in thirty-five countries on six continents and serve a richly diverse student body offering phenomenal opportunities for the nearly 50,000 students each year who make Nazarene institutions their schools of choice. The International Board of Education (IBOE) serves the Nazarene system of higher education in advocacy, support, evaluation, and networking. This system is resolute in guiding its institutions in shaping Christlike disciples and servant-leaders for lifelong service and global impact.[33]

However, it is important for this focus of life to not be totally removed from the cultural setting. In her consideration of African renaissance, Samantha Chambo recalls as "unfortunate" the early Christian efforts in southern Africa. During the time when her denomination began in Africa it "devalued" many "aspects of African traditional beliefs and culture," labeling them "idolatrous." When "congregants were encouraged to cut all ties" to their "idolatrous" African traditional beliefs and culture, many "chose to disconnect" while others "felt compelled to live in a syncretistic way." Yet "the rich spiritual background already present in African life by God's prevenient grace" could have been utilized as a "vehicle" to convey the gospel.[34]

---

32. Joseph Kisoi and Daryll Stanton, "A Philosophy of Education for the Church of the Nazarene in the Africa Region," *Didache* 12, no. 2 (2013).

33. International Board of Education, "IBOE Schools," http://nazarene.org/resource/iboe-schools (accessed 9 February 2016).

34. Samantha Chambo, "Holiness and the African Renaissance," in *Renovating Holiness*, ed. Josh Broward and Thomas Jay Oord (Nampa, ID: Sacra Sage, 2015), 91.

African Christian Universities' Prospects and the *Lev*
Motivating Spirit

The first prospect for African Christian universities relates to understanding the biblical concept of the *lev* as it connotes the "motivating spirit." Craig Dykstra describes education as "the work of bringing into consciousness the hidden dimensions embedded in and through our actions and relations and institutions, giving these dimensions names, and then helping each other take notice and live in their light." Dykstra particularizes this for Christian educators, noting, "Education in faith presupposes and depends on people's experiences of the Mystery of God." Because this experience takes place in fellowship, Christian education also presupposes and depends on communities whose ways of being make the experience of this "Mystery" possible.[35] But how does this happen? Dykstra suggests it is "through investigation, criticism, interpretation, and care." Christian universities provide "education in faith" which "may help people in a community of faith not only to see and grasp the inner character and hidden nature of the graceful Mystery that sustains their life together but also to experience it more profoundly."[36]

However, when speaking of the formation of character, Dykstra does not equate this with the ethics of secular institutions. Rather, he prefers to use the term "moral education" through which there is means "most fundamentally to become persons who see deeply into the reality of things and who love that reality – over time and across circumstances." Nevertheless, this involves "long, hard, patient formation of our desires; struggle with our fears; learning ways of thinking and speaking that disclose what is true and good; participation in traditional practices . . . and the shaping and testing of fundamental convictions."[37] Dykstra speaks of this happening in a "community of conviction" which is likely to be perceived as "intrinsically antagonistic" in the eyes of secular institutions of higher education. Even Christian higher education is in danger of being corrupted "since secular assumptions govern the structure of the curriculum, contemporary methods of inquiry, and virtually every other important dimension of the educational environment and process."[38]

---

35. Craig Dykstra, *Growing in the Life of Faith: Education and Christian Practices* (Louisville, KY: Geneva Press, 1999), xii.

36. Dykstra, *Growing in the Life of Faith*, xiii.

37. Dykstra, 132.

38. Dykstra, 135.

Choun and Lawson acknowledge that "Christian education does lean on modern educational research even as biblical studies use modern archaeology and other disciplines." Moreover, they concede that "Unfortunately, modern educational research largely belongs to secular scholars." However, they point out an important distinction: "Most Christian educators depend on secular research to explain how students learn ordinary information. Then they draw implications about how people assimilate spiritual truth."[39]

Lawrence Richards notes: "Christians are called to a reality which is at odds with the values and perceptions of our society . . . we continue to affirm the impossible dream of a community of faith which expresses Christ's own kingdom: the enfleshing of Jesus in man's world."[40] As he observes, "a Christian educator whose theology leads him to understand Scripture as a revelation of reality will find in that theology direction both for the educational process he will shape, and for the curriculum he designs." Furthermore, "the content, method, and goal of the educational enterprise will all be theologically determined."[41] Thus, it is essential for Christian educators to understand "how the biblical reality touches the life of the learner and [to design] learning processes that help him or her explore the 'lived meaning' of that truth."[42]

African Christian universities are in a unique position for shaping an African Christian worldview, appropriately framing both the temperament and the practice of the lives of students and staff. With expanded Christian worldviews they can demonstrate Christ's love to those around them. Dean Flemming inquired: "What impact did Paul's Christian conversion have on his worldview?" He concluded that Paul's Jewish worldview and beliefs "were not totally displaced," but were "profoundly" and "permanently transformed."[43] For Flemming, there is at least a fourfold process at work as one interacts with the world around oneself: it includes "affirming, relativizing, confronting and transforming."[44] It is appropriate for our Christian universities to guide our staff and students in affirming aspects of worldviews that visualize genuine knowledge of God as our Creator. Our Christian universities need to lead the

---

39. Robert J. Choun, Jr., and Michael S. Lawson, *Directing Christian Education: The Changing Role of the Christian Education Specialist* (Chicago: Moody, 1992), 16.

40. Lawrence O. Richards, "Experiencing Reality Together: Toward the Impossible Dream," in *Religious Education and Theology*, ed. Norma H. Thompson (Birmingham, AL: Religious Education Press, 1982), 199.

41. Richards, "Experiencing Reality Together," 203–204.

42. Richards, 207.

43. Dean Flemming, *Contextualization in the New Testament: Patterns for Theology and Mission* (Downers Grove, IL: InterVarsity, 2005), 121.

44. Flemming, *Contextualization*, 126.

pursuit of Paul's admonition to the Philippians (4:8) until our staff and students adhere to "whatever is true, whatever is noble, whatever is right, whatever is pure, whatever is lovely, whatever is admirable," "excellent" and "praiseworthy."

Moral Qualities

Second, from the standpoint of *lev* being the "seat" of a person's "moral qualities," the African Christian university can guide learners in exploring ways for the Bible to form and transform others into faithful disciples of Christ. What are our Christian universities exploring as ways to facilitate the formation and transformation of our staff and students into faithful disciples of Christ? As Dykstra points out: "Colleges and universities form students morally most thoroughly and most powerfully through the fundamental patterns of inquiry, learning, and teaching that they practice."[45]

Thomas Groome sees it as "unfortunate" to insinuate that one's "educating must transcend the influence of [one's] own spirituality, thus excluding what should be consciously present to [one] as a prime source of humanizing education." He is "convinced that the lack of a spiritual vision is an Achilles heel of the 'American experiment' in education."[46]

Christian universities are in the position to offer formal Bible survey classes as well as informal study groups which can bring staff and students together to discuss the meaning of biblical texts with openness to the voice of the Holy Spirit so they can receive contemporary understanding of Scripture.[47] Thereafter, these can lead others to respond appropriately to this biblical understanding of life, applying it to service not only in the university but also in the churches and the surrounding community.

Conscience

A third area of prospect concerns the usage of the term *lev* as one's "conscience." Accountability partners, among both staff and students, can provide a challenge to remain "wise in what is good, and innocent in what is evil" because it is God's desire for his people to be holy and blameless, as Paul emphasized to the church in Ephesus (Eph 5:27). At one point, David's life was filled with the

---

45. Dykstra, *Growing in the Life of Faith*, 139.

46. Thomas H. Groome, *Educating for Life: A Spiritual Vision for Every Teacher and Parent* (New York: Crossroad, 1998), 15.

47. Mark A. Maddix and Richard P. Thompson, "The Role of Scripture in Christian Discipleship," *Wesleyan Theological Journal* 46, no. 1 (Fall 2011): 135.

destructive consequences of his choices, as revealed in Psalm 51. His outlook was skewed, his attitudes fatigued. When he looked at himself, he saw failure, regret, disappointment, hopelessness. He was overwhelmed by his sin. So he pleaded for something he did not possess. He knew that he was not able to bring about the necessary change on his own. Notably the verb *yatsar* is not utilized in this psalm, which would imply doing, fashioning, or making. Instead, the verb *bara'* is used. David was not looking for remodeling.[48] The New Testament portrays the heart as the seat of the conscience, as in Romans 2. Paul observed of the Gentiles, "the requirements of the law are written on their hearts, their consciences also bearing witness, and their thoughts sometimes accusing them and at other times even defending them" (Rom 2:15). As Paul desired for the Roman believers, our Christian universities can assure faculty, staff and students learn that "Love must be sincere," and to "Hate what is evil" as well as "cling to what is good" (12:9). Like Paul, our Christian universities can also uphold the principle: "Do not be overcome by evil, but overcome evil with good" (12:21). And we can exhort our staff and students "to be wise about what is good, and innocent about what is evil" (16:19).

As Osmer and Schweitzer perceive, our religious education has to take on "the task of publicly advocating the human importance of religious education against its neglect in the philosophy of education as well as in the practice of education."[49] As they note, "the emerging self" of our young people "is intrinsically related to religious questions in several ways." Thus, our students will "inevitably raise questions that have, at least potentially, a religious meaning." Such religious questions that emerge as they develop are related to:

- Death and dying;
- Self and identity, including a higher "source" of affirmation;
- Morality: what is it? And why be moral in an unjust world?
- Religious pluralism, as personally experienced via media; and
- The idea of God, or a "God representation."[50]

As our staff and students find answers, they will shape their worldview into "something individual, something personal, something that makes sense within the context of their own lives and that appears meaningful in terms of their own personal experience, striving for coherence and unity even if in different ways" than for previous generations.[51] They can encourage one another to

---

48. Skip Moen, "Nearing the End (1)," *Hebrew Word Study: Skip Moen* (blog), 28 December 2014, http://skipmoen.com/2014/12/28/nearing-the-end-1/.

49. Osmer and Schweitzer, *Religious Education*, 260–261.

50. Osmer and Schweitzer, 262–265.

51. Osmer and Schweitzer, 266–268.

remain "attached" to Christ and engaged in his compassionate evangelism while remaining "detached" from those aspects of life which deter one from victorious Christian living.

Intellectual Function of Knowing

Fourth is the prospect in the context of the *lev* relating to the head or the brain as these relate to the "intellectual function of knowing." This is also the context of Paul's prayer for the saints in Ephesus in Ephesians 3:16–19. Christians acquire power through God's Spirit in their "inner being." The Ephesian Christians needed power "together with all the Lord's holy people, to grasp how wide and long and high and deep is the love of Christ," a love that "surpasses knowledge." Everyone has a "spiritual brain," and, as Barbara Bruce observes, "There is no question that mind and body are connected in a single being that has been created for the glory of God. The concept is quintessential to who and whose we are."[52] Thus, Christian education must be rooted in its biblical and theological commitments. Our Christian universities are accountable for their stated missions, which should include being guides to their communities in accepting, in nurturing, and in expressing, through service to the church and the world, a consistent and coherent Christian understanding of life.

The Bible is full of guidance for Christian living. Ronald Chadwick considers a number of key Bible words that help Christian educators focus on the biblical teaching–learning process. Chadwick offers eleven significant Old Testament terms (*alaph, be-en, chah-cham, dah-var, lamath, rah-ah, sah-chal, shah-nan, yah-dag, yah-rah, za-har*). In addition, he provides fourteen New Testament terms (*anangello, dianoigo, didasko, diermeneuo, ektithemi, hodegeo, katekeo, manthano, matheteuo, noutheteo, oikodoomeo, paideuo, paratithemi, suniami*).[53] The use of these terms may be summarized as follows:

Alaph is an Old Testament term which means "cleaving to." It carries the idea of "teaching by exposure or making something so familiar" that one adopts or holds onto it. *Be-en* means "separate." It indicates "differentiating, drawing conclusions, stepping from truth, divining, distinguishing and discriminating." *Chah-cham* means "being intelligent" or "wise." It implies "the ability to use facts in daily experience" as well as "applying doctrine to practical needs." *Dah-*

---

52. Barbara Bruce, *Our Spiritual Brain: Integrating Brain Research and Faith Development* (Nashville, TN: Abingdon, 2002), 19.

53. Ronald P. Chadwick, *Teaching and Learning: An Integrated Approach to Christian Education* (Old Tappan, NJ: Fleming H. Revell, 1982), 186–191.

var means "speak" and implies the use of speech to teach. *Lamath* is "the most common word for teaching" and for "learning." It must "become experienced." It suggests "stimulation to imitation or action." It carries the meaning of becoming "accustomed to something new." It is "subjective assimilation." *Rah-ah* means "see" and implies careful consideration "to the point of seeing a need and making provision" to meet that need. *Sah-chal* means to "show oneself attentive" and suggests looking at, pondering, and considering. It requires one to look close enough to gain insight in order to become "skilled in the subject." *Shah-nan* means to "sharpen" or "whet" the appetite or senses for learning. *Yah-dag* means knowing "by experience or by one's own observation." It is "a highly subjective knowing or taking note of things." *Yah-rah* carries the meaning of casting, throwing, or shooting as well as pointing out or directing someone in a new path. It is directive teaching. A final Old Testament term is *za-har* which indicates "shining" or "illuminating." In addition to "teach" it carries the meaning of "warning."

The first of the fourteen New Testament terms is *anangello* which suggests official reporting, proclaiming, or declaring, as demonstrated in John 16:13. *Dianoigo* is the "process of opening the mind and heart to spiritual truth." Of the eight times it is used in the New Testament, six times refer to God or Christ granting such understanding. *Didasko* is the "most common word for teaching." It focuses on the activity of teaching. *Diermeneuo* means "unfolding" or "opening" spiritual truth and is used in the sense of "translating" and "interpreting," as in Luke 24:27. *Ektithemi* means "setting forth," "expounding," or "explaining" in a logical order, especially in defending doctrines or reciting facts and narratives. It is only used four times in the New Testament. *Hodegeo* means "leading" or "guiding" in order to cause someone to "discover" practical doctrinal truth. *Katekeo* involves giving out information, communicating facts, reporting, or informing. The word "catechism" comes from this term. *Manthano* means learning by practicing, experiencing, or doing rather than through instruction. *Matheteuo* involves making disciples, which includes instruction in loyalty and devotion. This is the word used in Matthew 28:19. *Noutheteo* means "mind-shaping" and involves "training by word of encouragement," such as reproving, warning, or admonishing. *Oikodomeo* means "building" or "edifying," especially in the contexts of spiritual growth and maturity. *Paideuo* is used for giving guidance, instructing, or training. It can also be used in the correcting or disciplining sense, as in child-rearing. *Paratithemi* means placing beside or before, and involves putting something before someone in order that he or she might "mentally grasp it." Finally, *suniami* includes comprehending, gaining insight, or putting facts together "for usefulness and to completely understand." The most significant use is in Ephesians 5:17, where the Ephesians are to develop biblical concepts by putting "together biblical facts and understand God's will for their lives."[54]

Focus of Life

Finally, when applying this biblical concept of the *lev* as a "focus of life," African Christian universities must also function as a community of believers. Deuteronomy 6:5 is one of the places where God declares that his people must love him with all their *lev*. Here, the NIV interprets *levav* as "heart" in the setting of one loving Yahweh, "your" Elohiym, together with all the soul (*nephesh*) and might (*ma'od*). This idea of *lev* is carried over into the New Testament, as in Mark 12:30. When Nicholas Wolterstorff wrote about the Christian college, he described it as "a project of and for the Christian community . . . to share in God's work of renewal by being witness, servant and evidence."[55] Staff and students must not only be guided to come together in spiritual activities in the university setting, but they must also be guided in moving out to reveal personal holiness in all the operations of life.

Proverbs 4:23 urges: "Above all else, guard your heart, for everything you do flows from it," which indicates that the *lev* must be watched over "diligently" more than anything else. John Parsons observes: "This verse is saying that from the heart (*lev*) of a person a 'map' or 'chart' to life is drawn. As the heart is either pure or corrupt, so will be the course of one's life." So, he exhorts, "May God help you guard your heart and walk in the way of the true life."[56] This is consistent with Jesus's warning in John 14:6, "I am the way and the truth and the life: no one comes to the Father except through me."[57]

When responding to the question "Can virtue be taught?," David Tracy addressed aspects of education, character, and the soul, noting: "The life of the mind cannot live alone . . . Rather to think is to converse with the classics; to converse with the classics is to join the community of enquiry of the living and the dead. It is to recognize that we too can and must become part of that

---

54. Chadwick, *Teaching and Learning*, 186–191.

55. Nicholas Wolterstorff, *Educating for Shalom: Essays on Christian Higher Education* (Grand Rapids, MI: Eerdmans, 2004), 7.

56. John J. Parsons, "Keep Thy Heart with All Diligence," *Hebrew for Christians*, accessed 29 November 2015, http://www.hebrew4christians.com/Meditations/Keep_thy_heart/keep_thy_heart.html.

57. "Heart," *Easton's Bible Dictionary* (on Power Bible CD, 2011).

conversation."[58] Nevertheless, as Stephen Toulmin points out, in the context of the university "the term 'theology' cannot be read as the name of a separate discipline which exists alongside, and on a similar basis to, other disciplines." For Toulmin, the "issues of theology exist, and arise, *at the base of* all abstract academic disciplines equally." Thus, for example, "problems in ecology and psychoanalysis can be discussed *theologically*" for their "implications for religious life and experience."[59]

Still, as Roy Zuck has pointed out, students "learn best when teachers have established conditions favorable to the working of the Holy Spirit . . . relevant to their life needs." The "ultimate aim of Christian teaching" is expressed in 2 Timothy 3:17: "so that the servant of God may be thoroughly equipped for every good work." Thus, Christian education intends to move believers to "reach unity in the faith and in the knowledge of the Son of God and become mature, attaining to the whole measure of the fullness of Christ" (Eph 4:13). Paul told the Colossians, "He is the one we proclaim, admonishing and teaching everyone with all wisdom, so that we may present everyone fully mature in Christ" (Col 1:28). As Zuck has observed, "Christian teaching is concerned with spiritual transformation," which requires "spiritual change, with Christ-honoring results in every area" of life and "everyday experiences." Therefore, Christian universities must teach so that students first "come to accept Christ as their personal Savior, and then walk with him, grow in him, know him, and enjoy him."[60]

Conclusion

The application of the Old Testament concept of the *lev* to African Christian universities has been clearly brought out in this paper with specific reference to Africa Nazarene University in Kenya and Southern Africa Nazarene University in Swaziland. The paper notes that while African Christian universities face numerous challenges, they also have unique prospects for providing a holistic approach to higher education. This study has especially drawn on some of J. Barton Payne's observations of the *lev* as a "term that may stand for the

---

58. David Tracy, "Can Virtue Be Taught? Education, Character, and the Soul," in *Theological Perspectives on Christian Formation: A Reader on Theology and Christian Education*, eds. Jeff Astley, Leslie J. Francis, and Colin Crowder (Grand Rapids, MI: Eerdmans, 1996), 388.

59. Stephen Toulmin, "Theology in the Context of the University," in *Theological Perspectives on Christian Formation*, 400–401.

60. Roy B. Zuck, *The Holy Spirit in Your Teaching* (Wheaton, IL: Scripture Press, 1963), 116–120.

whole person." Five important areas of the *lev* as the "whole person" have been applied: the "motivating spirit," the seat of a person's "moral qualities," one's "conscience," the "intellectual function of knowing," and a "focus of life."

In achieving the "motivating spirit," African Christian universities can provide "education in faith" wherein there is means for students to become persons who see deeply into the reality of things and learn ways of thinking and speaking that disclose what is true and good. Christian educators partner with God in formation and transformation to produce the "moral qualities" that God expects. Formation of our "conscience" in the truth requires effort to acquire the necessary moral knowledge while taking a keen interest in application of ethical principles. As regards the "intellectual function of knowing," Christian universities must recognize that gaining moral knowledge should not be left to chance. With regard to the "focus of life" Christian universities must teach so that students first "come to accept Christ as their personal Savior, and then walk with him, grow in him, know him, and enjoy him."[61]

Bibliography

Balema, John. "Christian Higher Education in Africa: Past, Present and Future." *Africa Journal of Evangelical Theology* 24, no. 2 (2005): 153–164.

Benner, Jeff A. "Heart." Hebrew Word Definitions, Ancient Hebrew Research Center. Accessed 9 December 2015. http://www.ancient-hebrew.org/vocabulary_definitions_heart.html.

Bible Hub, "Leb." BibleHub. Accessed 9 December 2015. http://biblehub.com/hebrew/3820.htm.

Brown, Bill. "Top Ten Challenges Christian Students Face in College." *Journal of the Southern Baptist Convention*, 2012. Proceedings held at Cedarville University, March 21–23, 2012 in the CCCU Chief Academic Officers Conference, Nashville, USA.

Brown-Driver-Briggs Hebrew and English Lexicon. Unabridged Electronic Database, 2002, 2003 and 2006 by Biblesoft, Inc. (www.BibleSoft.com). Accessed 25 November 2015.

Bruce, Barbara. *Our Spiritual Brain: Integrating Brain Research and Faith Development*. Nashville, TN: Abingdon, 2002.

Carpenter, Joel, Perry L. Glanzer, and Nicholas S. Lantinga, eds. *Christian Higher Education: A Global Reconnaissance*, Kindle Edition. Grand Rapids: Eerdmans, 2014.

---

61. Zuck, *Holy Spirit in Your Teaching*, 116–120.

Chadwick, Ronald P. *Teaching and Learning: An Integrated Approach to Christian Education*. Old Tappan, NJ: Fleming H. Revell, 1982.

Chambo, Samantha. "Holiness and the African Renaissance." In *Renovating Holiness*, edited by Josh Broward and Thomas Jay Oord, 91. Nampa, ID: Sacra Sage Press, 2015.

Choun, Robert J., Jr., and Michael S. Lawson. *Directing Christian Education: The Changing Role of the Christian Education Specialist*. Chicago, IL: Moody, 1992.

Debeljuh, Patricia. *Ethics: Learning to Live*. Translated and adapted by Catherine Dean. Nairobi: Focus Publishers, 2006.

Dykstra, Craig. *Growing in the Life of Faith: Education and Christian Practices*. Louisville, KY: Geneva Press, 1999.

Easton's Bible Dictionary. "Heart" on the Power Bible CD, 2011.

Flemming, Dean. *Contextualization in the New Testament: Patterns for Theology and Mission*. Downers Grove, IL: InterVarsity, 2005.

Gearon, Liam. *MasterClass in Religious Education: Transforming Teaching and Learning*. London: Bloomsbury, 2013.

Groome, Thomas H. *Educating for Life: A Spiritual Vision for Every Teacher and Parent*. New York: Crossroad, 1998.

International Board of Education. "IBOE Schools." Accessed February 9, 2016. http://nazarene.org/resource/iboe-schools.

Kang, S. Steve and Gary A. Parrett. *Teaching the Faith, Forming the Faithful: A Biblical Vision for Education in the Church*. Downers Grove, IL: IVP Academic, 2009.

Kisoi, Joseph, and Daryll G. Stanton. "A Philosophy of Education for the Church of the Nazarene in the Africa Region." *Didache* 12, no. 2 (January 2013): 1–6.

Maddix, Mark A., and Richard P. Thompson. "The Role of Scripture in Christian Discipleship." *Wesleyan Theological Journal* 46, no. 1 (Spring 2011): 134–149.

McSwain, Larry L., and Paul D. Simmons. "Ethical Maturity and Spiritual Formation." In *Becoming Christian: Dimensions of Spiritual Formation*, edited by Bill J. Leonard, 59–72. Louisville, KY: Westminster John Knox, 1990.

Menken, Maarten J. J., and Steve Moyise, eds. *The New Testament and the Scriptures of Israel*. New York: T & T Clark, 2007.

Moen, Skip. "Nearing the End (1)." *Hebrew Word Study* (blog). Posted on 28 December 2014. http://skipmoen.com/2014/12/28/nearing-the-end-1/.

———. "Highway 60 from Be'er Sheva to Jerusalem." *Hebrew Word Study* (blog). Posted on 29 June 2013. http://skipmoen.com/2013/06/29/highway-60-from-beer-sheva-to-jerusalem.

Osmer, Richard R., and Friedrich Schweitzer. *Religious Education between Modernization and Globalization: New Perspectives on the United States and Germany*. Grand Rapids, MI: Eerdmans, 2003.

Parsons, John J. "Keep Thy Heart with All Diligence." *Hebrew for Christians*. Accessed 29 November 2015. http://www.hebrew4christians.com/Meditations/Keep_thy_heart.html.

———. "*Lev Tahor.*" Accessed 29 November 2015. http://www.hebrew4christians.com/Meditations/Lev_Tahor/lev_tahor.html.

Payne, J. Barton. *The Theology of the Older Testament*. Grand Rapids: Zondervan, 1962.

Pazmino, Robert W. *Foundational Issues in Christian Education*. Grand Rapids, MI: Baker, 1988.

Reeves, Rodney. *Spirituality According to Paul: Imitating the Apostle of Christ*. Downers Grove, IL: IVP Academic, 2011.

Richards, Lawrence O. "Experiencing Reality Together: Toward the Impossible Dream." In *Religious Education and Theology*, edited by Norma H. Thompson, 198–217. Birmingham, AL: Religious Education Press, 1982.

Stanton, Daryll Gordon. "The Importance of Regular Faculty Reviews." In *Education Leadership: Up One Level*, edited by Amy Crofford, 51. https://www.whdl.org/sites/default/files/publications/Education%20Leadership%20-%20Up%20One%20Level%20-%20May%202016.pdf.

———. "The Role of the Church in the Rehabilitation of the Lev." *Didache* 13, no. 2 (January 2014): 1–11.

Strong's Hebrew Dictionary. "Leb," 03820 on Power BibleCD, 2011.

Thayer, Joseph Henry. "Kardia." In *Thayer's Greek-English Lexicon of the New Testament*. Grand Rapids, MI: Associated Publishers and Authors, 1889.

Thomas, Robert L. "Leb." In *New American Standard Exhaustive Concordance of the Bible/Hebrew-Aramaic and Greek Dictionaries*. Lockman Foundation at Lockman.org, 1981.

Toulmin, Stephen. "Theology in the Context of the University." In *Theological Perspectives on Christian Formation: A Reader on Theology and Christian Education*, edited by Jeff Astley, Leslie J. Francis and Colin Crowder, 400–401. Grand Rapids, MI: Eerdmans, 1996.

Tracy, David. "Can Virtue Be Taught: Education, Character and the Soul." In *Theological Perspectives on Christian Formation: A Reader on Theology and Christian Education*, edited by Jeff Astley, Leslie J. Francis and Colin Crowder, 388. Grand Rapids, MI: Eerdmans, 1996.

Van der Ven, Johannes A. *Formation of the Moral Self*. Grand Rapids, MI: Eerdmans, 1998.

Van Der Walt, B. J. "The Challenges of Christian Higher Education on the African Continent in the Twenty-First Century." *Christian Higher Education* 1, no. 2 (2002): 195–227.

Van Dyke, John. *The Craft of Christian Teaching: A Classroom Journey*. Sioux Center, IA: Dordt Press, 2000.

Vikner, David W. "Challenges to Christian Higher Education in Asia." *Christian Higher Education* 2, no. 1 (2003): 1–13.

Wolterstorff, Nicholas. *Educating for Shalom: Essays on Christian Higher Education*. Grand Rapids, MI: Eerdmans, 2004.

Zuck, Roy B. *The Holy Spirit in Your Teaching*. Wheaton, IL: Scripture Press, 1963.

12

A New Model of Theological Training in Nairobi: Tyrannus Hall at the Nairobi Chapel

David Bawks
Minister, Tyrannus Hall Training Ministry, Nairobi Chapel, Nairobi, Kenya

Abstract

Theological education is a tremendous resource to advance the work of the church through preparing leaders and making disciples. From the early days of church history, the church has recognized that training in reading and interpreting the Bible, preaching, and ministry skills is an important prerequisite to serving as a pastor or church leader. Over the years, the form of this training has shifted, and currently a high percentage of theological education takes place in formal, degree-granting institutions. Degrees such as a bachelor of divinity, a master of divinity, and a doctor of ministry are highly valued in many churches. Nairobi currently boasts many premier institutions of theological higher learning, such as Daystar University, Africa International University, International Leadership University, and St Paul's University. Many of these institutions have been granted university status by the government, while others operate as diploma colleges. Nairobi Chapel has entered this sphere of theological education by launching a lay training institute called Tyrannus Hall. Tyrannus Hall, named after the building in Ephesus used by the apostle Paul to engage new believers in matters of faith in Acts 19, is seeking to train believers for both traditional ministry, such as pastoring, and marketplace discipleship in all sectors of society. This paper examines the philosophical underpinnings of Tyrannus Hall, arguing that new models of theological training are necessary to advance the kingdom of God and meet the current needs of the church in Kenya. This new training model is not meant to replace or eliminate the previous models, but seeks to add needed capacity and correct some of the shortcomings of formal education as it has traditionally been done. Theological training must be affordable, sustainable, relevant, and focused on discipleship.

Key words: theological education, Nairobi, Nairobi Chapel, Tyrannus Hall, education models.

Introduction

Theological education is both as old as the church and as recent as the most modern innovation. The church in Kenya has seen the necessity of investing in theological education, resulting in a wide range of available programs from informal training at the grassroots level up to the PhD. Churches are taking responsibility for the development of those who will spearhead their future networks and thus are seeking to improve the effectiveness of theological training. Nairobi Chapel has joined this movement in revitalizing the church through developing leaders who are trained, gifted, called, and proven for work. Tyrannus Hall, a new ministry training school of Nairobi Chapel, was instituted to accelerate and structure this training process. This paper explores the biblical basis for theological education, the current status of theological education in Nairobi, selected pioneering educational models, and new trends in educational technology in order to argue that new models like Tyrannus Hall are necessary to face the new challenges facing the Kenyan church.

Biblical Basis for Theological Education

As Christians, we have a very specific foundation for teaching. Before Christ ascended into heaven, he commanded his disciples, "Go therefore and make disciples of all nations, baptizing them in the name of the Father and of the Son and of the Holy Spirit, teaching them to observe all that I have commanded you" (Matt 28:19–20 ESV). Thus, teaching is a core component of our mandate as believers. Writing to Titus, Paul commands him to "teach what accords with sound doctrine" (Titus 2:1 ESV). Paul goes on to describe such teaching as showing "integrity, dignity, and sound speech that cannot be condemned, so that an opponent may be put to shame, having nothing evil to say about us" (Titus 2:7–8 ESV).

The goal of Christian teaching should be changed lives, lives that are growing closer to and becoming more like Christ. This requires excellence and a focus on God in all things: "whatever you do, do all to the glory of God" (1 Cor 10:31 ESV). In Romans, Paul discusses the principle of transformation: "Do not be conformed to this world, but be transformed by the renewal of your mind, that by testing you may discern what is the will of God, what is good and acceptable and perfect" (Rom 12:2 ESV). Education is an important part of this process.

Theological education is tied to a larger question: Who does ministry in the church? In Ephesians 4:11 Paul writes that God has given specific roles to the church: apostle, prophet, evangelist, pastor, and teacher. These are significant roles, with major gifts that must be exercised responsibly. The point of these special roles and positions in the church is not primarily to do acts of service. The purpose of these gifts is to equip God's people for acts of service – which requires recruiting, training, mobilizing, and empowering.

We must always remember that theological education points to a greater goal. As Ian Markham reminds us, "Theological education is not an end in itself, but a means to an end. We educate to transform the world; we educate to make a difference to congregations; we educate to enable mission that brings the gospel of our Lord Jesus to the world."[1] For those of us who have been given the gift of theological training, teaching is an essential component of the Christian life and comes with great responsibility. James writes, "Not many of you should become teachers, my brothers, for you know that we who teach will be judged with greater strictness" (Jas 3:1 ESV). Teaching is an undertaking that must be taken seriously.

The Church and Theological Education in Africa

In Nairobi, as indeed throughout Africa, theological education has been integrally tied to evangelism and missions. The rapid growth of the Christian church in Africa since 1900 has been accompanied by growth in theological training institutions, from informal church training programs up to PhD level. Peter Nyende writes that "the hundreds of Theological Institutions in Africa (including university Religious Studies Departments and Faculties of

---

1. Ian Markham, "Theological Education in the Twenty-First Century," *Anglican Theological Review* 92, no. 1 (2010): 165.

Theology) represent an appetite in Africa to have her clergy and church workers theologically educated or trained."[2] Many churches value highly degrees such as a bachelor of divinity, a master of divinity, or a doctor of ministry. James Amanze observes that "[t]heological institutions have become the backbone of Christian evangelism throughout Africa."[3] In addition to founding many colleges, some as joint ventures between different denominations, a key development has been "the creation of Associations of Theological Institutions in much of Africa whose objective is to come up with relevant theology for the African churches."[4] These developments are encouraging, but tremendous work still remains to meet the demand for theological education.

Along with the encouraging developments, more troubling features of theological education have been observed. Significant weaknesses have been exposed in many institutions of African theological education, especially within the curriculum utilized. Relevant and impactful theological education in Africa must employ a curriculum that is informed by the context of the training. J. Kwabena Asamoah-Gyadu writes: "The challenges arising out of new developments within religion and Christianity invites us to re-examine the traditional methods of education through the existing curricula of Biblical Studies, History and Mission, Pastoral Care and Counseling, Comparative Religion and Ethics and Philosophy. The re-examining must be conducted against the backdrop of the growth in African Christian presence both on the continent and in the West."[5]

Much of the training that occurs at these theological institutions is valuable and applicable, but questions have been raised about the underlying philosophy and influence on the curriculum used in these schools. Focusing on central and southern Africa during the colonial area through to independence (1960s), James Amanze notes several weaknesses in theological education, including

---

2. Peter Nyende, "Ethnic Studies: An Urgent Need in Theological Education in Africa," *International Review of Mission* 98, no. 388 (April 2009): 132.

3. James N. Amanze, "Paradigm Shift in Theological Education in Southern and Central Africa and Its Relevance to Ministerial Formation," *International Review of Mission* 98, no. 388 (April 2009): 122.

4. Amanze, "Paradigm Shift," 123.

5. J. Kwabena (Johnson Kwabena) Asamoah-Gyadu, "'Called to Make a Difference': Theological Education and a Mission in Twenty-First Century Africa," *Ogbomoso Journal of Theology* 15, no. 2 (2010): 2.

male dominance, opposition to African culture, and an overly Western traditional curriculum.[6] He gives the background of this situation:

> Essentially, theological education was an exact replica of the curriculum which was dominant in the mother churches overseas. Because of the missionaries' emphasis on European and American oriented theology, theological institutions during the colonial period and immediately after ended up producing Eurocentric theology which was out of touch with the African reality. The result was that much of the theology produced at this period was divorced from the aspirations and realities of African life and, therefore, irrelevant to the church in Africa.[7]

The gaps highlighted above are significant and undermine the value of such education. Fortunately, at least in some regions and schools, great strides have been taken in recent years to improve the curriculum. Amanze charts improvements in feminist theology, the HIV/AIDs crisis, growth in democratization, preservation of the environment, and development.[8] Nyende surveys a number of theological institutions across Africa and concludes that "in principle, theological institutions in Africa are striving, in the TE [theological education] they offer, to address Africa's context. Theological institutions which offer degrees and higher studies that do not address themselves in their curriculum to the African context would be the exception."[9] However, much still remains to be done. Nyende reminds us that "curriculum revision is a necessity in view of the constant movement and ever-evolving contexts."[10] This work is an ongoing task that can be improved but never completed.

---

6. Amanze, "Paradigm Shift," 123–124. He further explains, "The curriculum was dominated by biblical studies with emphasis on the literature of the Old and New Testament, biblical theology and biblical interpretation. Apart from biblical studies, a great deal of emphasis was placed on church doctrines covering much of the patristic period, scholastic theology, theology of the Reformation, history of Christian mission, sacramental theology, the planting of the churches in Africa, homiletics, Christian ethics, pastoral studies, the liturgy and, in some instances, other world religions such as Islam. Little attention, if any, was paid to cultural studies, gender issues, the environment, socio-economic development, ecumenical studies, globalization, and the like" (124).

7. Amanze, "Paradigm Shift."

8. Amanze, 126–130.

9. Nyende, "Ethnic Studies," 137. He does highlight one particular gap in all the institutions he analyzed, namely, a lack of ethnic studies.

10. Nyende, "Ethnic Studies," 137.

Technology and Other Changes in Education

Tremendous changes have been taking place in the field of education worldwide. The rising cost of university education has caused many to question the value and structure of the typical university. At the same time, the rise of the Internet, mobile phones, and other technological advances have begun to make their mark on education. Students have become aware of the increasing educational options available to them, and this is changing their expectations of an educational experience. The Online Computer Library Center (OCLC) report on education, entitled *At a Tipping Point*, notes, "We are tipping from the age of students as directed learners to an era of students as empowered education consumers and eager education evaluators."[11] Traditional schools must ensure they provide value for what they charge, or risk being left behind.

One change currently taking place in the educational arena is the rise of massive open online courses, known as MOOCs. OCLC calls it "perhaps the most radical alternative to traditional education in 200 years."[12] Premier schools such as Harvard and the Massachusetts Institute of Technology have put many of their courses online, at no cost. The primary limitation is that these free courses do not offer validated credits, only the learning opportunity itself. Currently, some of these changes are being felt especially strongly in the West, but ripple effects are moving across the world, and are reaching African educators. As Amanze highlights, "There is a growing awareness in theological circles that we live today in an era of global communications, Internet, information superhighways and intercontinental travel to the extent that the world is conceived as a 'global village.'"[13] Technology continues to develop at a dizzying rate and affords tremendous potential for educational advancement. Especially as the Internet continues to expand and reach into all aspects of society, teaching will likely be increasingly online.

New Educational Models

Theological education today must incorporate the biblical imperatives of ministry, the cultural situation, and the technological changes currently taking place. J. Kwabena Asamoah-Gyadu argues, "most of the time the gap between

---

11. Cathy De Rosa et al., *At a Tipping Point: Education, Learning and Libraries: A Report to the OCLC Membership* (Dublin, OH: Online Computer Library Center [OCLC], 2014), 4, http://www.oclc.org/content/dam/oclc/reports/tipping-point/215133-tipping-point.pdf.
12. De Rosa et al., *At a Tipping Point*, 9.
13. Amanze, "Paradigm Shift," 126.

what is presented in the classroom and the challenges faced by students is simply too wide for theology to make any impact on society."[14] This gap is a significant weakness, a huge liability that must be addressed by anyone doing theological education. Fortunately, many have risen to the challenge and formed new structures and models of training.

New education models can take a myriad of forms and unique aspects. As Donn Morgan writes, "there has been a blurring of the definition of theological education. Some of which has been intentional. 'Theological education' no longer refers to seminary education alone, but to efforts on the part of the whole church to learn from its rich traditions."[15] Asamoah-Gyadu argues "for a new form of theological curriculum that enables theological institutions to turn out students who have a more prophetic ministry within the context of the Protestant principle of the 'Priesthood of all Believers.'"[16] This prophetic ministry would build on a strong biblical and theological foundation to speak into the current realities of life across Africa.

Colin Smith, formerly of Carlile College in Nairobi, points out the need to engage urban as well as suburban and rural settings: "within Nairobi, as with many other cities, the most renowned theological institutions are inevitably situated within the city's affluent suburbs and its peri-urban hinterland."[17] He goes on to write, "While much theological education in Africa rightly seeks to engage with the context of African tradition and the traditional values, cosmology, and belief systems of rural communities there remains a gap in the theological process if those at the socio-economic margins of rapidly expanding urban societies find their voices and experiences are unheard in the process of theological education."[18] Relevant theological education, in Nairobi and elsewhere, must continue to evaluate all aspects of the culture and context to ensure its training is appropriate for the needs and outcome of the local church.

Other teaching models, such as Theological Education by Extension, have gained credibility and support in recent years. These programs offer similar content to the full-time residential models of theological education but allow for distance learning, online learning, and mixed models that include intensive periods of classroom instruction with personal study between these periods.

---

14. Asamoah-Gyadu, "Called to Make a Difference," 5.

15. Donn F. Morgan, "As Through a Glass Darkly: Defining Theological Education in the Twenty-First Century," *Anglican Theological Review* 90, no. 2 (2008): 257.

16. Asamoah-Gyadu, "Called to Make a Difference," 13.

17. Colin Smith, "De-Suburbanising Theological Education in Nairobi," *Ministerial Formation* 108 (January 2007): 17.

18. Smith, "De-Suburbanising Theological Education in Nairobi," 17.

Some are offered by correspondence, others through workbooks, and some are completely online. Kinsler writes, "There is no question that TEE and Diversified Theological Education offer enormous possibilities for widespread programs of theological education, now that alternatives to the schooling model have attained recognition and accreditation within the mainstream."[19] He goes on to describe one new education program taking place in the United States:

> An even more radical expression of alternative theological education is called Word and World. It has emerged in the last five years as a movement among theologically oriented social activists to bring together the seminary, the sanctuary, and the street in ways that are "radically biblical and biblically radical." Many of those who have given birth to this movement have experienced or even continue to teach in traditional seminaries, but they acknowledge the inadequacy of these institutions to generate commitment to and skills for justice and peace work. The new model offers one or two one-week "schools" each year, modeled on Dietrich Bonhoeffer's underground seminary (Finkenwald), anti-war Bible-study weekends with William Stringfellow and Daniel Berrigan, the Freedom Schools of the civil rights movement, base communities animated by liberation theology, and women-church experiments and other movements for gender justice and inclusion.[20]

Such creative alternatives tremendously boost the scope, reach, and impact of theological education. These alternative models can reduce the cost, time commitment, and admission requirements – educating many students left behind by previous structures of education. Kinsler argues that these alternative models should even be elevated above older models, to expand theological education:

> Historically, theological institutions have tried to compete in resources and prestige with other institutions of higher learning, which is the model that 19th Century missionaries took with them to the far corners of the world. It may now be time to reconsider that model, however successful it may have been, and prioritize an emerging model of Diversified Theological Education that

---

19. Ross Kinsler, "Doing Ministry for a Change? Theological Education for the Twenty-First Century," *Ministerial Formation* 108 (January 2007): 12.
20. Kinsler, "Doing Ministry for a Change?," 12–13.

works – at all levels – with the marginalized peoples of all our countries and to commit ourselves to Sabbath-Jubilee spirituality in the struggle for the other world that God makes possible.[21]

Theological Education in Nairobi Today

The number of universities and schools of higher learning have exploded in Nairobi over the past several years. In March 2016, the website of the Kenyan Commission for University Education (CUE) listed seventy registered institutions, including constituent colleges and those with letters of interim authority. Theological institutions have also greatly increased. Of the total number listed by CUE, seventeen were chartered private universities, and many of these were premier theological institutions, such as Daystar University, Africa International University, St Paul's University, and Africa Nazarene University.[22] Eleven private universities were chartered between 2006 and 2013.[23] Many other smaller Bible or mission colleges also operate, offering certificates and diplomas. Students come from all over Africa to study in Nairobi. Even with this growth in higher education, there is still a huge unmet need, as the number of students finishing high school greatly outpaces the number of available slots in tertiary institutions.

While some schools are doing well, financial challenges have ensnared many Christian institutions of higher learning, including Africa International University, the International Leadership University, and Carlile College. Scholarship funding has dropped significantly, especially following the global economic recession of 2008. For many schools, costs have also gone up, making it difficult to pay staff and recruit students. Over-reliance on outside funding has become unsustainable, and thus schools are scrambling to raise tuition fees and find alternative sources of income. Government regulations

---

21. Kinsler, "Doing Ministry for a Change?" The following quote explains what Kinsler means by "the other world": "Our world is being run by a complex convergence of corporate economic globalization, U.S. imperialism bent on policing and controlling the countries and resources of the world, and increasing concentration of wealth among the Group of Seven/Eight – with concomitant intensification of poverty in the South, with terrible physical and spiritual consequences for both poor and rich, with the emergence of what has been called global Apartheid. The good news is that there is an increasing clamor for alternatives, an insistence that 'Another World Is Possible!' While the world we know is ruled from the top-down, by the rich and powerful, this other world is emerging from the bottom, among the poor and weak" (13).

22. Commission for University Education (CUE), "Accredited Universities in Kenya," November 2015, http://www.cue.or.ke/images/phocadownload/Accredited_Universities_Kenya_Nov2015.pdf.

23. CUE, "Accredited Universities in Kenya."

and requirements for higher institutions in Kenya are also a constraint on the educational systems and structures, especially for Christian institutions. This has led many schools to restructure their cost schedules and recruitment procedures. For some of these schools, this combination of factors has led to a reduced theology department with dropping student intakes even as other subject areas, such as business, IT, or education, grow in student numbers.

Tyrannus Hall

Nairobi Chapel, located on Ngong Road near the Nairobi Showground, is one of the major and trendsetting churches of Nairobi. The full history of Nairobi Chapel extends back even before Kenya achieved independence, but traces its current story to 1989 when the Nairobi Baptist Church sent Pastor Oscar Muriu and several families to help grow the church. This growth was so successful that they have since divided into a number of daughter churches and planted other churches all over Nairobi, Kenya, and Africa. Another defining feature of Nairobi Chapel is its intentional leadership development, including a complex leadership training process. This training process is an intensive, multi-year program incorporating the following steps: intern, pastoral trainee, ministry director, pastor, associate pastor, and finally senior pastor. In the past, this sometimes included studying on a master's program and spending time overseas to gain cross-cultural ministry experience.

Nairobi Chapel entered the sphere of adult theological education by launching a lay training institute called Tyrannus Hall in May 2015. This enterprise is best understood within the context and against the background of the larger church. The mission statement of Nairobi Chapel is "growing D.E.E.P. to reach W.I.D.E." These are acronyms which stand for the following:

Daily devotions	Witness (to one million people)
E-groups (small groups)	Impact (6 sectors of society)
Engagement in ministry/service	Disciple (100,000 people)
Pulpit (preaching)	Establish (300 churches)[24]

Thus, Nairobi Chapel seeks to maintain a balance between reaching out and developing within. The first four characteristics, summarized by "Deep," are the internal elements which provide spiritual discipline for those within the church. The next four, "Wide," are the means by which the church reaches

---

24. "Our Mission," Nairobi Chapel, 2016, http://nairobichapel.net/about-us/our-mission/.

out to evangelize and bring in others. The process of achieving this mission is shown in Figure 12.1, called the "Transformational Track," or "T-Track."[25]

NAIROBI CHAPEL TRANSFORMATION TRACK

[Diagram: The Transformational Track showing the progression through church involvement]

- **5 WOWS**: Welcome, Worship, Fellowship (Sambaza Time), Sermon, Post Service Fellowship
- **1ST SERVICE** — I WILL BE BACK — *Come Get to Know Us* — **KARIBU & RUDI**
- **REGULAR ATTENDEE** — THIS IS MY CHURCH
- **PLUG-IN**: God, Community, Church, Destiny
- **OUTREACH & EVENTS** — *Come Worship with Us* — **REACH** — **CONNECT** — *Come Grow with Us*
- **NETWORKS**: EOBO (EACH ONE BRING ONE)
  - **W** Witness to 1,000,000 people
  - **I** Impact the 6 sectors of society
  - **D** Disciple 100,000 people
  - **E** Establish 300 church plants
- **I'M IN**
- **DEEP**:
  - **D** Daily devotions
  - **E** E-groups
  - **E** Engagements
  - **P** Pulpit
- **eGROUPS** — THIS IS MY FAMILY
- **6 SECTORS OF SOCIETY**: Church & Religion, Education & Family, Business & Commerce, Arts & Media, Science & Medicine, Politics & Governance
- **SEND** — **GROW** — *Come Lead among Us*
- **FRONTLINE ENGAGEMENTS** — HERE I AM SEND ME — *Rise to Your Calling* — **TYRANNUS HALL**
- **SHEPHERD LEADERS** — I'M RESPONSIBLE FOR OTHERS
- **BIG 5**: Word, Prayer, Fellowship, Service, Evangelism
- **GO YE THEREFORE**

Figure 12.1: The "Transformational Track"

The process of personal growth at Nairobi Chapel follows a progression from being invited to church, attending your first service, becoming a regular attendee, going through a ten-week discipleship program called "Plug-In,"[26] joining an "e-group" (mid-week small group), and going through a further discipleship program involving the "Big 5" (Word, prayer, fellowship, service, and evangelism). At this point, members are invited to positions of leadership and are considered to be the "shepherd leaders" of the church. The only

---

25. "T-Track," Nairobi Chapel, 2016, http://nairobichapel.net/adult-church/t-track/.

26. "Plug-In" is a ten-week program which uses the *Mizizi* book, written by Muvuno pastor MuriithiWanjau – a "course that combines typical learning assignments following a workbook with experiential practical learning activities" (Muriithi Wanjau, *Mizizi: Growing Deeper in Your Faith* [Nairobi: Clear Vision Media, 2005], 137). This is an intensive program that integrates a number of elements, and it has been chosen as the means by which attendees can become members. Mizizi bills itself as an "exciting church-based discipleship model that is designed to help people into radical followers of Jesus" (137).

remaining point of growth is to become a frontline engager, which could refer to any number of ministries in the areas of marketplace discipleship, social justice, missions, and more. Tyrannus Hall provides the training expected to reach this level and impact the six sectors of society listed in the "T-Track" diagram. Note that this track is not a perfect model of everyone's progression – people enter at different levels or skip various steps – but it is meant to reflect the general pattern of Christian growth at the church.

Tyrannus Hall, named after the building in Ephesus used by the apostle Paul to engage new believers in matters of faith in Acts 19, is seeking to train believers both for traditional ministry, such as pastoring, and marketplace discipleship in all sectors of society. In the development of Tyrannus Hall, gaps were identified in the growth process of a church member. The leadership of Nairobi Chapel realized that listening to Sunday sermons and participation in small groups are not enough to grow members fully. Staff members returning from theology school weren't always well prepared for ministry, but sometimes were better trained for academics. Additionally, as the staff team grew, sending staff members to theology school became too expensive.

Tyrannus Hall has adopted the following mission statement: "Tyrannus Hall trains and equips people in faith, skills, and character for Christ-like living."[27] The training focuses on three areas: (1) the cognitive, growing people's understanding of faith, the kingdom of God, and the relevant subject matter; (2) practical skills, learning to be able to do something; and (3) character, living with integrity, humility, holiness, and other features of a victorious Christian life. Tyrannus Hall training aims to be *affordable, sustainable, relevant*, and *focused on discipleship*.

The lay training courses of Tyrannus Hall are intended to be accessible in terms of cost, location, and duration to those who would never ordinarily attend a Bible college or the theology courses offered at a university. Some courses are offered on Sunday morning, and others on evenings during the week. Most courses are ten weeks long, while some are shorter – for example, six weeks long. These courses are especially focused on affordability: for example, the ten-week courses offered in February 2016 cost 5,000 Kenyan shillings (around 50 USD at that time) per course, and the six-week course cost 3,500 Kenyan shillings (around 35 USD). Courses offered in January 2017 maintained the same pricing. This is a fraction of the cost of a course at most alternative theological colleges or universities in Nairobi. If members of the

---

27. "Tyrannus Hall," Nairobi Chapel, 2016, http://nairobichapel.net/tyrannus-hall/.

church are not able to attend traditional theological education, the church should *bring theological education to them.*

The lay training courses include the following: Financial Stewardship, Discovering and Fulfilling Your Purpose, Prayer, Navigating Biblical Texts, Navigating the New Testament, Exploiting 21st-Century Leadership Theories, and Pursing Justice. The selection of topics is made through a discussion between the leadership committee of Tyrannus Hall and interested volunteer facilitators, taking into account preferences expressed by church members. While some of these courses would not be out of place in a formal theological institution, others would be more difficult to find. These topics are also more responsive to the needs of the church body, which are expressed through congregational surveys. As there is no formal validating structure, the flexibility in both course content and structure is very broad. Tyrannus Hall courses are unique because, unlike most of the formal theological training opportunities in Nairobi, they take place within the context of a local church body. This allows for a closer alignment with practical ministry on the ground.

In addition to the lay training courses geared toward members of the congregation, departments are being developed at Tyrannus Hall in areas such as leadership, youth ministry, children's ministry, leading worship, and sound in worship (technical aspects of sound engineering and production). The background to this is that Nairobi Chapel currently has a strong internship program, with over 500 students having graduated over the last twenty-five years. Going by the name "Kinara," this internship is a one- or two-year program that requires classes during the week, reading, ministry reports, and hands-on experience in the assigned ministry department. Tyrannus Hall is now forming an umbrella structure for all of the training ministries of Nairobi Chapel, and will provide structure and a more developed curriculum process for those coming to be trained within the ministry departments of the church. Another major training arm of Nairobi Chapel is the church-planting school, which trains pastors to lead churches across Africa and the world.

The ministry training described above would resemble formal training in some ways, with the advantage of weekly ministry assignments within an active church body. For example, someone entering the program for children's ministry would go through a one- or two-year training course that included theory classes but also ministry projects and participation within the children's team at Nairobi Chapel. Going through this program would not require a participant to find a practical application for the classes, as the two aspects would already be closely coordinated. Upon completing this program, the participant would already have extensive experience working in a children's ministry, unlike in some formal degree programs. As so aptly put by Asamoah-Gyadu, "The question that confronts theological education today . . . is how to restructure Christian theological training so that it takes care of the experiential aspects of ministry."[28] Tyrannus Hall is seeking to answer this question and provide a sustainable model for ministry training that will grow and strengthen the church in Nairobi. This training model is not meant to eliminate models like degree programs, but seeks to overcome some of the shortcomings of a degree or diploma program as it has traditionally been done.

Limitations of Tyrannus Hall

Tyrannus Hall is not a perfect solution to the challenge of theological training, and it suffers from various weaknesses and limitations. For those who require accredited programs, Tyrannus Hall will not serve them well. Formal, government-recognized programs have the advantage of clear, documented standards and a longer history. Courses at Tyrannus Hall will have to develop their own value and reputation over time, through the outcomes and experience of those who go through the program. Tyrannus Hall doesn't have all the resources of a full university – a well-stocked library of books, access to journals, study areas, and so on. Each model must be recognized for what it can and cannot do; Tyrannus Hall will not replace all university training in Kenya, but it serves a specific role for a specific target group.

Another weakness of Tyrannus Hall is that it is highly volunteer-reliant. If well-qualified people are not available to facilitate, classes are also not available. Certain subjects will end up being harder to offer than others, depending on the expertise of the volunteers available at Nairobi Chapel. As Tyrannus Hall becomes larger and more established, expenses will also rise and eventually more paid staff will be necessary. This has the potential to take Tyrannus Hall down the same road of financial pressure that other institutions have traveled. For it to succeed and realize its larger goals, great care must be taken to maintain the mission and distinctiveness of Tyrannus Hall.

Way Forward

Theological education has many stakeholders. Churches should be the custodians of theological education and must be actively engaged throughout the entire education process. Universities must continually evaluate their

---

28. Asamoah-Gyadu, "Called to Make a Difference," 13.

curricula, structures, and training to ensure their objectives are being met. Churches and universities should also seek opportunities for collaboration and partnership, and to see how they can each make up for the weaknesses and limitations of the other. Churches can provide ministry engagements for students, and universities, and other training institutes can provide resources, curriculum, trained staff, and venues that churches may lack.

Relationships are absolutely central to theological education. Education is not primarily about the accumulation of credit hours and degrees, or the decimal points of a grade point average, but about development as people. This development involves the growth of character, communication, and personality. Another core value of education is critical thinking. Many Christians accept whatever their parents, church, or tradition tells them to believe, resulting in incoherent and illogical concepts of God, ministry, and the nature of the Christian life. Meaningful theological education must challenge these often untested and ill-founded assumptions. In the evangelical tradition, the Bible is hailed as the source and foundation of all doctrine and practice, but many have very little idea of what the Bible actually says, much less what it actually means. Solid training must provide a strong biblical foundation and skills for interpreting and responsibly applying the Bible.

How should the effectiveness of theological training be measured? Is it based on the employability of graduates? The spiritual growth of the participants? Or the impact made on the surrounding society? Ian Markham suggests that, instead of merely measuring the growth or financial capacity of a particular school or program, "Successful leadership should be judged by the impact made on the wider denomination" (such as the Episcopal Church, the context he is focusing on).[29] More research should be done on the effectiveness of university education, seminary training, TEE, and models like Tyrannus Hall. Such research can provide a more detailed way forward, and highlight the features that are most effective within each educational approach. Most likely, the theological education of the future will take on a hybrid nature, incorporating different aspects of different programs in use today, but the "which and how" aspects need to be further studied and explored.

Within theological education in the United States, Markham has noticed a disturbing inverse correlation between theological education and church growth: "the traditions that spend most on theological education are declining, while those who spend much less are getting stronger."[30] To combat this trend,

---

29. Markham, "Theological Education in the Twenty-First Century," 165.
30. Markham, 157.

he argues that a strong theological foundation must be prioritized, and teaching must be done in a way that "weaves theology together with the insights learned from congregational studies, globalization, and technology."[31] Asamoah-Gyadu mentions a similar trend in some African churches, saying, "Indeed many of the African independent/initiated churches are skeptical of the sort of 'bookish theology' that is propounded in theological seminaries and colleges. Yet it is the growth of these churches that has extended the boundaries of the church in Africa."[32] Theological education does not guarantee church growth, but, if done well, contributes deeply to the health, maturity, and vitality of the church. Asamoah-Gyadu concludes, "Whether the church in Africa can rise up to the challenge or not would depend to a very large extent on the proper contextualization of theological education so that theology as done in Africa does not remain bookish but answers the critical questions that African Christians are asking in the light of their experiences."[33] For the church in Nairobi to thrive, different models of theological education are needed to train the people of God and speak into the contextual realities.

Conclusion

New models of theological education are necessary to meet all the needs of church ministry, leadership, and discipleship. Given the brief survey above of the value of theological education, the current state of theological education, technological changes, and the situation in Nairobi, creativity and innovation are required to bring theological training to the place it needs to be. Tyrannus Hall provides an alternative model of theological education that is meant to complement existing models and provide accessible training to those who may not otherwise receive it. As theological education continues to grow, churches and theological institutions should explore more meaningful ways to engage and partner together in theological education, thus expanding God's kingdom and equipping God's people in accomplishing God's mission.

---

31. Markham, 158.
32. Asamoah-Gyadu, "Called to Make a Difference," 5.
33. Asamoah-Gyadu, 14.

Bibliography

Amanze, James N. "Paradigm Shift in Theological Education in Southern and Central Africa and Its Relevance to Ministerial Formation." *International Review of Mission* 98, no. 388 (April 2009): 120–131.

Asamoah-Gyadu, J. and Kwabena (Johnson Kwabena). "'Called to Make a Difference': Theological Education and a Mission in Twenty-First Century Africa." *Ogbomoso Journal of Theology* 15, no. 2 (2010): 1–16.

Commission for University Education. "Accredited Universities in Kenya." *Commission for University Education*, November 2015. http://www.cue.or.ke/images/phocadownload/Accredited_Universities_Kenya_Nov2015.pdf.

De Rosa, Cathy, Joanne Cantrell, and Diane Cellentani. *At a Tipping Point: Education, Learning and Libraries: A Report to the OCLC Membership.* Dublin, OH: Online Computer Library Center (OCLC), 2014. http://www.oclc.org/content/dam/oclc/reports/tipping-point/215133-tipping-point.pdf.

Kinsler, F. Ross. "Doing Ministry for a Change?: Theological Education for the Twenty-First Century." *Ministerial Formation* 108 (January 2007): 4–13.

Markham, Ian. "Theological Education in the Twenty-First Century." *Anglican Theological Review* 92, no. 1 (2010): 157–165.

Morgan, Donn F. "As Through a Glass Darkly: Defining Theological Education in the Twenty-First Century." *Anglican Theological Review* 90, no. 2 (2008): 255–265.

Nyende, Peter. "Ethnic Studies: An Urgent Need in Theological Education in Africa." *International Review of Mission* 98, no. 388 (April 2009): 132–146.

"Our Mission." Nairobi Chapel, 2016. http://nairobichapel.net/about-us/our-mission/.

Smith, Colin. "De-Suburbanising Theological Education in Nairobi." *Ministerial Formation* 108 (January 2007): 14–24.

"T-Track." Nairobi Chapel, 2016. http://nairobichapel.net/adult-church/t-track/.

"Tyrannus Hall." Nairobi Chapel, 2016. http://nairobichapel.net/tyrannus-hall/.

Wanjau, Muriithi. *Mizizi: Growing Deeper in Your Faith.* Nairobi: Clear Vision Media, 2005.

13

From the Classroom to the Pulpit: Navigating the Challenges

Elizabeth Mburu[1]
Adjunct Associate Professor, International Leadership University

Abstract

From the advent of the missionary-led Bible schools to the establishment of departments, schools, and faculties of theology in both Christian and public universities, theological education in Africa has undergone many challenging phases. However, despite this rich history and the fact that Africa was regarded as the most Christian continent by the year 2000, the constant cry in Africa is that we lack an audible voice in the theological conversation that is taking place across the globe. Although some changes have begun to take place, African theologians are often viewed as deficient in developing contextually relevant and biblically grounded theological systems. This has led to a deficiency in empowering both the African academy and the church of Christ in its African expression. There is a dichotomous thinking and lifestyle, particularly in times of crisis and need.

What factors have led to this failure? To address this issue, an empirical study of three schools of theology in universities in Nairobi, Kenya, was conducted. The research questions focused on the effectiveness of the education

---

1. I acknowledge the help of Ruth Wachira-Ndungu, who worked as my research assistant to disseminate the questionnaires and tabulate the data.

received in the classroom across four criteria relating to contextual relevance of curriculum, training of faculty, adequacy of resources, and research, writing, and publishing.

The study concludes that there is inadequate deliberate contextualization of curriculum in both its development and its delivery; while qualifications of faculty are adequate, there is need for more "home-grown" faculty; there is a scarcity of resources, hence the need for creative solutions; and, finally, the faculty in general are deficient in research, writing, and publishing.

Key words: contextualization, theological training, worldview, curriculum.

Introduction

Theological training in higher education in Africa has gone through many challenging phases. From the advent of the missionaries and the missionary-led Bible schools to the establishment of departments, schools, and faculties of theology in both Christian and public universities, the experiences have been diverse. However, despite this rich history, the constant cry is that Africa lacks an audible voice in the theological conversation that is taking place across the globe. Africa was regarded as the most Christian continent in the world by the year 2000,[2] and yet it is viewed as impoverished with regard to its contribution in theology. Although some changes have begun to take place, African theologians are often viewed as aping the West rather than striving to develop home-grown contextually relevant and biblically grounded theological systems.

The failure to do this in virtually all disciplines of theology has led to a deficiency in empowering not just the African academy, but, more seriously, the church of Christ in its African expression. African traditional practices, such as witchcraft and polygamy, are still rife on the continent. For instance, it is not uncommon to hear of pastors consulting witchdoctors in a bid to acquire more "power" for the pulpit. Moreover, there appears to be negligible transformation of congregants if the statistics surrounding corruption and impunity on the continent are to be taken into consideration. According to a report released in 2014 by Transparency International, Kenya ranks at the bottom of the index with regards to public perception on corruption.[3] This is despite the fact that

---

2. See Wilbur O'Donovan, *Biblical Christianity in Modern Africa* (Waynesboro, GA: Paternoster, 2000), 1.

3. Transparency International Kenya, "Annual Report 2013–2014," https://tikenya.org/wp-content/uploads/2017/06/transparency-international-kenya-annual-report-2013-2014.pdf.

Kenya is at least 80 percent Christian.⁴ Many people are "Sunday Christians," or at least exhibit a Christian orientation when in a Christian environment. However, when faced with choices that are not of an inherently spiritual nature, they reflect a dichotomized orientation that indicates, at the very least, that the content of Christian faith has not been internalized.

Magesa observes that many Christians "operate with two thought-systems at once, and both of them are close to each other. Each is only superficially modified by the other."⁵ This compartmentalization is what leads to a dichotomous thinking and lifestyle, particularly in times of crisis and need. From the classroom to the pulpit, theological education in Africa lacks the impact that it ought to have and has therefore failed to achieve many of its goals and objectives. The question remains: What factors have led to this failure? Could the fault lie with the training that has been given to the ministers of the church and those involved in teaching in the more formal theological academic arena in Africa?

The intention of this paper is to explore the challenges of theological training in higher education in Africa, focusing mainly on the effectiveness of the theological training received in the classroom across four specified criteria, namely:

- Contextual relevance: Are the theological programs contextually relevant and current?
- Faculty: Are the theological faculty adequately trained?
- Resources: Are the resources adequate to facilitate an effective teaching–learning process?
- Research, writing, and publishing: Are research, writing, and publishing an important component of the theology department?

Contextual Relevance

As a result of the re-socialization that took place regarding social, economic, political, religious, ethical, and artistic systems, much confusion has arisen as to the place of "African ways" in Christianity. Hillman states that "Some Christians, confusing Euro-American cultural forms and practices with the good news of Jesus Christ, are unable even to imagine how any African

---

4. See United States Department of State: Bureau of Democracy, Human Rights and Labor, "Kenya 2012 International Religious Freedom Report," accessed 23 January 2017, https://www.state.gov/documents/organization/208372.pdf.

5. Laurenti Magesa, *African Religion: The Moral Traditions of Abundant Life* (Maryknoll, NY: Orbis, 1997), 6.

religious forms and practices might be compatible with Christianity, much less how they could be signs of saving faith."[6] This is indeed a sad state of affairs. However, an even bigger mistake has been to try to ignore what is innately held by the African and constitutes an integral part of who he or she is. At the same time – and this must be acknowledged – many mistakes have been made in the attempt to incorporate African religious and cultural practices with Christianity. This is an unfortunate situation given the recent trend in the growth of the church globally: the southern hemisphere, particularly Africa, is demonstrating a dramatic increase in the number of Christians being added to the church.

In addition to this, the increasing resources on African Christian theology have raised questions concerning the understanding of theology as static. The question therefore is whether a theological understanding or system in a Western (or other) context should be transferred to an African context without regard for the differences in context. Although some goals of theological education are generic and apply globally, the specific goals of theological education cannot be uniformly adopted across the globe but must be contextualized to meet the needs represented in each part of the world. These needs relate to social, economic, political, and theological aspects. Theology must be relevant to the context in which it is being taught and applied, and this obviously means that an African Christian theology would raise questions that a Christian theology from a different environment would not.

Granted, there are debates as to whether one can rightly identify and isolate a theology that is uniquely African. One must understand that, while Christian theology has a commonality throughout the world where Christianity is practiced, there are aspects of our Christian theology that are influenced by our cultural contexts. This means that theology in a Western context may manifest itself differently from theology in an African context. Adopting Kato's definition, contextualization is simply "making concepts or ideas relevant in a given situation."[7] It therefore accurately reflects that the modes of expression of the biblical message are not static, but dynamic. This implies that an African Christian theology is valid. However, in articulating an African Christian theology, which is the rightful end product of the contextualization process, Kunhiyop notes that certain issues must be addressed: first, the religious worldview of the African should be acknowledged; second, it must be made

---

6. Eugene Hillman, *Toward an African Christianity* (New York: Paulist Press, 1993).

7. Byang H. Kato, "Contextualization and Religious Syncretism in Africa," in *Biblical Christianity in Africa*, Theological Perspectives in Africa 2 (Achimota, Ghana: Africa Christian Press, 1985), 23.

clear that this worldview is not lost when an African becomes a Christian; third, it must raise and discuss those issues that are relevant to African Christians in the philosophy, methodology, and teaching materials used; fourth, it must situate abstract thinking in concrete reality, and so should be productive and relevant; and fifth, it must be comprehensible to all Christians and not just to a select group of intellectuals.[8] Contextualization is of paramount importance in our higher institutions if theology is to become relevant in Africa. Kunhiyop mentions that a proper articulation of an African Christian theology must be relevant to African issues. This raises a crucial question: Are the goals in our theological departments/schools/faculties contextualized to the African situation, or are they generic? And are these goals clearly articulated or even understood by those in our classrooms?

Methodology

To help answer the questions raised in the introductory part of this paper, a preliminary survey of three departments of theology in selected universities in Nairobi was conducted. All three are Christian universities that were originally seminaries/Bible schools.

The findings that are incorporated in this paper are based on the responses of thirty-nine students from a sample population of forty-five respondents, and ten lecturers from a sample population of fifteen respondents. In terms of demographic information for the students, a large majority (61.5%) fell in the under-40 age group, with 43.6 percent of the respondents aged 30 and under. Only 10.3 percent were aged between 41 and 50, with the larger percentage of 25.6 percent coming in at 50 and above. This is to be expected given that most were in the undergraduate programs (59%) while the rest were in the master's (25.6%) and doctoral programs (15.4%). The responses are, therefore, mainly from an undergraduate perspective. The disciplines represented amongst the lecturers were Bible/Theology, Biblical Studies, Intercultural Studies, and Missiology. As far as the level of education is concerned, about an equal number were at master's and PhD levels. This is to be expected given that all the institutions have undergraduate students and require a lecturer to be only at master's level.

---

8. Samuel Waje Kunhiyop, *African Christian Theology* (Nairobi: HippoBooks, 2012), xv–xvi.

Findings and Discussion

When students were presented with a question on the general goal of theological programs, respondents cited the equipping of students with biblical and theological principles as well as skills to impact the world positively; to equip students for ministry within their contexts, such as urban, rural, mission, and chaplaincy; to shape servant leaders for strategic global impact; to shape mission-minded servants, referring to ministers of the gospel with a burden to reach the lost; and to enable students to identify Africa's challenges and come up with relevant solutions. A few did not indicate their views. Either they did not understand the question, or they did not know what these goals were, even though they were actively involved in a theological program.

Clearly, these institutions have largely succeeded in accurately communicating the general goals of theological education to their African audience. Whether this is done specifically, or the students pick it up as they move along in the program, is not clear. However, only 12.9 percent of the students referred to goals that specifically reflect the African context. It is evident from this that African students in theological programs generally understand why they are undertaking the program of study, but do not necessarily relate this to their specific African context. This may be a major factor in the "disconnect" between the classroom and the pulpit.

Most of the responses of the lecturers were also general, such as the equipping of Christ-centered leaders who will transform the church and society. However, at least 40 percent of the lecturers said the goal was of a more contextual nature, which included the equipping of leaders so that they can help fulfill the Great Commission and provide solutions to the problems facing Africa; offering quality relevant, contextual, and sustainable graduate and undergraduate programs; and producing church leaders who are biblically sound and able to address contextual issues from a biblical perspective. So, while the lecturers may themselves have a more contextually oriented goal in mind, this is not clearly understood by the students, even though these goals seem to filter down to the course content (as noted below).

One of the problematic factors in designing any curriculum is ensuring that the courses address the needs of the African church and society – that is, the issue of contextualization. Most students (97.4%) felt that the courses were successful in addressing these needs. Moreover, the percentage of content delivery that is geared specifically for application to the African context correlates to this. Most students (66.6%) felt that more than 50 percent of the course content reflected this contextualization component. This was corroborated by the lecturers, 80 percent of whom answered in the affirmative regarding whether the courses addressed the needs of the African church and society, seeing at least 60 percent of the course content as addressing the African context.

If, as appears to be the case, contextualization is taking place in the classroom, this is indeed a positive finding. However, what still needs to be addressed is why it is not effectively being incorporated beyond the classroom. Is it going beyond the cognitive level to the point where the student can incorporate it in his or her ministry and daily life? What other underlying issues might be preventing a transformation of church and society?

Theological educators must not only understand the worldview of the Bible but also be deliberate about communicating it. This is a major foundation in avoiding the dichotomous approach that is exhibited even by graduates of theological institutions in Africa. A biblical worldview is the orientation of the self to all of life that undergirds the expression of our identities as redeemed human beings in relationship with God and others, which expression, primarily embodied through behavior, is consistent with the biblical metanarrative in all its aspects.[9] The goal is to ensure that, as the students move through the various stages of the educational process, they begin to develop a Christian worldview that is both clearly articulated and lived out because it has been internalized. As Nash warns, "Worldviews are double-edged swords. An inadequate conceptual scheme can, like improper eyeglasses, hinder our efforts to understand God, the world, and ourselves. The right conceptual scheme can suddenly bring everything into focus."[10]

What about worldview in general? Is there such a thing as an "African worldview?" Questions have been raised as to the validity of this concept, given the variety of cultures and ethnic groups represented on the continent. The following comment by Rabaka gives us clarity in addressing these objections:

> The African worldview theory is essentially a combination of the classical and contemporary, continental and diasporic African overarching outlook on human experience and the natural and phenomenal world. It is distinguished from the worldviews of other peoples in so far as it is grounded in and grows out of African history and culture. African peoples' beliefs about

---

[9]. Certain elements borrowed from James W. Sire, *Naming the Elephant: Worldview as a Concept* (Downers Grove, IL: InterVarsity, 2004).

[10]. Ronald Nash, *Worldviews in Conflict: Choosing Christianity in a World of Ideas* (Grand Rapids, MI: Zondervan, 1992), 33.

God, nature, and major life rituals – such as birth, puberty, adulthood, marriage, elder-hood, and death – exhibit enough commonalities to warrant being called an African worldview. These commonalities in many areas of the life-worlds and lived experiences of African peoples render interminable philosophical disputes and semantic discussions as to whether there exists a general or universal African worldview utterly unnecessary and unrewarding.[11]

However, it must be pointed out that, even though there is uniformity in worldview at some level, thereby justifying this category, there are also differences that are the result of immersion in different subcultures. Culture includes the values and social mores of a society, as well as all the learned patterns of behavior that make that society unique. It is dynamic and includes aspects that cannot be seen, as well as the visible ones. Most people in Africa today have a cultural background that is diverse, with key elements ranging from the traditional to the modern because of the exposure to a variety of values and ideas.

All too often, people are not aware of the deep influence culture has on their thinking, emotions, and behavior. A study of one's own culture, as well as the subcultures within the larger culture, is invaluable for helping one begin to recognize what is truly biblical and what is culturally influenced. Being able to peel the layers away until one comes to the core of what is truly biblical is not easy, but it is well worth the effort: this is what guides one in forming a Christian worldview. While a study of one's own culture is extremely useful, this should not be taken as final. Understanding other cultures helps to clarify even further what is negotiable in interactions and what is not. A common error in intercultural communication is to assume that one's worldview is the right one, and that any other view of life is faulty. Intercultural studies are therefore a vital tool in helping one understand other cultures, so that one can interact wisely with others, and not be critical in areas that do not count.

Consequently, to effectively address African contextual issues, theological educators must not only understand the worldview of the Bible; they must also take into consideration the worldview of the students they are teaching. While we live in the twenty-first century, and even though Western secularism has invaded the continent, there is nevertheless continuity with the African traditional worldview in most contexts. As Gehman perceptively points out:

---

11. Rabaka, "African Worldview Theory," *Encyclopedia of Black Studies*, 2004, http://www.credoreference.com.proxy.globethics.net/entry/sageblackst/african_worldview_theory.

"Scholars too easily assume the uniform process of secularization wherever economic and social changes accompany urbanization and westernization. They assume a total acceptance of scientific reality, which would make religion irrelevant. But in fact the many new indigenous religious movements in Africa undermine this assumption. While secularization is taking place in urbanized Africa, we cannot assume that this eliminates the traditional religious worldview. The continual eruption of new religious movements confirms this."[12]

Unfortunately, the African traditional worldview is often seen as a hindrance to the process of theological education, and students are often expected to almost erase this background when they come into the classroom – a "tabula rasa" approach. There has often been the assumption that this background is injurious to the theological endeavor. While this may be true, and the brief section on syncretism below does point out this danger, one must also consider that the presuppositions or assumptions that undergird the worldview of African students may help rather than hinder the process.

For instance, when students were asked about ways in which African traditional beliefs, which form a crucial component of worldview, hinder or help theological education, a large number (43.6%) of the respondents said that African traditional beliefs help particularly in understanding some theological concepts, such as the existence of one God in the Bible. This concept was likened to the African belief in one Supreme Being. Several respondents felt that this understanding helped the students better understand other areas, such as evangelism and the teachings in the Bible on angels and demons. An added benefit was the motivation for scholars to do research on how best to reach traditionalists. Aspects of African traditions like oral literature, proverbs, songs, and folktales were also felt to be helpful. Given that a basic educational philosophy is to move from the known to the unknown, allowing the African worldview its rightful place in the classroom can only yield positive results.

A minority of the respondents (27.1%) said that African traditional beliefs hinder theological education, and they gave various reasons pertaining to syncretism. For instance, the role of the living dead in the lives of the living, the belief in witchcraft and superstition, polygamy, and so forth, were viewed as a pollution of the Christian faith. Some respondents felt that some African traditions are oppressive toward women. The practice of traditional rituals in marriage and burial ceremonies was also seen as a hindrance to theological

---

12. Richard J. Gehman, *African Traditional Religion in Biblical Perspective*, rev. ed. (Nairobi: East African Educational Publishers, 2005), 6.

training. Interestingly, some (25.6%) of the respondents felt that this was a "both/and" situation and cited reasons such as those given above.

The lecturers' responses were largely in accord with those of the students. Regarding whether African traditional beliefs hinder or help theological education, 20 percent of the respondents said they help in several ways, such as enabling Africans to easily understand the God of the Bible because of their belief in a Supreme Being. This was seen to serve as an entry point to the gospel. Other positives included the fact that a converted African brings a sincere and intense reverence for the ancestors (which is negative) which is then focused on God in a positive way. Aspects of African traditions, like oral literature, proverbs, songs, and symbols, were also cited as being useful in theological education in helping understand the different genres of the Bible. Interestingly, a larger percentage, 40 percent, believed that the beliefs hinder theological education through tendencies such as valuing instant help and the relief that comes from dependence on magical powers. This was compared to what may appear to be delays in answers to prayers offered to the God of the Bible, which may cause students not to be objective in their theological studies. Moreover, certain beliefs could be contrary to biblical teachings, especially those in relation to traditional rituals like burial. Other reasons included the risk of syncretism, such as professing Christians continuing to visit witchdoctors for assistance, and the ignorance that prevails among some Christians regarding such beliefs. At the same time, a large number held the view that this was a "both/and" situation (40%), their reasons revolving around those given above.

Clearly, it is not advisable to ignore the background of the students as it provides a positive springboard from which to introduce many theological ideas. At the same time, it is vital to recognize that this background can be a hindrance to theological education and to therefore put in place measures to counter any perspectives that might undermine the integrity of the theological endeavor and encourage the dichotomous orientation to life that is so prevalent today. What is necessary is the alignment of the African worldview with the biblical metanarrative. For instance, the belief in the living dead or divinized ancestors must be evaluated from Scripture. If an African student is not taught how to incorporate his or her worldview in the learning process, it is likely that biblical truths will not be internalized.

Moreover, we live in an age when culture, and, by extension, worldview, is undergoing change at an extremely rapid pace. For instance, the African audience today straddles not only rural and urban spaces – that is, geographical – but also digital spaces. The Internet has changed the way the world functions and the information that is being transmitted and received constantly across the globe has implications for how contextualization in theological education ought to be carried out. Given the trends in Africa today, there is need to concentrate on the contextual needs represented by the 35-and-under age group, as this constitutes not only the largest group in the African population, but also the most technologically up-to-date. In an orality colloquium held at Daystar University (October 2015), Chong pointed out that the digital space implies that individuals occupying completely different geographical spaces may in fact have more in common than those living in the same locality.[13] This implies that different generations of African students must be approached according to the space they predominantly occupy.

This has implications for the evaluation and subsequent revision of curricula. Teaching a curriculum that is even two years old is detrimental to the effectiveness of theological education, as some aspects of it may be outdated by the time of delivery. While the core content may still be viable – though even this is subject to change – the learning objectives, illustrations, assignments, and even teaching methods that will enable a successful teaching-learning process will need to be periodically reviewed to meet the needs of a rapidly changing society within the right contextual framework. Indeed, even addressing methods of evangelism amongst different age groups in our classrooms is challenging. While the older generation may be comfortable with traditional methods such as paper tracts, the younger generation is looking to digital methods of evangelism that can easily be communicated via smartphones, computers, tablets, and so on. The GodTools app developed by Cru (formerly Campus Crusade for Christ) is one such effort to bridge the gap and make theological education more relevant in different contexts. The data showed that most lecturers reviewed their course syllabi within a period not exceeding two years, giving a very encouraging picture of their sensitivity to contextual issues.

However, caution must be exercised to avoid syncretism. Before 1960, not much was done to relate Christian theology to the African context. Theology was therefore viewed by many as an imposition.[14] In a bid to resolve this inconsistency, theologians over the past few decades have recommended many different strategies. One of the errors that has resulted is that of syncretism. In general, African Traditional Religion has three basic components: belief

---

13. Calvin Chong, "Participatory Multimodal Communications and Learning: A Case Study from Singapore Bible College" (Paper presented at Orality Colloquium, Nairobi, 14 October 2015).

14. Wilbur O'Donovan, Jr., *Biblical Christianity in African Perspective*, 2nd ed. (Carlisle: Paternoster, 1995), 5.

in the Supreme Being, the spirit world, and mystical powers.[15] Scholars have attempted to join some of these elements to the teachings of the Bible. This has filtered down to the development of new religious movements in the rapid growth of African Initiated Churches. Unfortunately, as they attempt to make sense of the world, these movements have mixed Traditional Religions with elements of Christianity, resulting in a syncretistic blend that can no longer rightly be called Christianity.[16] As Kato noted many decades ago, "Africans need to formulate theological concepts in the language of Africa. But theology itself in its essence must be left alone. The Bible must remain the basic source of Christian theology. Evangelical Christians know of only one theology – Biblical Theology – although it may be expressed in the context of each cultural milieu."[17] This implies that while African religious and traditional beliefs can and should be used in some measure to formulate an understanding of Christian theology in an African context, they must not be allowed to supersede biblical revelation.[18] Whatever else theological education communicates concerning relevance to different cultures and subcultures within Africa, it must be in alignment with the biblical metanarrative.

Training of Theological Faculty

Kato pointed out as far back as 1973 that seminary and graduate training in theology were top priorities, since church leadership stood at the top of the list of the needs of the African church.[19] Since then, not only have many African scholars received the opportunity to study abroad, but several seminaries and graduate schools have been established to cope with the demands of a rapidly expanding church. In Kenya alone, there are numerous seminaries and departments/schools in universities offering evangelical theological training. The problem that he identified – that men and women looking for

---

15. Gehman, *African Traditional Religion*, xi.

16. Gehman, 6.

17. At the time of Kato's work, there was already a growing interest in the use of African religions as sources for an African theology. The danger he identified, even at that time, was the move away from a clear understanding of the unique nature of biblical revelation such that other sources would be viewed as equal to the Bible and therefore Christianity would lose its status as the unique way of salvation. Byang H. Kato, "Theological Anemia in Africa," in *Biblical Christianity in Africa: Theological Perspectives in Africa 2* (Achimota, Ghana: Africa Christian Press, 1985), 12.

18. The study of comparative religions, so popular in African universities, becomes dangerous when biblical revelation and African theology are put on an equal footing.

19. Kato, "Theological Anemia in Africa," 13.

advanced training had nowhere to turn within Africa – is no longer an issue. From the preliminary survey, at least an equal number of lecturers were at the master's and doctoral levels (either completed or continuing), showing that they had undergone at least a tertiary level of theological training. This is a very positive finding given the need identified above. The question therefore is, What opportunities for further training had they received since attaining their degrees, particularly those at master's level? Except for those who already had a PhD and who felt that that was sufficient, 40 percent indicated that they were currently enrolled in a master's or PhD program. At least 10 percent indicated that they were not able to enroll for PhD studies due to lack of finances, while another 10 percent said that such opportunities were rare. The majority therefore had access to further theological training.

There are now numerous opportunities for this training to be "disseminated" and, as noted above, many have in fact graduated and continue to graduate from these institutions. The question that needs to be addressed is whether there is an appreciable corresponding impact – on the church, society, and academia in general. Unfortunately, the continuing influx of Western-trained faculty in many African institutions, particularly those that still employ a missionary model, contributes to a dichotomized understanding of what theology in both its abstract and its practical aspects really means. While diversity in the teaching faculty is desirable, and indeed necessary, what is at stake as far as this study is concerned is whether there is a "critical mass" of faculty who understand the African situation. It would have been useful to examine the curriculum that was undertaken by the teaching faculty in these institutions to determine whether the learning objectives required by a faculty member in Africa were addressed at all. As O'Donovan points out, the modern educated person in Africa must contend with two worlds: "On one side, there is the strong influence of a traditional rural African culture, which has existed for many centuries. On the other side, the beliefs, practices, values, and worldview of the modern, scientific, educated world of western Europe and North America have an increasingly important influence in their lives."[20] It is likely that if the faculty member received a Western education, the issues addressed in the classroom would relate to that context, ignoring the other side of the coin of an African student's life. Even though a student might opt to address an African issue to correct this deficiency, the financial resources necessary to travel back to his or her country of origin, as well as the library resources relevant to carry out the research, are often limiting factors.

---

20. O'Donovan, *Biblical Christianity in African Perspective*, 3.

In relation to the percentage of their training that covered African context and realities, 30 percent of lecturers' responses indicated between 0 and 25 percent, while 20 percent put it at 26–50 percent. What this data shows is that although 40 percent of the respondents got at least 50 percent and above exposure to African context and realities, about half of the respondents got less than 50 percent exposure, with most of this group falling below 25 percent. The implication is that most of these lecturers had to acquire the skill of contextualization on their own – a challenging venture even when there is a formal setup to guide the progress. It is commendable that most of these even incorporated reading resources and content that related to African realities, as reported in the section on adequacy of resources below. Interestingly, when asked how relevant their training was for African theological education, 10 percent said it was relevant at the PhD level but not at the BA/MA level, 20 percent were unsure, while 70 percent thought it was very relevant. This is an interesting finding given the data above.

In addition, if "culturally effective" methods of teaching were not employed in the training process of the current faculty, was the teaching–learning process as effective as it could have been? A study done by Dorothy Bowen amongst post-secondary school students (four theological colleges and three government secondary schools) revealed that the learning style of most African students was field dependent (91%) as opposed to field independent. Field-dependent students view things globally, corresponding to a holistic view of life. Field-independent students view things analytically, corresponding to an analytical approach to life. Interestingly, the theological students scored more highly than the secondary school students in this regard. An additional finding of the study was that African students were more group-oriented than individualistic. A parallel study was conducted by Elie Buconyori, whose intent it was to confirm Bowen's results. His results corroborated Bowen's but, in addition, he found that there were more field-dependent students from a rural background than from an urban one.[21] The implications for both teaching and learning in the African context are tremendous. A curriculum structure and delivery that ignores the holistic model and the community framework is not likely to be successful.

Chong adds an additional dimension: in his presentation, he argued that participatory multi-modal and omni-channel communication is what is most effective in the teaching–learning process. By multi-modal, he means multiple

---

21. As reported by O'Donovan, 9.

media and channels of communication.[22] This is a crucial finding given the global and group orientation of students in Africa. Teaching methodology that develops content in multiple forms, such as word or text, audio, visual/video, and performances, and then propagates that content via different channels will therefore be extremely beneficial. Integration of these modalities, along with cooperative learning, is likely to yield tremendous benefits. Faculties that receive training covering all these aspects are likely to be more successful in Africa, as there is a high probability that they will deliver it in the same way. Moreover, they are likely to view their training as far more relevant for their context because both the content and the modalities of delivery resonate with them.

Given that most (80%) of the lecturers indicated that they had a background in education courses, it would have been beneficial to investigate the teaching methodology they employed as far as curriculum development and delivery were concerned. Since they indicated clearly that the African context was taken into consideration in the teaching–learning process, could it be that the mode of delivery was lacking? If they did not receive an education that used culturally effective methods of content preparation and delivery, it is not likely that they would do any differently.

Adequacy of Resources

It has been noted by numerous African scholars that there is an almost complete lack of resources that originate from a contextualized, African understanding of biblical truths and their subsequent application. African scholars frequently decry the lack of "Africanization" in the resources that are available to us. At the same time, theological training must develop learners in at least four areas – the head, the heart, the hands, and the surrounding context. The head deals with the fundamentals of the church – namely, the Bible, theology, history, and ethics. The heart relates to the inner landscape of an individual, such as character and spiritual maturity, while the hands have to do with ministry or professional skills and competencies. The surrounding context relates to the cultural environment and change.[23] Given this reality, it is indeed a daunting task for African writers to provide what is needed. Part of the challenge stems from the expense in publishing and the difficulty in accessing funds for the process. However, there are many rising opportunities for publication of articles

---

22. Chong, "Participatory Multimodal Communications and Learning."
23. See also Chong.

in journals that are housed on the continent. Although it is often a lengthy process, the results are well worth it. A few institutions are now beginning to develop institutional-based journals, primarily as a publishing outlet for their lecturers.

Unfortunately, there is not only scarcity of resources originating from African scholars, but also inadequacy of resources in general, particularly current resources. Although publishing houses are now available on the continent, these are still not able to meet the demands. Interestingly, when students were asked about the adequacy of the library, specifically whether it was well stocked with books and journals, an almost equal number stated "yes" as stated "no." Those who stated that it was not adequately stocked cited shortage of books, journals, and computers, and difficulty in finding books on certain topics. The fact that some of the books and journals were out of date was also mentioned. A small number (2.6%) also noted that the books were authored by theologians from the West and therefore were not contextually relevant. Given the diversity in levels represented (from undergraduate to doctoral), it is possible that this disparity in opinion was due to increasing exposure as to what constitutes good standards in a library. While an undergraduate student might feel that what was on offer was sufficient, a doctoral student, who had more specialized needs, might not. A crucial factor in assessing adequacy of library resources obviously has to do with contextualization. What percentage of the resources covered African context and realities? While this was not a question that could be put to the respondents, given that it required the input of the more technical library staff, it would have been useful to conduct such an analysis.

Indeed, the lecturers' responses also needed to be investigated further. As to whether the libraries were well stocked, 50 percent responded in the negative, stating that the books and journals were either not current or inadequate. At least 10 percent of this number noted that there was a scarcity of journals and books that addressed the African situation. Moreover, even though 50 percent answered in the affirmative, 10 percent noted that there were no current journals. Responding to the question on whether textbooks and journals were current or not, at least half of the students said that they were current, which corresponds to the responses on the adequacy of the library. The lecturers, on the other hand, had a higher percentage (60%) saying they were not. This disparity can only be understood with respect to different disciplines. It may be possible that some disciplines had more up-to-date resources; for example, leadership, being a relatively new field, would obviously have more current books.

Still on the adequacy of resources, students were asked what percentage of required reading texts addressed the African context. This question correlates to the one above on the percentage of course content that covered these aspects. More than half of the respondents put it below 50 percent, but at least 40 percent of them responded that it was over 50 percent. Of the respondents that put it under 50 percent, most gave the lower end of this range. Similarly, 60 percent of the lecturers stated that less than 50 percent of the required reading covered the African context. Again, most were in the lower end of this range. This finding supports the response that authorship on the African context, particularly by African authors, is lacking. On a positive note, the availability of resources on the African context seems to be increasing, in the form of both journals and books.

Online resources are an avenue that can be used to boost access to much-needed learning and instructional materials. The cost involved in importing books from outside Africa is usually prohibitive for many institutions and the demands from accrediting bodies cannot often be met, making use of online resources a viable solution. For instance, the Commission for University Education in Kenya requires that most of the books in the libraries of institutions in Kenya be current to truly be relevant in supporting teaching, learning, research, and community service via the existing programs.[24] All the institutions surveyed had an online system in place, which was a positive development. On the effectiveness of the online system for accessing resources, most of the students said that it was effective (71.8%). The lecturers' responses, however, differed slightly, coming in at only 60 percent. Those who felt that it was not effective said that there was no way of accessing books online, the Internet was not always accessible, and computers were few. However, it is important to point out that while e-resources have gained impetus across Africa, thus providing a solution to the problem of importation, many institutions still lack the infrastructure, and, in many cases, the funds, to access this service consistently.

Research, Writing, and Publishing

A related problem, therefore, has to do with research, writing, and publishing, from a uniquely African perspective. The output in these areas is frequently seen as inadequate; even though the data shows that the situation is improving

---

24. Commission for University Education (CUE), "Standards and Guidelines," 65. www.cue.or.ke/index.php/downloads/category/6-standards-and-guidelines, pdf.

and that students do indeed get exposure to the relevant resources, it is still well below what it should be. The evidence lies in our libraries! Although the last few years have seen an increase in the articles and books written by African authors, it is still not sufficient. This question of research and publishing is one that is directly affected by the model followed by African institutions. Are they more teaching-based, or do they lean more toward research? The Commission for University Education in Kenya leaves room for the establishment of both models.[25] Is there a bias toward one or the other, or does a balance exist? This can easily be verified by the research output of the institution per department. In many cases, faculty are not given an opportunity to participate in research, whether through time specifically allotted for it, training provided, or even funds designated for specific research projects. Moreover, even if all these are in place, it is often difficult to successfully publish an article because of the competitive nature of the journals, given that they are mainly based in the West. Getting an outlet for one's work is often a daunting task.

An implication of this challenge is that it will filter down to the students and the problem will be passed down to the next generation of scholars and practitioners. Indeed, when students were asked if they had opportunities to publish their work, almost 37 percent said that the opportunities were limited or non-existent. A more concerning finding from the data surrounding this question is that most did not seem to have any idea what publishing meant. This was evident in responses that referred to there being no printing machine, the year book, interacting with scholars, guidance and reference materials, and research courses. This may be a resultant problem with the faculty, who may not have encouraged students to actively participate in research and publishing. What was surprising was that at least 61.5 percent of the faculty felt that they accomplished this through research-based assignments and courses in research and academic writing. A very small percentage (2.6%) said that they encouraged students to join societies such as Africa Society for Evangelical Theology, which is interested in research. Fortunately, there was at least an indication (2.6%) that some of the institutions required students to publish before confirming them as PhD candidates. The fact that only 35 percent of the students responded in the affirmative regarding whether the institution had a specific outlet for publishing, also contributes to this problem. On the positive side, at least half of the respondents stated that they had opportunities to participate in theological seminars or conferences, which are crucial vehicles in the production and dissemination of research.

---

25. CUE, "Standards and Guidelines."

It appears that the faculty in general lacked accurate information on, or even direction in, what publishing is. Their responses with regard to how they encouraged students to actively participate in research, writing, and publishing reflected the student responses: 60 percent of the respondents said they did that by giving students research-related assignments. While this is a crucial first step, if the lecturers do not go beyond this, students will be left with the impression that that is all that is entailed in research and publishing. However, at least 10 percent said that master's and PhD students were encouraged to research and publish articles in academic or peer-reviewed journals or publish books for use in churches, schools, and so on. Another 10 percent said that students were encouraged to publish their theses and make presentations at the Africa Society of Evangelical Theology. Interestingly, 10 percent said that the undergraduate students were not able to research and publish since they were already struggling with the writing of term papers! This may be an institutional problem as most lecturers gave negative responses when questioned about the opportunities they had for doing research. Only 40 percent indicated that they were actively engaged in research and publishing; however, even this was limited due to lack of resources, a problem cited by other respondents as well. Only 10 percent said they did research through the Africa Society of Evangelical Theology. This inertia is unfortunate given that at least 50 percent of the respondents said that the institutions had a specific outlet for publishing. However, the majority (80%) pointed out that there were no funds specifically allocated for research, showing that this lack of prioritization – due to either ignorance or lack of available funds – may constitute the major problem in research and publishing.

This area is a major shortcoming in African theological education given the increasing need for contextualized resources. There needs to be a paradigm shift at both institutional and individual level where this area of research and publishing is concerned. An incentive for publishing that is now gaining momentum in many universities is the requirement for publication for ranking purposes.

What Next?

Clearly, although there are many positive things in our theological education, challenges remain. If the general context as noted in the introduction is anything to go by, the internalization or even the transfer of concepts acquired in the classroom to the life or ministry context is not as effective as it should be. The four criteria addressed – contextual relevance, training of faculty, adequacy of resources, and involvement in research, writing, and publishing – provide some information on the way forward.

Contextual Relevance

Although some contextualization is taking place in the classroom, this needs to be engaged in more deliberately and at a deeper level. Goals for the African context must be spelt out clearly and students guided to understand through their coursework how these goals are being achieved. The worldview of the students must be viewed as a positive factor in the learning process even as students are taught how to weigh their worldview against the biblical worldview to avoid syncretism. Both geographical and digital spaces must also be considered. Any education that does not challenge the students to engage their worldview is not likely to lead to an internalization of values and concepts. Moreover, contextual relevance must go beyond the course content to the modes of delivery. All these must be incorporated into the curriculum development process and must feature prominently in the learning outcomes.

Training of Faculty

We must focus on getting "home-grown" faculty. Faculty trained on the continent, for the continent, are likely to be more effective than those trained outside. Moreover, if contextual relevance forms a key foundation of the training they receive, they, as the next generation of theological educators, will be better equipped to pass it on. Another key step is sharing faculty and learning best practices. Those institutions that appear to train for the African "market" can serve as key resources.

Adequacy of Resources

Given the shortage of resources across the continent, it would be prudent for institutions to develop relationships with each other so that resources can more easily be shared. Having an online resource that hosts material from African scholars that could easily be accessed across the continent would be an added benefit. Those institutions that are ahead should be the first to lend a helping hand to struggling institutions. Networking is key. Organizations like Network for African Congregational Theology (NetACT)[26] can make it their goal to have an online library with minimal membership fees. With the affordability of cell phones in Africa, particularly smartphones, networking can be done with relative ease.

Research, Writing, and Publishing

Research, writing, and publishing can be encouraged through providing access to funds for research and publishing. There is also a need for faculty to be sensitized on the need to provide resources for African theological education if true transformation is to be an expected outcome of our training. Again, organizations like ASET and NetACT are crucial for organizing research forums and networking with publishing houses for the publication and dissemination of research. For instance, ASET has consistently worked with *Africa Journal for Evangelical Theology* (*AJET*) and is now working with Langham Publishers. We foresee great strides ahead in the area of African authorship.

Bibliography

Adeyemo, T. *Salvation in African Traditional Religion*. Nairobi: Evangel, 1979.

Chong, Calvin. "Participatory Multimodal Communications and Learning: A Case Study from Singapore Bible College." Paper presented at Orality Colloquium, Nairobi, 14 October 2015.

Commission for University Education (CUE), "Standards and Guidelines," 65. www.cue.or.ke/index.php/downloads/category/6-standards-and-guidelines, pdf.

Gehman, Richard J. *African Traditional Religion in Biblical Perspective*. Revised edition. Nairobi, Kenya: East African Educational Publishers, 2005.

Hillman, Eugene. *Toward an African Christianity*. New York: Paulist Press, 1993.

Kato, Byang H. "Contextualization and Religious Syncretism in Africa." In *Biblical Christianity in Africa: Theological Perspectives in Africa* 2. Achimota, Ghana: Africa Christian Press, 1985.

———. "Theological Anemia in Africa." In *Biblical Christianity in Africa: Theological Perspectives in Africa* 2. Achimota, Ghana: Africa Christian Press, 1985.

Kunhiyop, Samuel Waje. *African Christian Theology*. Nairobi: HippoBooks, 2012.

Magesa, Laurenti. *African Religion: The Moral Traditions of Abundant Life*. Maryknoll, NY: Orbis, 1997.

Mbiti, John S. *African Religions and Philosophy*. Nairobi: East African Educational Publishers, 1969; reprinted, 1992.

---

26. This is an organization based in South Africa with member institutions from South, East, and West Africa.

Mugambi, J. N. K. *African Christian Theology: An Introduction*. Kenya: Heinemann, 1989.

Nash, Ronald. *Worldviews in Conflict: Choosing Christianity in a World of Ideas*. Grand Rapids, MI: Zondervan, 1992.

O'Donovan, Wilbur, Jr. *Biblical Christianity in African Perspective,* 2nd edition. Carlisle: Paternoster, 1995.

———. *Biblical Christianity in Modern Africa*. Waynesboro, GA: Paternoster, 2000.

Parinder, G. *African Traditional Religion*. London: SPCK, 1962.

Rabaka. "African Worldview Theory." In *Encyclopedia of Black Studies*, 2004. Retrieved from http://www.credoreference.com.proxy.globethics.net/entry/sageblackst/african_worldview_theory.

Sire, James W. *Naming the Elephant: Worldview as a Concept*. Downers Grove, IL: InterVarsity, 2004.

———. *The Universe Next Door,* 5th edition. Downers Grove, IL: InterVarsity, 2009.

Turaki, Yusufu. *Foundations of African Traditional Religion and Worldview*. Nairobi: WordAlive, 2006.

United States Department of State: Bureau of Democracy, Human Rights and Labor. "Kenya 2012 International Religious Freedom Report." Accessed 23 January 2017. https://www.state.gov /documents/organization/208372.

14

Toward the Propagation of KAG Christian Schools in Kenya: An Investigation of Stakeholder Perceptions

Rev Isaac Kasili
Dean, School of Education, KAG East University, Nairobi, Kenya

Abstract

This research investigated the perceptions of stakeholders toward establishing successful church-based Christian schools for Kenyan Assemblies of God (KAG) churches. The research question was: What are the perceptions of existing models of Christian schools in Kenya that may lead to the establishment by KAG churches of successful church-based Christian schools? A mixed-methods design for the purpose of triangulation of divergent data sources was used in this research. A case-study procedure was used to investigate three existing Pentecostal Christian primary schools and to collect data to assist in developing effective church-based Christian schools for KAG. Data was collected using the following instruments: a focus group, semi-structured interviews, and questionnaires. The researcher used appropriate procedures to analyze data collected by each research instrument. The researcher looked for emerging themes and recurrent events and categorized them. Research participants were twenty-four KAG pastors, forty parents from the KAG, all administrators and teachers from the three selected schools, and five executive members (EC) of the KAG leadership.

Literature findings revealed that, in the past, training in the Bible was intentional: education had specific goals and objectives to fulfill. The early church gave priority to teaching, and the Bible was a major part of the school curriculum. The Reformers regarded Christian education as a core part of every education system. Stakeholders want KAG churches today to start schools that will similarly serve as centers of excellence both academically and spiritually. The alumni of such KAG schools would be ambassadors of Christ everywhere they went, and could transform Kenyan society in morals, values, and leadership.

Key words: Christian schools, stakeholders, KAG, missionaries, education system, Bible-based curriculum.

Introduction

Think about the following questions: Is evil in our society increasing or has it always been like this? Is the media making us think that evil is on the rise when it is not? Are morals deteriorating very fast? Are Kenyans still practicing Christian values? Is Kenyan society 80 percent Christian?

A recent survey carried out by the East African Institute revealed shocking information about the young people of Kenya. The report states that 85% of the youth value faith values most compared to other values. 73% of youth are afraid of standing up for what is right. Approximately 50% believe it doesn't matter how one makes money as long as one does not end up in jail. 47% admire those who make money by hook or crook, and 35% would easily take or give a bribe.[1]

Public education institutions in Kenya, especially primary and secondary schools, are currently faced with many challenges. Shortages of teachers, inadequate learning materials, over-enrollment, deteriorating morals, and undisciplined students are just a few of them.[2] The series of strikes by students that hit many public schools in Kenya in recent years is evidence of deteriorating morals. According to an Afrol News report, more than 300 secondary schools

---

1. "Kenya Survey Youth Report," *Daily Nation*, 19 January 2016, https://www.nation.co.ke/news/Kenyan-youth-have-no-qualms-with-corruption-survey-shows/1056-3038800-pb8ydw/index.html.

2. Lee-Anne Benoit, "An Overview of the Kenyan Education System: Issues and Obstacles to Learning," accessed 10 October 2013, https://studymoose.com/kenya-education-essay.

went on strike in Kenya between May and August 2008.³ The trend of strikes and misbehavior did not stop in 2008. Reuben Githinji reported on 16 October 2012 that "students of more than seven schools in Embu had gone on a rampage demanding to be allowed to go for midterm break."⁴

The situation in public schools is likely to be affected by the current Kenyan Constitution, which prohibits preaching and witnessing in public schools. An analysis of the new constitution carried out by Kenya Christian Church (KCC), an umbrella organization of all Protestant churches in Kenya, concluded that Islam had been given priority over other religious groups by being allowed to have Kadhi's courts.⁵ As a way of preparing magistrates and judges for the Kadhi courts, Islam might be given more emphasis than Christianity in public learning institutions.

Who has the solution to these challenges? Christians, the church, the government, the judicial system, or . . .? In this paper I challenge my audience to re-think an old idea or concept that may contribute toward solving the social, political, and religious problems affecting our Kenyan society. The findings in this paper suggest a way to create an increasingly transformed and redeemed society.

Christian Education during the Pre-Reformation and Reformation Period

Developments in Christian education took place during the pre-Reformation period. This indeed was a period of Renaissance, or revival, of learning. Many people studied the Greek language, which in turn helped them to study the Greek New Testament. Benson reports that as they studied the New Testament, they encountered the Christian church of the apostolic period.⁶

The pre-Reformation period also saw the rediscovery of the Bible. Those who had long remained illiterate were now able to read the Bible and they began to appreciate it. Benson observes, "The Bible is the only book with sufficient knowledge needed by man."⁷

This period ushered in the Reformation, when a school system based upon the idea of universal education was established. The school system integrated

---

3. Afrol News report, 23 July 2008.
4. Reuben Githinji, "Strikes of Students in Secondary Schools in Kenya," accessed 12 October 2013, https://allafrica.com/stories/201210161251.html.
5. Kenya Constitution chapter 10 caps 170.
6. Clarence Benson, *A Popular History of Christian Education* (Chicago: Moody, 1943), 67.
7. Benson, *Popular History*, 68.

Protestant doctrine in its curriculum.[8] The Reformers contributed greatly to education. Luther urged the state to make education compulsory for every child.[9]

Philip Melanchthon, a teacher at the University of Wittenberg, Germany, influenced the curriculum of this university, adopting Protestant doctrines; this worked so successfully that many new universities copied this model. Melanchthon influenced and mentored thousands of students who enrolled in the university and who then, in turn, went out as teachers, carrying his ideals wherever they went.[10]

John Calvin proposed a system of education that could be used in Switzerland.[11] Another Reformer who contributed toward the growth in education was John Knox, who led the Reformation in Scotland. He recognized the value of religious training for children and young people. Not only were teachers in schools responsible for offering Christian education, but so were parents in their homes as well.[12] Ulrich Zwingli in Switzerland believed that Christian education was important because the truth had the power to change people or prevent them from doing evil.

The Reformers believed that any education system without Christian education was not enough. Because of its importance, Christian education was taught in three places: the home, the church, and schools.

The Catholic Counter-Reformation strengthened the education system of the time by establishing good Christian schools and universities which provided both religious and secular education.[13]

The General Benefits of Church-Based Christian Schools

Church-based Christian schools have made a great impact on society in general, an impact which dates back to the pre-Reformation period. Sifuna and Otiende noted that during the medieval period there were four types of

---

8. Marvin J. Taylor, *An Introduction to Christian Education* (Nashville/New York: Abingdon Press, 1966), 24.

9. Elmer L. Towns, ed., *A History of Religious Educators* (Grand Rapids, MI: Baker, 1975), 107.

10. Towns, *History*, 159.

11. Eleanor Daniel, John W. Wade, and Charles Greshman, *Introduction to Christian Education* (Cincinnati, OH: Standard, 1980), 40.

12. Towns, *History*, 163.

13. Benson, *Popular History*, 94.

church-oriented schools: parish, chantry, monastic, and cathedral.[14] These schools offered instruction in reading, writing, simple arithmetic, music, and religious doctrine. Mark Fakkema comments that during the Middle Ages, education was done by the church and for the church.[15]

The Reformation brought changes to education. It created an appetite in people to learn so that they could read the Bible on their own. The result, as reported by Sifuna and Otiende, was that "various denominations developed their own theologies of education. They also established their own schools and sought to commit the young members of the church to defend the faith against rival creeds."[16]

The Reformers and the Puritans were convinced that the goal of education was "for moral and religious growth in the life of every student."[17] However, the influence of the church in education in the West started diminishing after the Reformation. Fakkema observes that "The aims of education slowly acquired the emphasis of training for democratic living, for social efficiency and for useful pursuits in the world at large. Religion was no longer the center of the curriculum."[18] In the twentieth century, the Christian school movement was established to help restore the diminishing influence of the church in America.[19]

The education offered by Christian schools is different from that offered by public schools. The two types of education differ in purpose, content, and control of education. Public education benefits the student, government, and society in general, while Christian education benefits the student, the nation, society in general, and also the kingdom of God.[20] The Christian school curriculum goes beyond that of non-Christian schools. The Christian school curriculum stresses biblical thought, with all subjects taught from

---

14. Daniel N. Sifuna and James E. Otiende, *An Introductory History of Education* (Nairobi: Nairobi University Press, 1992), 86.

15. Mark Fakkema, "The Christian Day Movement," in *An Introduction to Evangelical Christian Education* (Chicago: Moody, 1964), 371.

16. Sifuna and Otiende, *Introductory History*, 105.

17. Leland Ryken, "Reformation and Puritan Ideals of Education," in Joel A. Carpenter and Kenneth W. Shipps, *Making Higher Education Christian: The History and Mission of Evangelical Colleges in America* (Grand Rapids, MI: Christian University Press, 1987), 40.

18. Fakkema, "Christian Day Movement," 372.

19. Robert G. Slater, "A 'Christian America' Restored: The Rise of the Evangelical Christian School Movement in America, 1920–1952" (PhD diss., University of Tennessee, 2012), 4, accessed 17 June 2014, http://trace.tennessee.edu/cgi/viewcontent.cgi?article=2528&context=utk_graddiss.

20. Tom Stewart, "What Is the Difference between Christian Education and Public School Education?" https://www.whatsaiththescripture.com/Fellowship-christian-education.html, accessed 17 June 2014.

the perspective of the Word of God.[21] The non-Christian school curriculum stresses humanism. As far as the public school system is concerned, the control of education is in the hands of the nation, while the Christian school properly understands that God has placed that control in the hands of Christian parents/leadership.

Christian schools of the Kenyan Assemblies of God (KAG) should therefore focus on the main purpose of Christian schools in general. With such a focus KAG schools can make an impact in their neighborhoods and transform communities. KAG Christian schools should resist the temptation to follow the patterns of education in the West, which eventually placed academic knowledge above spiritual truth.

Church-Based Christian Schools across Africa and in Kenya

The history of education in many African countries is associated with the history of Christian missions. In almost every African country, Christian missionaries from America and Europe established Christian schools. Apart from learning in order to obtain employment, students in these schools learned the Word of God and a number of them converted to Christianity.[22]

Bermar describes the impact of mission schools in parts of Africa: "In 1942, 97% of Nigeria's student population was enrolled in missionary schools. In 1950, missionary schools accounted for 97% of the total enrollment in Ghanaian schools. In 1945, there were 5,360 mission-run schools for Africans in South Africa and only 230 state-sponsored schools."[23]

Missionaries introduced *kusoma* Christianity in Uganda, where churches were used as schools. According to Anderson, Christians commonly used to say that they went to church to read (*kusoma*) rather than to pray (*kusali*).[24] The first African Catholic bishop in Uganda purposed to establish schools within walking distance for children.[25]

As to when education started in Kenya, Daniel N. Sifuna reports: "In Kenya education was introduced by Krapf in 1884 at Rabbai mission station and Frere town. Its main purpose was: fulfilling religious aims and preparing educated workers for white settlers. At the end of the First World War about 15 mission

---

21. Stewart, "What Is the Difference."
22. Stewart, "What Is the Difference," 273.
23. Edward H. Bermar, "African Response to Christian Mission Education," *African Studies Review* 17, no. 3 (Dec 1974): 527–540.
24. William B. Anderson, *The Church in East Africa 1840–1974* (Nairobi: Uzima, 1988), 111.
25. Anderson, *The Church in East Africa*, 140.

groups were well established in Kenya. Roman Catholic Mission and Church Missionary Society (CMS) were leading in offering African education."[26]

Otiende and others point out that the purpose of mission stations and schools was primarily to spread Christianity.[27] To this end "the missionaries established networks of schools in villages where they offered a very simple education in reading, writing and arithmetic alongside the religious education leading to baptism and church membership."[28] In addition to teaching Christian values, the colonial government and Christian missionaries used education to inculcate Western values in the minds of those who were intended to be loyal to them.

As the twenty-first century began, a new movement took place in Kenya that focused on offering universal primary education. The government also worked to involve religious groups in new education-related public policies. The focus on religious-sponsored education was spearheaded by World Bank's World Faiths Development Dialogue (WFDD) which worked with Catholic and Protestant churches as they celebrated the Millennium.

One of the documented impacts of this movement in Kenya was the opening of Rongo Christian Academy. The school was built by the Christians of Rongo community without any foreign support. Its purpose was to evangelize the community and prepare servant-leaders who would spur development in the local village and grow the church internationally.[29] The philosophy of Rongo Christian Academy was in agreement with that of other evangelical schools. Geoffrey Walford presents a picture of evangelical Christian schools: "They share an ideology of biblically-based evangelical Christianity that seeks to relate the message of the Bible to all aspects of present-day life whether personal, spiritual or educational. Teachers within these schools have a personal relationship with Jesus Christ and believe that the Holy Spirit is active in their lives and the world . . . The schools aim to provide a distinctive Christian approach to every part of school life and the curriculum."[30] If today's church-based Christian schools remain focused on this important function, Kenyan society will be transformed.

---

26. Daniel N. Sifuna, *Development of Education in Africa: The Kenyan Experience* (Nairobi: Initiative, 1990), 121.

27. J. E. Otiende, S. P. Wamahiu, and A. M. Karugu, *Education and Development in Kenya: A Historical Perspective* (Nairobi: Oxford University Press, 1992), 42.

28. Sifuna, *Development of Education*, 50.

29. Amy Stambach, *Faith in Schools: Religion, Education and American Evangelicals in East Africa* (Stanford: Stanford University Press, 2010), 142.

30. Geoffrey Walford, *Private Education: Tradition and Diversity* (New York: Continuum, 2006), 87–188.

However, the current issues affecting young people in Kenya indicate that most parents are not adequately teaching their children at home, and that is because they are not available for them. In 2015, a few media organizations in Nairobi engaged the public to discuss the causes of indiscipline in schools. Ninety percent of the respondents cited the failure of parents to teach their children in the home as the main reason for disciplinary problems.[31]

Local churches and Christian schools must not simply watch as the situation worsens; they can reinforce the teaching children do receive at home. Gangel and Hendicks observed that most church-sponsored schools emerged from the primary vision of a local church, making them an integral part of the church's overall Christian education program.[32]

Methodology

This research investigated the perceptions of stakeholders toward establishing successful church-based Christian schools for Kenyan Assemblies of God (KAG) churches. The research question was: What are the perceptions of existing models of Christian schools in Kenya that may lead to the establishment by KAG churches of successful church-based Christian schools? A mixed-methods design for the purpose of triangulation of divergent data sources was used in this research. A case-study procedure was used to investigate three existing Pentecostal Christian primary schools and to collect data to assist in developing effective church-based Christian schools for KAG. Data was collected using the following instruments: a focus group, semi-structured interviews, and questionnaires. The researcher used appropriate procedures to analyze data collected by each research instrument. The researcher looked for emerging themes and recurrent events and categorized them. Research participants were twenty-four KAG pastors, forty parents from the KAG, all administrators and teachers from the three selected schools, and five executive members (EC) of the KAG leadership.

Kenya Assemblies of God (KAG), which forms the case for this paper, has about 4,000 churches in Kenya distributed among every county. The church's focus is evangelizing the people groups in Kenya, such as Muslims. Its annual budget for missions stands at about a quarter of the total income.[33]

---

31. BibliaHusema Radio, *Public Debate on Causes of Indiscipline Cases among Youth*, 31 August 2015.

32. Kenneth O. Gangel and Howard G. Hendricks, *The Christian Educator's Handbook on Teaching* (Grand Rapids, MI: Baker, 1988), 320.

33. Kenya Assemblies of God 2011–2016 financial report booklet.

The findings are presented thematically as follows.

Results and Discussion

1. Perceptions of Executive Members

Using an interview guide,[34] the author sought first the reasons for KAG starting church-based Christian schools. The responses were presented under three main themes: quality of education, discipleship and evangelism, and safety. All the executives, represented by 100 percent (N=5),[35] gave quality education and discipleship as the main reasons for starting KAG schools. The respondents also specified the expected outcome of their schools. KAG/EM[36] 1 said, "They want to produce Christian leaders in the society, to expose children to the gospel and be filled with the Holy Spirit." KAG/EM 3 said, "We want to mentor our children and have them be born again." Forty percent (N=2) of the respondents cited safety of children as a reason for starting KAG schools, reiterating that their children need a secure environment. KAG/EM 2 said the current happenings in the world pose a great danger to children, hence the need to start KAG schools.

The respondents were asked to indicate how they wanted KAG church-based Christian schools to be different from other schools; all (N=5) said that KAG schools would be different mainly in the area of curriculum. In addition, Christian values, Bible study, devotions, and prayers should be incorporated into the learning system. The schools should be not only for academic purposes but also evangelistic centers.

Regarding the contributions that the church-based Christian schools would make to Kenyan society, all the respondents (N=5) said the Christian schools would contribute toward the transformation of society. Respondents used terms like "influence," "model," and "transform" to describe the impact that the Christian schools would make in society.

The author also sought to find out how the kingdom of God would benefit from church-based Christian schools; all respondents (N=5) agreed that the kingdom of God would grow. They expressed powerful sentiments, such as the idea that some of the students in these schools would be future pastors, Bible-school teachers, and university professors. Through witnessing in schools,

---

34. Please refer to appendix A at the end of the chapter.
35. N refers to number of participants
36. KAG/EM means executive members of the Kenya Assemblies of God top leadership.

many would be likely to be born again and would acknowledge Christ in their generation.

The author then asked how KAG churches would benefit from church-based Christian schools. All the respondents said the local churches would grow numerically and economically. The impact of the churches would be felt in the community as they evangelized the communities around them. One executive, KAG/EM 2, said the impact would be not only local but global, because the product (alumni) of the schools would carry the seed of the gospel planted in them to the places they went to.

The respondents were required to identify one thing that would characterize church-based Christian schools in ten years' time. All the respondents (N=5) expressed great hope in Christian schools. Respondent KAG/EM 1 said, "I can see Christian students who are growing in Christ. I can see Christian students who are examples in the community. I can see students who love and serve God." Respondents KAG/EM 2 and KAG/EM 3 said that all counties in Kenya would have at least one KAG church-based Christian school in the next ten years.

In summary, all the KAG executive members interviewed felt that KAG church-based Christian schools would serve as centers of excellence both academically and spiritually. The young people in Kenya would be discipled and prepared to serve as ambassadors of Christ everywhere they went. These schools would benefit KAG local churches and all Kenyan communities.

2. Perceptions of Pastors

In seeking to establish the perceptions of KAG pastors from Nairobi County regarding the development of successful KAG church-based schools, six pastors from each of the four sections in Nairobi County formed a group. The sections were Dagoret, Ngong South, Kayole, and Outering. Each participant in a group freely answered the five questions presented in the focus group discussion guide (see appendix B at the end of this chapter).

On the reasons for starting KAG church-based Christian schools, three main themes were noted from the responses from the four groups. Sixty-seven percent of the respondents from each group mentioned discipleship as one of the reasons for starting schools. Seventeen percent from each group gave evangelism and offering quality education respectively. Table 14.1 shows the results.

Table 14.1: Perceptions of Pastors on Starting Up KAG Christian Schools

Groups	Themes		
	Discipleship	Evangelism	Quality education
Dagoret	66.7%	16.7%	16.7%
Ngong South	66.7%	16.7%	16.7%
Kayole	66.7%	16.7%	16.7%
Outering	66.7%	16.7%	16.7%

According to the pastors, several aspects would differentiate KAG church-based Christian schools from other schools. Eighty-three percent of respondents (N=5) from Dagoret focus group identified the area of curriculum; seventeen percent mentioned transformation. KAG schools should incorporate biblical teachings in the curriculum. Fifty percent and seventeen percent of Ngong South focus-group respondents cited curriculum and transformation respectively.

On the other hand, fifty percent, thirty-three percent, and seventeen percent of Kayole-section respondents identified curriculum, discipline, and quality education respectively as key areas. Sixty-seven percent, seventeen percent, and seventeen percent of respondents of Outering-section focus group gave priority to curriculum, discipleship, and transformation respectively. Table 14.2 shows the results of the respondents.

Table 14.2: Question 2 Group Interview Responses

Groups	Themes						
	Discipleship	Discipline	Quality Education	Transformation	Curriculum	Professionalism	
Dagoret	-	-	-	17%	83%	-	
Ngong South	-	17%	-	17%	50%	17%	
Kayole	-	33%	17%	-	50%	-	
Outering	17%	-	-	17%	67%	-	

Third, the author sought the contributions that would be made by KAG church-based Christian schools to Kenyan society. The main themes that featured from the respondents were transformation, service to community, evangelism, discipleship, and curriculum. Eighty-three percent of respondents from Dagoret section said the schools would transform Kenyan society, while seventeen percent said the schools would provide services to society. Fifty percent, thirty-three percent, and seventeen percent of respondents from Ngong South section identified transformation, evangelism, and service to society respectively as key contributions. From Kayole section, sixty-seven percent mentioned transformation, while thirty-three percent cited evangelism as major contributions to society. In the case of Outering, fifty percent, thirty-three percent, and seventeen percent mentioned transformation, curriculum, and discipleship respectively as major contributions. Table 14.3 shows the results.

Table 14.3: Question 3 Group Interview Responses

Groups	Themes				
	Discipleship	Transformation	Curriculum	Evangelism	Service
Dagoret	-	83%	-	-	17%
Ngong South	-	50%	-	33%	17%
Kayole	-	67%	-	33%	-
Outering	17%	50%	33%	-	-

The fourth question sought to establish how the kingdom of God would benefit from KAG church-based Christian schools. Two major themes emerged from the interview: fulfilling the Great Commission and kingdom growth. Fifty percent of all respondents from each focus group said the KAG Christian schools would contribute toward the fulfillment of the Great Commission (Matt 28:19–20). The remaining fifty percent said that, as children and staff of the church-based Christian schools preached the gospel, people would be born again, and as a result the kingdom of God would grow.

It was necessary to find out how KAG local churches would benefit by starting church-based Christian schools. Five themes emerged from the responses of the four groups: discipleship, job creation, financial growth, quality education, and numerical church growth. Table 14.4 shows the responses per theme.

Table 14.4: Benefits for KAG Local Churches

Groups	Themes				
	Discipleship	Job creation	Financial growth	Quality education	Church growth
Dagoret	50%	17%	17%	17%	-
Ngong South	17%	-	17%	-	67%
Kayole	17%	-	-	17%	67%
Outering	-	17%	33%	-	50%

Fifty percent of respondents from Dagoret section said the local churches would build strong disciples. Seventeen percent said members of the local churches would get jobs. Another seventeen percent said children of church members would get quality education, and the remaining seventeen percent said the church would gain financially.

In the case of Ngong South respondents, sixty-seven percent identified church growth as a main benefit. Seventeen percent each settled for financial growth and discipleship. Sixty-seven percent of Kayole-section respondents said the local churches would grow numerically, seventeen percent said that children would receive quality education, and the remaining seventeen percent identified discipleship.

For Outering respondents, fifty percent said the local churches would grow numerically, thirty-three percent cited financial gain, while the remaining seventeen percent pointed to job creation.

In summary, the focus-group responses revealed that the main reasons for starting KAG church-based Christian schools are to evangelize, disciple, and offer quality education to Kenyan children. The responses further revealed that KAG schools would be different from other schools in matters of curriculum. The schools would incorporate the Bible and its teachings in the curriculum. The KAG schools would transform Kenyan society in morals, values, and leadership, among other things. Finally, yet importantly, the kingdom of God would grow, as people would be born again through the ministry of the schools. In addition, the church would grow both numerically and financially.

3. Perceptions of Church Members (Parents)

The perceptions of parents from four sections in Nairobi District toward the development of successful KAG church-based Christian schools were sought. A questionnaire was given to forty parents, ten from each section. This represents 100 percent. A 70 percent consensus in each question or theme was regarded as significant to determine the conclusions.

Items 1–3 in the questionnaire investigated the need for KAG church-based Christian schools. 97.5 percent (N=39) totally agreed that KAG churches should begin church-based Christian schools. 92.5 percent (N=37) totally agreed that Kenyan communities needed church-based Christian schools. Another 92.5 percent (N=37) totally agreed that issues affecting the community could be effectively addressed in church-based Christian schools. Table 14.5 summarizes the responses for items 1–3.

Table 14.5: Responses to Items 1–3

Item	Statement	Frequency	Percent
1	KAG churches should begin church-based Christian schools	39	97.5
2	Kenyan communities need church-based Christian schools	37	92.5
3	Issues affecting the community can be effectively addressed in church-based Christian schools	37	92.5

In summary, the KAG parents strongly believe that their churches should begin church-based Christian schools. They too think that Kenyan communities need church-based Christian schools. In addition, they believe that issues affecting Kenyan society can be effectively dealt with in church-based Christian schools.

Conclusion

Kenyan society needs transformation. There is moral degradation, corruption almost everywhere, and a lack of quality education in schools. Church-based Christian schools can contribute toward a positive transformation of society.

Christian schools were started long ago (pre-Reformation period) and advanced during the Reformation. The main reason for starting these schools was to create moral and God-fearing societies. The teachers integrated the Protestant faith into the curricula of their schools. Missionaries from America

Appendix B: Focus Group Interview Guide for Pastors

RQ 4: Perceptions of KAG pastors toward the development of successful KAG church-based Christian schools.

1. What are the reasons for KAG churches starting church-based Christian schools?
2. In what ways should KAG church-based Christian schools differ from other schools?
3. What contributions can KAG church-based Christian schools make to Kenyan society?
4. How will the kingdom of God benefit from KAG church-based Christian schools?
5. How will KAG local churches benefit by starting church-based Christian schools? Explain.

and Europe then introduced Christian schools in Africa. The schools became centers of evangelism, discipleship, and quality education. Some of us, or our parents, can today testify that missionary schools indeed produced men and women who transformed Kenya.

This study reveals the need for churches in Kenya to begin church-based Christian schools. The study also indicates that Kenyan communities need Christian schools; and that the problems affecting society could be effectively dealt with in Christian schools. The future of this nation could be bright, great, and promising if the churches in Kenya began church-based Christian schools.

If the churches are to establish schools, they must ensure that evangelism, discipleship, and educative processes are effective so that the desired goals are realized. Could theological schools like KAG East University have an input? Teachers and administrators in church-based schools must be able to witness, disciple, and effectively teach the students. Our Bible schools should prepare teachers and administrators of church-based schools. Are our theological institutions serving the needs of the church and society?

Bibliography

Anderson, William B. *The Church in East Africa 1840–1974*. Nairobi, Kenya: Uzima Press, 1988.

Baur, John. *2000 Years of Christianity in Africa: An African History 62–1992*. Nairobi, Kenya: Pauline Publications, 1994.

Benoît, Lee-Anne. "An Overview of the Kenyan Education System: Issues and Obstacles to Learning." Accessed 10 October 2013. https://studymoose.com/kenya-education-essay.

Benson, Clarence. *A Popular History of Christian Education*. Chicago: Moody, 1943.

Bermar, Edward H. "African Response to Christian Mission Education." *African Studies Review* 17, no. 3 (December 1974): 527–540.

Carpenter, Joe A., and Kenneth W. Shipps, eds. *Making Higher Education Christian: The History and Mission of Evangelical Colleges in America*. St Paul, MN: Christian University Press, 1987.

Daniel, Eleanor, John W. Wade, and Charles Gresham. *Introduction to Christian Education*. Cincinnati: Standard Publishing, 1980.

Fakkema, Mark. "The Christian Day Movement." In *An Introduction to Evangelical Christian Education*. Chicago: Moody, 1964.

Gangel, Kenneth O., and Howard G. Hendricks. *The Christian Educator's Handbook on Teaching*. Grand Rapids, MI: Baker, 1988.

Githinji, Reuben. "Strikes in Secondary Schools in Kenya." Accessed 12 October 2013. https://allafrica.com/stories/201210161251.html.

15

Spirituality, Work Conditions, and Job Satisfaction of Distance Education Personnel in Kenya's Christian Institutions of Higher Education

Rosemary Wahu Mbogo
Dean, School of Education, Arts, and Social Sciences,
Africa International University, Karen, Kenya

Abstract

This paper outlines the findings of a dissertation study conducted in 2011 to explore the relations of spirituality, work conditions, and job satisfaction of distance education personnel (also referred herein as extension studies personnel) in Kenya's Christian higher education. The study was conducted among six Christian universities, three accredited and three licensed by the Commission for University Education (Kenya) to operate as universities. All six universities are based in Nairobi. Of the three research questions in the original research, this paper addresses only two: (1) What are the perceptions of administrators and faculty of extension studies on factors associated with their job satisfaction? and (2) In what ways do administrators and faculty of extension studies seek to enhance their job satisfaction?

The study adopted a mixed-methods approach using the qualitative paradigm, specifically, the grounded theory approach. Qualitative data was collected from twenty purposefully selected respondents using semi-structured interviews. Emerging categories were analyzed through a process of open, axial, and selective coding using NVIVO 9 until a theme was reached. This ultimately led to the generation of grounded theory indicating that job satisfaction is influenced by interrelated multidimensional and multilayered factors emanating from organizational, relational, personal, and spiritual forces. Organizational factors included organizational structure, policy issues, logistical issues, financial issues, and workload issues. Different dimensions of work relations emerged as related to job satisfaction, including the relationships of personnel with extension students and supervisors/leaders, and cross-cultural relations at work. Personal factors including personality traits, family responsibilities, backgrounds, and competences of extension studies personnel influenced their job satisfaction. Personnel also explained that spirituality played an important role in overcoming work-related stress generally in life and particularly through spiritual disciplines. Finally, personnel explained that they enhanced their own job satisfaction by seeking further education, practicing spiritual disciplines, attending professional workshops and seminars, confiding in colleagues, and communicating their ideas or complaints to supervisors/leaders.

Key words: job satisfaction, work conditions, spirituality of personnel, higher education, Christian higher education, administrators, faculty members.

Introduction

Distance education has become common all over the world, evidenced by the growing numbers of traditional institutions of higher learning that have begun to launch extension sites, establish cohorts, or modify residential programs to be accessible to learners in the marketplace.[1] In this paper, the terms "extension education" and "distance education" are used synonymously to refer to alternative (nontraditional) delivery modes of learning applied by institutions of higher learning to facilitate the education of students who are working or have obligations inhibiting their availability for a full-time, residential, and rigid schedule (nontraditional students).

---

1. Hilary Perraton, *Open and Distance Learning in the Developing World* (London: Routledge, 2000).

In Kenya, traditional institutions of higher learning ventured into distance education slightly over two decades ago.[2] Theological institutions and Christian universities have been following suit. The last two decades have been marked by growth due to the high demand for extension education in ministerial and other training,[3] but there have been numerous challenges in the administration and implementation of extension programs.[4] These challenges are mainly impacting the administrative personnel and faculty members who are directly and indirectly administering and teaching in the programs, using nontraditional methods among nontraditional learners. This paper seeks to address two research questions:

1. What are the perceptions of administrators and faculty of extension studies on how spirituality and work conditions are associated with their job satisfaction?

2. In what ways do administrators and faculty of extension studies seek to enhance their job satisfaction?

Literature Review

According to Locke,[5] job satisfaction is "a pleasurable or positive emotional state resulting from the appraisal of one's job or job experiences." It refers to "an attitudinal variable that can be a diagnostic indicator of how a person is doing in one of the major domains of his or her [work] life . . . Job satisfaction can be indicative of good work adjustment and positive well-being."[6] Job satisfaction constitutes the perceptions of workers as to how well their jobs meet their fundamental needs.

Job satisfaction has been found to be associated with various variables, including spirituality and work conditions such as salary, promotion opportunities, job variety, autonomy, and supervision. "Christian higher

---

2. Perraton, *Open and Distance Learning*, 47, 75.

3. D. W. Breneman, "Entrepreneurship in Higher Education," *New Directions for Institutional Research* 129 (2005): 3–9, accessed 25 June 2007 from Academic Search Premier.

4. S. L. Broskoske and F. A. Harvey, "Challenges Faced by Institutions of Higher Education in Migrating to Distance Learning" (paper presented at the National Convention of the Association for Educational Communications and Technology, October 2000), 37–42, accessed 25 June 2007 from Academic Search Premier, Publication no. 143.

5. E. A. Locke, "The Nature and Causes of Job Satisfaction," in *Handbook of Industrial and Organizational Psychology*, ed. M. D. Dunnette (Chicago: Rand McNally, 1976), 1304.

6. P. E. Spector, *Job Satisfaction: Application, Assessment, Cause, and Consequences* (Thousand Oaks, CA: SAGE, 1997), 72.

education" refers to a tertiary-level education that is committed solely to scholastic pursuit that is guided and influenced by, and focused on, Christian tenets. It is a "Christ-centered" tertiary-level education whose aim is "to discover all that is true, how it is true, how it relates to everything else and ultimately, how it all relates to Jesus Christ."[7] It is therefore necessary to consider how personnel perceive spirituality to relate to their job satisfaction. According to McGrath, the term "spirituality" is derived from the Hebrew word *ruach* and has a variety of meanings, including "spirit," "breath," and "wind."[8] In its application, the term refers to an inward empowerment for something. The concept of Christian spirituality introduces the person of Christ. Therefore, "Christian spirituality" refers to empowerment which draws people to relate to Christ. "Spirituality . . . arises from a creative and dynamic synthesis of faith and life, forged in the crucible of the desire to live out the Christian faith authentically, responsibly, effectively, and fully."[9] Hence, Christian spirituality is relational, encompasses all of life, and should play a significant role in the job satisfaction of Christian workers.

Brown and Sargeant[10] conducted a quantitative study to investigate the relationship between job satisfaction and organizational and religious commitment among full-time workers at Akra University (a pseudonym) based on a number of demographic factors. A total of 542 employees who worked at the Caribbean university were purposively sampled. Data revealed that (1) the longer employees stayed at their institution, the higher the levels of organizational commitment and extrinsic job satisfaction; (2) workers with doctoral degrees had higher levels of job satisfaction and religious commitment than individuals with a high-school diploma; and (3) administrators and sector managers had higher levels of intrinsic job satisfaction and religious commitment than those in other occupational areas.[11]

Lazar[12] conducted a quantitative study to investigate the impact of spirituality on the job satisfaction of female Jewish Israeli hospital nurses. Spiritual values (sacredness of life, altruism, and idealism) were significantly

---

7. D. Litfin, *Conceiving the Christian College* (Grand Rapids, MI: Eerdmans, 2004), 66.

8. A. E. McGrath, *Christian Spirituality: An Introduction* (Malden, MA: Blackwell, 1999), 9.

9. McGrath, 9.

10. D. Brown and M. A. Sargeant, "Job Satisfaction, Organizational Commitment, and Religious Commitment of Full-Time University Employees," *Journal of Research on Christian Education* 16 (2007): 211–241, accessed 25 April 2010 from ATLA.

11. Brown and Sargeant, "Job Satisfaction," 221.

12. A. Lazar, "Spirituality and Job Satisfaction among Female Jewish Israeli Hospital Nurses," *Journal of Advanced Nursing* 66, no. 2 (2010): 334–344, doi: 10.1111/j.1365-2648.2009.05172.x.

related to job satisfaction. After controlling for age and religiousness, the results of multivariate hierarchical regression analysis showed that "the dimensions of spirituality made a statistically significant and unique contribution to the prediction of job satisfaction."[13]

Walker, Jones, Wuensch, Aziz, and Cope[14] conducted a study to investigate the relationship between employees' sanctifying of their work and job satisfaction, organizational commitment, and intent to leave a job. Data confirmed the first hypotheses that "perceiving one's job in a sacred light adds explanatory power to individuals' levels of job satisfaction above and beyond that of the demographic variables, including general religiosity."[15]

Clark, Leedy, McDonald, Muller, Lamb, Mendez, Kim, and Schonwetter[16] conducted a correlational study to determine, among other things, the relationships of spirituality (SPR), integration of spirituality at work (INT), level of self-actualization (ACT), and employee job satisfaction (JOB).

Duggleby, Cooper, and Penz[17] conducted a mixed-methods study to examine the relationships between hope and spiritual wellbeing, global job satisfaction, and general self-efficacy. The findings indicated that direct hours of contact and job satisfaction scores had a statistically significant negative relationship ($r = -.35$, $p < .05$). Those who preferred Roman Catholicism had significantly higher job satisfaction scores than those who did not, and those who indicated they were spiritual rather than religious had significantly higher levels of self-efficacy scores (GSES). Qualitative analysis indicated that respondents had hope which gave them strength and power for each day.

Perrone, Webb, Wright, Jackson, and Ksiazak[18] conducted a mixed (quantitative and qualitative) study to explore the relationship of spirituality, work, and family roles to life satisfaction among gifted adults. In their

---

13. Lazar, "Spirituality and Job Satisfaction," 339.

14. A. G. Walker, M. N. Jones, K. L. Wuensch, S. Aziz, and J. G. Cope, "Sanctifying Work: Effects on Satisfaction, Commitment, and Intent to Leave," *International Journal for the Psychology of Religion* 18, no. 2 (2008): 132–145, accessed 25 April 2010 from ATLA.

15. Walker et al., "Sanctifying Work," 140.

16. L. Clark, S. Leedy, L. McDonald, B. Muller, C. Lamb, T. Mendez, S. Kim, and R. Schonwetter, "Spirituality and Job Satisfaction among Hospice Interdisciplinary Team Members," *Journal of Palliative Medicine* 10, no. 6 (Dec 2007): 1321–1328, accessed 20 October 2008, Academic Search Premier.

17. W. Duggleby, D. Cooper, and K. Penz, "Hope, Self-Efficacy, Spiritual Well-Being and Job Satisfaction," *Journal of Advanced Nursing* 65, no. 11 (2009): 2376–2385, doi: 10.1111/j.1365-2648.2009.05094.x.

18. K. M. Perrone, L. K. Webb, S. L. Wright, Z. V. Jackson, and T. M. Ksiazak, "Relationship of Spirituality to Work and Family Roles and Life Satisfaction among Gifted Adults," *Journal of Mental Health Counseling* 23, no. 3 (2006): 253–268, accessed 13 April 2009 from ATLA.

qualitative analysis, the most common responses on the impact of spiritual beliefs on life satisfaction were that their "spiritual beliefs contributed positively to life satisfaction, and that spiritual beliefs helped them cope with difficult life events or hardships."[19]

Methodology

After gathering qualitative data through face-to-face interviews or equivalent telephone interviews for two respondents not reachable physically, the first step I took was to transcribe the data verbatim. NVIVO 9 was used to create nodes, to ensure that the ideas of the respondents, and not my personal biases, were captured.[20] Memos were taken throughout the process and were eventually tabulated to allow "constant comparison"[21] of concepts from the respondents. By focusing on the categories and providing data for each category, the process continued "until no new properties emerged."[22] The categories were saturated and sorted for theoretical sampling. Through sorting and diagramming, I formed an initial analytic framework and eventually arrived at a major theme through selective coding.[23] I used the theme to generate grounded theory, a process of "taking comparisons from data and reaching up to construct abstractions and simultaneously reaching down to tie these abstractions to data."[24]

Factors Related to Job Satisfaction

Participants perceived several factors to be related to their job satisfaction. These can be grouped in four categories: organizational (work conditions and work characteristics) factors, relational factors, personal factors, and spiritual factors.

---

19. Perrone et al., "Relationship of Spirituality," 262.
20. K. Charmaz, *Constructing Grounded Theory: A Practical Guide Through Qualitative Analysis* (Thousand Oaks, CA: SAGE, 2006); U. Flick, *An Introduction to Qualitative Research*, 3rd ed. (London: SAGE, 2006).
21. M. D. Gall, J. P. Gall, and W. R. Borg, *Educational Research: An Introduction* 8th ed. (New York: Allyn & Bacon, 2006), 469.
22. Charmaz, *Constructing Grounded Theory*, 96.
23. Flick, *Introduction*; Charmaz, *Constructing Grounded Theory*.
24. Charmaz, *Constructing Grounded Theory*, 181.

Organizational Factors

Organizational factors include several work conditions that were associated with the job satisfaction of administrators and faculty members of extension studies in the six institutions. These factors are primarily related to unique aspects of working in the extension programs. The personnel of extension studies identified several factors that related to their job satisfaction both positively and negatively, including structural issues, policy issues, financial issues, and logistical issues.

Structural Issues

Many respondents indicated that one of the challenges they faced while working with extension programs was lack of structure. This was more of a challenge for the administrators than for the faculty. Lack of structure interfered with effective supervision. For example, one respondent asserted: "I am supposed to report directly to the registrar, but the registrar is not very familiar, unfortunately, with a lot of these processes, because the university has just grown in a bang within the last three years. So the registrar is not very familiar with these procedures that we go through. So what I do is that I supervise myself, unless if I have to consult."

Extension programs were reported to be part of rapid expansions in all of the institutions involved in the study. Thus, supervisors seemed not to be keeping pace with what was happening. Some felt that the structural challenges affected the quality of services offered to extension students, indicating that those services were "inferior" and lacked clear supervisory roles. One respondent explained that he reported to three supervisors. Lack of clear structure implied that extension studies personnel felt that they performed some other departments' responsibilities.

Policy Issues

In some way, structural shortcomings were perceived to have contributed to and to have been caused by lack of clear policy to run extension programs. There was no policy to govern the involvement in extension programs of full-time faculty in the regular program. Therefore, faculty involvement was based on willingness of individual faculty members. This frustrated the efforts of administrators of extension studies. Participants from four out of the six schools alluded to the challenge of faculty involvement. One observed: "I find it challenging to work with the faculty. You know, faculty are very independent people, and they feel committed to the students more than to the system because that is where they enjoy their work. You find they are not willing to go an extra mile [in administrative tasks]."

Similarly, administrators who had supervisory roles lacked policies to govern them in dealing with extension students.

Another area related to policy issues was the perceived inequitable treatment of personnel. Some respondents indicated that ambiguity in the institutions' systems had caused decisions to be made unfairly. For example, one participant indicated: "Rather than have a job group that requires [specific credentials] . . . because someone has come and has room for negotiation for offers and counteroffers . . . they get what is naturally unusual [special treatment] in any one's interpretation. Everybody may not know, but when they do, they feel hurt and they feel that the system is not fair. There is discrimination." The consequences of this scenario were ill-feeling and even brought divisions among the personnel, resulting in the formation of social cliques.

Logistical Issues
Respondents indicated that job satisfaction was impacted by logistical concerns that affected the provision of instructional materials and other resources in serving dispersed students.

With regard to instructional materials, a respondent said that extension students complained of the poor quality of service they received: "So they complain that they are left out from the mainstream communication and things that are happening. The other [complaint] is [about] access to the library and computer lab because they feel they have paid fees and should have access."

Another logistical challenge involved the mode of delivery of programs, which are mostly in modular format. This limited interaction time with students, ultimately impacting on student guidance and supervision. One respondent asserted: "The basic thing, first of all, is time. We have very little time to interact with the students, to guide them and for academic advising to give them academic counseling. So time constraint is an issue we have to gamble with."

Additionally, extension students were dispersed across different locales all over Kenya. A respondent explained: "Dealing with the extension programs is not easy. Very few missionaries will agree to go out . . . especially with evening classes." One respondent from the same institution said that one challenge was that many of the faculty members, whether missionaries or not, did not want to drive at night.

Financial Factors

"Financial constraints" was top of the list for a number of respondents who referred to the construct as mainly related to job satisfaction. In five out of the six schools, financial challenges were associated with personnel remuneration, availability of qualified personnel, limited learning resources, and the development and growth of the institutions. One respondent indicated that financial constraints hampered her work because they reduced the quality of the programs: "The remunerations are not [very] attractive. So I am not able to get qualified staff. When you get someone with a PhD and tell them the salary you offer, they say no, no, no – they turn away. So we end up using sub-standard faculty. And that becomes dissatisfying because you know the quality is not where it is supposed to be."

Lack of qualified personnel seemed to be a main outcome of limited finances. Another respondent indicated that his school had experienced high turnover due to poor remuneration.

Unfortunately, financial constraints seemed to hamper the development of the institutions. Another respondent indicated that the situation was similar in her institution, where publicity was forfeited on the grounds of lack of finances. Another also expressed concern because the financial situation had made the institution dependent on the "free" services of missionaries. He said: "Sometimes we give courses not because the courses are needed by the students but because those who are available are not paid by the school." He further explained that such programs would not attract more students to the institution because they were irrelevant.

Social Responsibilities

A factor that seems to have influenced the perceptions of personnel regarding satisfaction with salary was their social responsibilities, particularly family responsibilities. For example, one indicated that being a family member carried financial obligations. Although he had been able to meet some of his financial obligations, he indicated that a rise in his salary would be of help to his family. Another lamented that his low income had made him dependent on his wife. He wished he were able to provide both for his family and for other needy people in the community: "Even making a living for my wife is difficult. I have to get support from my wife. My wife should feel that my income supports her. I am stressed and I stress her to make ends meet. We need to widen our perception of our resources, to meet our needs and the needs of others. They come for monetary help not for prayers. I can be the one who prays and gives."

Similarly, another indicated that she would appreciate a salary rise to be able to give her children a quality education. She explained that she "moonlighted" in order to make ends meet. Another used a sense of humor when explaining that institutions transitioning from small Bible institutes to Christian universities were used to dependence on "free" missionary services, and abused the concept of service at the expense of personnel needs.

Work Characteristics

Respondents pointed out some work characteristics that positively influenced their job satisfaction. Many of them pointed to the significance of their work. For example, one felt that his work contributed to the development of leaders and met a real need in society. At another school, one indicated that "because most of these people [extension students] apply what they have learnt almost immediately," serving extension students motivated her.

Similarly, another respondent explained that extension studies programs allowed a mode of delivery that was "user-friendly," helping students who would not study full-time to further their education. This aspect encouraged her to keep serving extension students. Many faculty members indicated that their relationships with students or their impact on students positively impacted their job satisfaction. Nevertheless, the overall workload of extension studies personnel seemed to challenge their ability to cope with work stress or to maintain a positive outlook on their work.

Workload

Personnel of extension studies from all of the participating institutions explained that their workload was related to their job satisfaction. This component was particularly mentioned by coordinators of extension studies and by faculty who were involved in administration. A respondent explained that one of the challenges that extension studies personnel faced was related to the fast growth of their departments without corresponding growth in personnel. This forced personnel to multitask as administrators, academic advisors, and teaching assistants.

Another similarly felt his workload was heavy. He explained his frustration because of the conflict between his roles as a teacher and an administrator: "As a teacher I need to focus on my classes, I need to be organized. Administration brings conflicts in teaching my classes because some people [extension students and extension faculty] look for me even when I am getting prepared for a class. Unless I am given fewer classes, there is collision, and I feel my preparation is not adequate compared to other lecturers."

Full-time coordinators of extension programs who had no teaching responsibilities also indicated that the workload was large. One said that the institution had responded to her request for more help by hiring a student worker, but she complained that student workers were not usually available when most needed, due to their student schedule.

Three respondents who were primarily administrators without teaching responsibilities indicated dealing with crises as a factor that added to the complexity of their workload. From three different universities, they explained that sometimes they had scheduled classes, but the department responsible did not have teachers by the time the courses were to begin. They described that as their most stressful time – when they had to call each student to explain and reschedule. Hence, crisis management seems to have been a contributor and possible cause of heavy workload for the extension studies personnel.

Workload was increased by the nature of the students with whom extension personnel dealt. Respondents explained that they dealt with chronologically mature extension students who needed more attention than regular, younger students.

Relational Factors

The second category of factors related to the job satisfaction of extension studies personnel was relational factors. These factors included challenges related to working with extension students, supervisors, and colleagues. From the respondents' data, it appeared that relationships in different dimensions affected the job satisfaction of personnel. These relationships were seemingly interdependent, and included working with distant learners and working with colleagues and supervisors in multicultural contexts.

Working with Distant Students

Extension students were different from regular/residential students because they were more mature, juggled many responsibilities, and needed more attention. A respondent elaborated, saying that extension students "have other responsibilities . . . these are people whose parents are aging, someone is dying in the middle of their program, [they have] their own kids, some are parents. There are so many issues to deal with outside the academic program." She felt that these students demanded more time from her.

Moreover, these students expected to be considered in light of their personal experiences. Serving extension students demanded sacrifice: "So when you serve an extension student, . . . it is giving more. It demands sacrifice. If a student comes just before lunch time (which in Kenya is normally from 1 p.m. to 2 p.m.), you may not tell them to wait until 2 p.m., because some are working and have jobs and quickly come over their lunch hour to seek assistance."

However, relationships with students were perceived to contribute positively to job satisfaction of personnel. A respondent indicated that he drew satisfaction from interacting with his students. Two others also indicated that they drew satisfaction from the feedback they received from students, the fact that they were immediately applying what they had learned, and that their knowledge was "working."

Working with Colleagues

One of the factors associated with personnel job satisfaction was related to working with their colleagues, whether hierarchically or horizontally. One of the most frequently recurring phrases used by the respondents to describe their horizontal work relations with colleagues was "teamwork." Many respondents indicated that there was a team spirit among their colleagues that helped them in three ways: support, feedback, and encouragement. Some pointed to the willingness of colleagues to assist them, and vice versa. Another explained that her colleagues helped in areas where she lacked skills and thus completed her abilities. Moreover, respondents indicated that they received encouragement from their colleagues.

Hierarchically, those with supervisory roles indicated that their work relations with juniors were motivating. A supervisor explained that her relationships with administrative juniors kept her motivated to continue with her work, even in the midst of insurmountable stress at work. She explained, "In terms of my juniors, I have the administrative staff in the academics and I have the faculty. I work very well with my administrative staff. We have good rapport. I thank God. Maybe that is why when I come to [work] tired I feel very happy." She, however, also indicated that she faced challenges with faculty. Apparently, working with supervisors seemed to pose challenges for the juniors. For example, a respondent lamented that a lack of first-hand experience with extension students on the part of institutional leaders and supervisors made them delay making decisions. This brought antagonism among their clients, the distance students.

A main relational aspect was the cross-cultural diversity of the personnel. This was especially true for the institutions that had faculty who were missionaries from international agencies. For example, one indicated that some missionaries had dual responsibilities, implying they were not totally focused on working for the institution. She felt that such faculty dictated their terms and made scheduling of courses a challenge to her: "Because the missionaries are kind of on appointment and they are not on pay, they open up to other things, . . . they have other things. And sometimes those other things may take [priority] in some situations . . . The missionary will come and say, I am available on this and this date, because I have my other missionary duties on this and this date. So you can only schedule them when they are available." She explained that this created discontent among other faculty members, who felt they had no choice. Another explained that some of the missionaries were not willing to teach extension students, due to extraneous situations such as driving at night or teaching off-campus. A respondent from a different school was puzzled that missionaries seemed to overlook school policies.

Personal Factors

Personal factors related to the job satisfaction of extension personnel included their personality traits, social responsibilities, and work competencies. Personality traits were clearly evident as respondents explained what impacted their job satisfaction. Using the Big Five mode of categorization of personality traits, the respondents seemed to exhibit two main traits: openness and conscientiousness.

Openness
In relation to openness, many of the respondents, especially those who were involved in administration of extension studies, tended to be creative, constantly proposing new ideas to the institutional leaders. One of these mentioned more than five programs or initiatives he was undertaking for his institution. He explained that he proposed and implemented new initiatives as a form of service to his institution. In another school, a respondent also shared about his initiatives to change the way some things were done in his institution. He felt that this was his contribution to the "kingdom."

Conscientiousness
In relation to conscientiousness, many respondents also indicated that their job satisfaction was connected to their achievement. One mentioned that he was fulfilled in his work because the extension programs he administered had offered services to many students, including those in senior positions in their respective places of work. Many of the personnel, who were involved in administration or programs, whether on full-time or part-time bases, seemed to be individuals who were achievement-oriented.

Competence

Another aspect that was related to the job satisfaction of extension studies personnel involved their competencies to handle various tasks on the job. One indicated that job satisfaction was enhanced when "you know what you are supposed to do and therefore you have confidence with what you are doing." She explained that knowing her job well motivated her to work. Two respondents from two different institutions felt that the refresher courses offered by their universities gave them skills and competencies needed to do their job. Another indicated that his lack of technological skills was disadvantageous to him, and he wished his institution would invest in building the capacity of personnel.

Spiritual Factors

Spirituality was one of the key elements related to the job satisfaction of the extension studies personnel. All respondents indicated that spirituality played a key role in their job satisfaction. One may wonder why spirituality did not emerge as an intervening variable in work conditions and work characteristics. Spirituality seemed to be a core value of the workers which indirectly impacted their job satisfaction by helping them to perceive work in sacred terms and as a mandate given by God, empowering them to deal with challenging and stressful work situations, and causing them to give themselves sacrificially beyond the call of duty.

One explained that his spirituality had led him to his understanding of the meaningfulness of work: "I get it from the Word of God, knowing what work is all about . . . I have the concept of work." This understanding helped him to appreciate his work. Another explained that, as a Christian, she had to be consistent both at home and at work. Her Christian identity helped her to take work beyond a human mandate or physical incentives: "Spirituality is more [about] your relationship with God and the fact that if you have a relationship with God, your life is a package. Therefore, whatever happens, is part of it . . . I am Christian and that's it, and so whether I am at home or church I am a Christian. That in essence is my identity, for who I am defines what I do, whether at home or wherever. I approach my work as Christian; it's part of my identity."

Many respondents used the term "service" to describe how spirituality was connected to their perception of work. One elaborated: "I believe my spirituality helps me to find job satisfaction. I am here to serve." Many respondents also used the words "timing" and "place" to explain their feeling that God had not only called them to do their jobs of ministry, but had also intended for them to work in their respective institutions at that time or season.

Additionally, spirituality helped personnel to overcome work challenges and stress. One explained that, because of stress and poor remuneration, "if it was just a job I would not have satisfaction. When I think of ministry, I forget – I forget the stress. Ministry has little to do with the money." Spirituality seemed to intervene through reflection and the practice of spiritual disciplines. Finally, personnel indicated that spirituality enabled them to give themselves to their work sacrificially. One indicated that "situations demand sacrifice – teaching in the morning, evening, and meetings during the day," in addition to his administrative responsibilities.

Personnel Initiatives to Enhance Job Satisfaction

The second research question in this paper asked: In what ways do extension studies personnel enhance their job satisfaction? Extension personnel were asked to explain their personal initiatives to enhance their job satisfaction.

Observance of Spiritual Disciplines

One of the most frequently mentioned answers was related to the practice of spiritual disciplines. One respondent explained that he enhanced his spirituality by praying and reading the Word of God. Another asserted that, even before he joined the institution, he practiced spiritual disciplines, and had purposefully decided to maintain the same stance even at his work.

Personal and Career Development

Another common response was that personnel had taken the initiative to further their education for the purpose of building their competencies and skills. Five respondents indicated they were PhD students aiming to improve their competencies, while three others reported they were intending to enroll in doctoral studies, but were currently involved in refresher nonformal courses or academic courses in areas of interest.

Additionally, personnel indicated that involvement in professional conferences enhanced their job satisfaction. One explained that participation in professional workshops and conferences was beneficial because of discussions with professionals from other institutions. She explained how hearing other professionals recount familiar challenges encouraged her to share her experiences. She also learned from the experiences of others.

Interactions with Supervisors

Finally, respondents explained that openness with supervisors or leaders had helped them deal with some challenges. A participant explained that she had requested a meeting with her supervisors to discuss her enormous workload. She explained her belief that people cannot "read" her thoughts, having no explanation of her own experiences. Another also indicated that dialogue with supervisors had caused the supervisors to understand his heavy workload and to understand when he did not meet deadlines.

Summary

Data analysis indicated that the job satisfaction of extension studies personnel in Kenya's Christian higher education was related to an intricate combination of factors that had a direct and indirect effect on administrators and faculty of extension studies. Organizational, relational, and personal factors were all interwoven into spirituality factors, and were all perceived to be related to job satisfaction. Spirituality factors enabled personnel to overcome work stress caused by structural issues, policy issues, logistical issues, and work conditions; relational stress from interactions with students, colleagues, and supervisors; and, by inference, personal stress emanating from personal and family responsibilities. Spirituality enabled personnel to have spiritual dispositions that formed the framework for understanding their jobs as sacred. Moreover, satisfaction with the work itself, with work relations, and with personal factors amalgamated with spirituality factors to contribute positively to the job satisfaction of extension studies personnel. Figure 15.1 shows a conceptual framework to illustrate the theoretical interconnectedness of the different constructs.

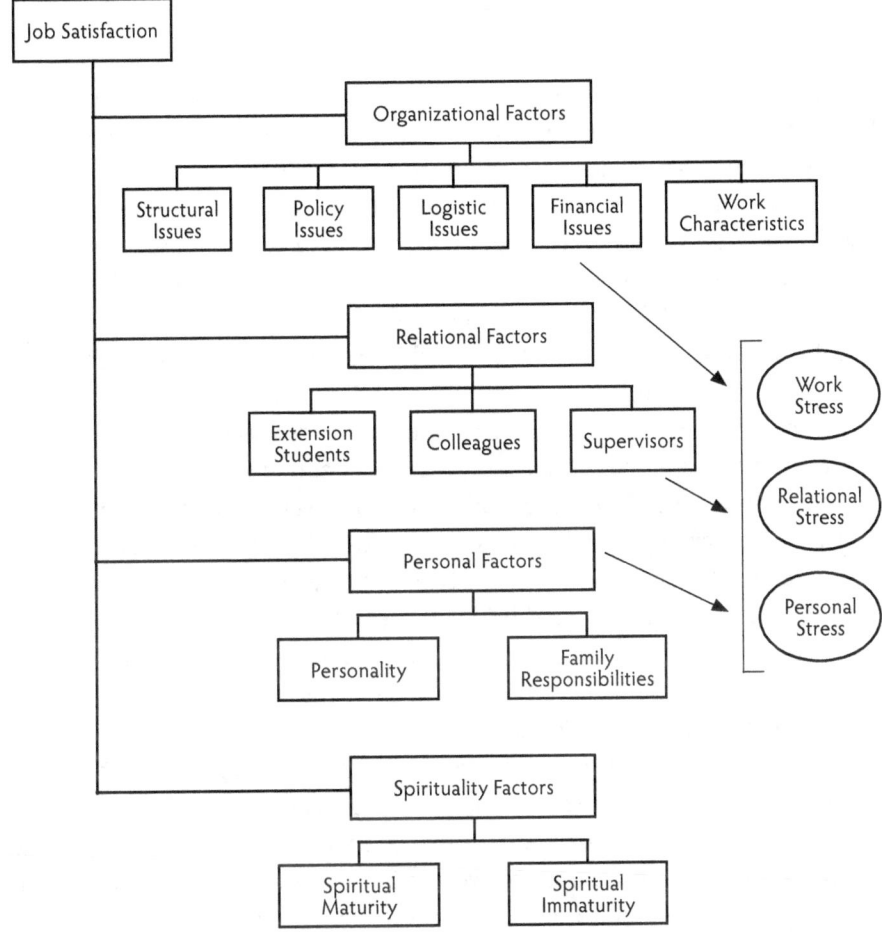

Figure 15.1: Model for the Factors Related to Job Satisfaction

Grounded Theory

From the foregoing discussion on main themes that emerged from the study, grounded theory was generated: The job satisfaction of extension studies personnel of Christian universities in Nairobi is associated with interrelated multidimensional and multilayered factors emanating from organizational, relational, personal, and spiritual forces. Spirituality seemed to have an overarching role in facilitating personnel's ability to deal with work, relational, and personal stress through reflection and action.

Implications for Institutional Leaders

The qualitative data in this study indicated that personnel were overwhelmed by the complexity of administering and teaching in extension studies programs. Hence, the workloads of administrators, administrating faculty members, and faculty teaching in extension programs need to be reviewed.

Leaders need to review traditional policies for workload to consider issues of travel to meet extension students, flexibility to communicate through technology, and different teaching methodologies, among other issues. Training needs to be offered for technical facets and support needs to be provided to handle these areas. For administration roles, leaders need to clearly define the workloads of personnel and to provide additional support where necessary. In this case, in addition to employing adequate personnel, the use of interns from various schools could alleviate some workload problems.

Leaders may need to address disparities between missionaries and local personnel. For example, in dealing with proposals from overseas missionaries, local personnel need to be involved. Giving local personnel the opportunity to contribute to these ideas would bridge some of the gaps that make them feel their ideas are less favored. Improving local personnel's salaries would also deal with some ill-feeling because of underpayment and constant comparison between them and the missionaries.

Additionally, opportunities for promotion should be made available to all equitably, both to local personnel and to missionaries. Criteria for promotion need to be clarified with personnel to avoid misunderstandings. Instituting programs that provide dialogue between missionaries and local personnel for the purpose of cross-cultural exchange and synergy could enhance honest relationships between local personnel and missionaries.

Honest discussions about differences, challenges, aspirations, and intentions could cultivate relationships that glorify God and build the community of God's people.

Bibliography

Breneman, D. W. "Entrepreneurship in Higher Education." *New Directions for Institutional Research* 129 (2005): 3–9. Accessed 25 June 2007 from Academic Search Premier.

Broskoske, S. L., and F. A. Harvey. "Challenges Faced by Institutions of Higher Education in Migrating to Distance Learning." Paper presented at the National Convention of the Association for Educational Communications and Technology,

October 2000, 37–42. Accessed 25 June 2007 from Academic Search Premier, Publication No. 143.

Brown, D., and M. A. Sargeant. "Job Satisfaction, Organizational Commitment, and Religious Commitment of Full-Time University Employees." *Journal of Research on Christian Education* 16 (2007): 211–241. Accessed 25 April 2010 from ATLA.

Charmaz, K. *Constructing Grounded Theory: A Practical Guide Through Qualitative Analysis.* Thousand Oaks, CA: SAGE, 2006.

Clark, L., S. Leedy, L. McDonald, B. Muller, C. Lamb, T. Mendez, S. Kim, and R. Schonwetter. "Spirituality and Job Satisfaction among Hospice Interdisciplinary Team Members." *Journal of Palliative Medicine* 10, no. 6 (2007): 1321–1328. Accessed 20 October 2008, Academic Search Premier.

Duggleby, W., D. Cooper, and K. Penz. "Hope, Self-Efficacy, Spiritual Wellbeing and Job Satisfaction." *Journal of Advanced Nursing* 65, no. 11 (2009): 2376–2385. doi: 10.1111/j.1365-2648.2009.05094.x.

Flick, U. *An Introduction to Qualitative Research.* 3rd edition. London: SAGE, 2006.

Gall, M. D., J. P. Gall, and W. R. Borg. *Educational Research: An Introduction.* 8th edition. New York: Allyn & Bacon, 2006.

Lazar, A. "Spirituality and Job Satisfaction among Female Jewish Israeli Hospital Nurses." *Journal of Advanced Nursing* 66, no. 2 (2010): 334–344. doi: 10.1111/j.1365-2648.2009.05172.x.

Litfin, D. *Conceiving the Christian College.* Grand Rapids, MI: Eerdmans, 2004.

Locke, E. A. "The Nature and Causes of Job Satisfaction." In *Handbook of Industrial and Organizational Psychology*, edited by M. D. Dunnette, 1297–1349. Chicago: Rand McNally, 1976.

McGrath, A. E. *Christian Spirituality: An Introduction.* Malden, MA: Blackwell, 1999.

Perraton, H. *Open and Distance Learning in the Developing World.* London: Routledge, 2000.

Perrone, K. M., L. K. Webb, S. L. Wright, Z. V. Jackson, and T. M. Ksiazak. "Relationship of Spirituality to Work and Family Roles and Life Satisfaction among Gifted Adults." *Journal of Mental Health Counseling* 23, no. 3 (2006): 253–268. Accessed 13 April 2009 from ATLA.

Spector, P. E. *Job Satisfaction: Application, Assessment, Cause, and Consequences.* Thousand Oaks, CA: SAGE, 1997.

Walker, A. G., M. N. Jones, K. L. Wuensch, S. Aziz, and J. G. Cope. "Sanctifying Work: Effects on Satisfaction, Commitment, and Intent to Leave." *International Journal for the Psychology of Religion* 18, no. 2 (2008): 132–145. Accessed 25 April 2010 from ATLA.

List of Contributors

Fredrick Otieno Amolo is an ordained minister and educator of the Church of the Nazarene, having served for eight years in full-time pastoral ministry and two years in youth ministry. He received his MDiv from Nairobi Evangelical Graduate School of Theology and is currently taking his PhD at Kenyatta University. He is a lecturer at Africa Nazarene University where he has served for the past six years.

David Bawks is a minister with Nairobi Chapel, having served in Kenya since 2008. He graduated from Wheaton College, IL with a Bachelor of Arts in Biblical/Theological Studies and History, then went on to complete a Master of Divinity at Africa International University. Previously, he taught at Carlile College and led the Nairobi Chapel Tyrannus Hall training ministry. Currently he leads a new church plant at Nairobi Chapel Karen.

Bill Black is Senior Lecturer in the Faculty of Theology at St Paul's University. He has also served as lecturer and Deputy Dean at the Makarios III Patriarchal Orthodox Seminary in Nairobi. Bill received his MDiv at Gordon-Conwell Theological Seminary and his PhD from the University of Cambridge. He served as an ordained Presbyterian minister for twenty-one years in the US, UK, Ethiopia, and Kenya before converting to Eastern Orthodoxy in 2011. From 2018 Bill will be based in Kisumu and serve as an assistant to the Bishop in the Diocese of Kisumu and Western Kenya.

Joseph Galgalo is an ordained minister in the Anglican Church of Kenya and an honorary Canon of All Saints Cathedral, Nairobi. He holds a PhD in Systematic Theology from the University of Cambridge. He is the current Vice Chancellor of St Paul's University in Kenya, a position he has held since 2010.

Johana Kariuki Gitau studied at the University of Nairobi and the international Leadership University where he obtained a Master of Divinity. He is an ordained pastor with the Worldwide Gospel Church of Kenya in Nairobi and is currently pursuing a doctorate in Theological Studies at the International Leadership University.

Ndung'u John Brown Ikenye lectures in Counseling Psychology and Pastoral Theology at St Paul's University in Limuru, Kenya. He is a clinical psychologist in private practice for individuals, marriages, families, and organizations.

He is also currently Director at the Institute of Leadership, Counseling, and Congregation Development, and Archdeacon in the Anglican Diocese of Thika. Prof. Ikenye holds a PhD in Counseling, Personality, and Culture from Northwestern University, USA; a DMin in Counseling and Psychotherapy; and an MTS in Pastoral Psychology from Garrett-Evangelical Theological Seminary, USA.

Patrick Mburu Kamau is a lecturer who has served in the School of Religion and Christian Ministry at Africa Nazarene University in Nairobi, Kenya, since 2008. He has been the coordinator of the Master of Arts in Religion degree at the same university since 2011. He holds a PhD in Religion from Kenyatta University, in which he focused on interfaith relations, and is an ordained minister in the Church of the Nazarene.

Isaac Wamalwa Kasili is an ordained pastor with Kenya Assemblies of God. Currently he is a lecturer and a dean of the School of Education at KAG EAST University. He received his BA in Bible and Theology from East Africa School of Theology, his MA in Biblical Studies from Global University, and his PhD in Theological Studies, with special emphasis on education, from Pan Africa Theological Seminary in Lome, Togo.

Rosemary Wahu Mbogo is a Senior Lecturer of Education at Africa International University, and the Dean of the School of Education, Arts and Social Sciences (SEAS). She holds a PhD in Educational Leadership and Administration from Biola University (USA). Her research interest is in the areas of assessing leadership and administration of Christian higher education, out of which she has authored several books and academic articles. She is married to Dr Stephen N. Mbogo of Africa Enterprise, with whom she keeps abreast on mission work. Together they are blessed with two children.

Elizabeth Mburu is an adjunct associate professor of New Testament and Greek in the School of Theology, International Leadership University, Kenya, where she previously served as the head of department. She pursued her doctoral studies at Southeastern Baptist Theological Seminary in Wake Forest, North Carolina, USA. Currently she teaches Greek, New Testament Studies, Hermeneutics, and Worldview studies. She is also actively involved in research and publishing in the same areas and is particularly interested in developing intercultural models in hermeneutics. She serves on the editorial teams of the Africa Bible Commentary and the Africa Society for Evangelical Theology, and is a curriculum evaluator for the Association of Christian Theological Education in Africa (ACTEA).

Gift Mtukwa was born and raised in Harare, Zimbabwe, and currently lives in Nairobi, Kenya. He is an ordained minister with the Church of the Nazarene, teaches Bible and Theology in the School of Religion and Christian Ministry at Africa Nazarene University, and is the Lead Pastor at the University Church of the Nazarene. He holds a Bachelor Degree in Theology, a Master of Arts in Religion from Africa Nazarene University, and a Master of Arts in Theology from the University of Manchester. He is currently pursuing a PhD in Biblical Studies at the University of Manchester.

Hermann Yokoniah Mvula attended Africa Nazarene University in Nairobi, Kenya, where he obtained both bachelor and master degrees in Theology. Mvula obtained his doctoral degree at Chancellor College of the University of Malawi. His field of research interests is political and public theologies, ethics, and governance. Currently, he is a lecturer in Biblical Studies (Old Testament Theology and Ethics) at Chancellor College of the University of Malawi, where he headed the Department of Theology and Religious Studies for two years.

David K. Ngaruiya is an Associate Professor at the International Leadership University where he has served in various capacities, such as Deputy Vice Chancellor for Research, Extension, and Development. He holds a PhD in Intercultural Studies from Trinity Evangelical Divinity School. He served as chair of the Africa Society of Evangelical Theology (2015–2016). He has published journal and book articles and served as co-editor and contributor to the book *Communities of Faith in Africa and African Diaspora* (Pickwick Publications, 2013).

Rickson Nkhata is a member of the Faculty of Theology at Southern Africa Nazarene University in Manzini, Swaziland. He has a Bachelor of Theology and Master of Arts in Religion from Africa Nazarene University and is currently pursuing a Doctor of Ministry there. He is an ordained minister in Church of the Nazarene where he has also pastored several churches for over twenty-five years.

Mary Thamari Odhiambo has been involved in missions in community development for over ten years. She currently serves as the Country Director for Life In Abundance (LIA) Kenya program and has previously led development projects in rural and urban informal settlements. She has also worked as adjunct faculty in development studies at PAC University, teaching gender mainstreaming and NGO coordination courses. Mary holds a Master in Missions from Africa International University and is a PhD candidate in

Anthropology and Development at the University of Birmingham. Her research in rural Kenya is focused on women's negotiations of gender relations in the context of strained livelihoods.

Rodney L. Reed is a missionary educator who has served at Africa Nazarene University in Nairobi, Kenya, since 2001. Currently he is the Deputy Vice Chancellor of Academic Affairs, a position he has held since 2010. Prior to that he served as the Chair of the Department of Religion for nine years. He holds a PhD in Theological Ethics from Drew University and is an ordained minister in the Church of the Nazarene.

D. G. Stanton is an ordained missionary and educator of the Church of the Nazarene, having served for thirty-five years in eastern and southern Africa. He received his EdD from California Coast University (Santa Anna). Currently he is Senior Lecturer in the Department of Religion at Africa Nazarene University in Nairobi, Kenya, where he has served for the past twenty years. Previously he trained and mentored pastors and Christian religion educators in South Africa, Tanzania, and Zambia.

Langham Literature and its imprints are a ministry of Langham Partnership.

Langham Partnership is a global fellowship working in pursuit of the vision God entrusted to its founder John Stott –

> *to facilitate the growth of the church in maturity and Christ-likeness through raising the standards of biblical preaching and teaching.*

Our vision is to see churches in the majority world equipped for mission and growing to maturity in Christ through the ministry of pastors and leaders who believe, teach and live by the Word of God.

Our mission is to strengthen the ministry of the Word of God through:
- nurturing national movements for biblical preaching
- fostering the creation and distribution of evangelical literature
- enhancing evangelical theological education

especially in countries where churches are under-resourced.

Our ministry

Langham Preaching partners with national leaders to nurture indigenous biblical preaching movements for pastors and lay preachers all around the world. With the support of a team of trainers from many countries, a multi-level programme of seminars provides practical training, and is followed by a programme for training local facilitators. Local preachers' groups and national and regional networks ensure continuity and ongoing development, seeking to build vigorous movements committed to Bible exposition.

Langham Literature provides majority world preachers, scholars and seminary libraries with evangelical books and electronic resources through publishing and distribution, grants and discounts. The programme also fosters the creation of indigenous evangelical books in many languages, through writer's grants, strengthening local evangelical publishing houses, and investment in major regional literature projects, such as one volume Bible commentaries like *The Africa Bible Commentary* and *The South Asia Bible Commentary*.

Langham Scholars provides financial support for evangelical doctoral students from the majority world so that, when they return home, they may train pastors and other Christian leaders with sound, biblical and theological teaching. This programme equips those who equip others. Langham Scholars also works in partnership with majority world seminaries in strengthening evangelical theological education. A growing number of Langham Scholars study in high quality doctoral programmes in the majority world itself. As well as teaching the next generation of pastors, graduated Langham Scholars exercise significant influence through their writing and leadership.

To learn more about Langham Partnership and the work we do visit **langham.org**

The Africa Society of Evangelical Theology (ASET) is a professional society, founded in 2009 for the purpose of fostering evangelical theological scholarship and to facilitate collegial relationships among scholars and practitioners of the Christian religion in Africa. It is a registered society in the country of Kenya that sponsors an annual conference with current members drawn from several African countries and the United States. Among its objectives are to encourage research among African scholars of Christianity to provide a platform for that research to reach a wider audience within Africa and around the world, to create a context where evangelical perspectives on issues facing the African church and society are addressed and to create a context for fellowship and networking among its members. Its core values are: (1) Faithfulness to the Bible, (2) Professional ethics, (3) Creative and critical thinking, (4) Christ-like humility, (5) Community of scholars encouraging, respecting, and learning from one another, and (6) Development and inspiration of young scholars.

To learn more about ASET, please see its Facebook page at:
www.facebook.com/AfricaSocietyOfEvangelicalTheology

Or contact any of the following offices:

- Secretary: asetsecretary@gmail.com
- Program and Arrangements: asetprograms@gmail.com
- Publications: asetpublications@gmail.com
- Communications: asetcommunications@gmail.com

www.ingramcontent.com/pod-product-compliance
Lightning Source LLC
Chambersburg PA
CBHW060555230426
43670CB00011B/1826